Study Guide

to accompany

Child Development

Ninth Edition

John W. Santrock
University of Texas at Dallas

Prepared by
Wayne Benenson
Illinois State University

McGraw Hill

Boston Burr Ridge, IL Dubuque, IA Madison, WI New York San Francisco St. Louis
Bangkok Bogotá Caracas Lisbon London Madrid
Mexico City Milan New Delhi Seoul Singapore Sydney Taipei Toronto

McGraw-Hill Higher Education
A Division of The ***McGraw-Hill*** *Companies*

Study Guide to accompany
CHILD DEVELOPMENT, NINTH EDITION
JOHN W. SANTROCK

Published by McGraw-Hill Higher Education, an imprint of The McGraw-Hill Companies, Inc., 1221 Avenue of the Americas, New York, NY 10020.

This book is printed on acid-free paper.

2 3 4 5 6 7 8 9 0 CUS/CUS 0 3 2 1

ISBN 0-07-241295-X

www.mhhe.com

CONTENTS

How to Use the Study Guide

This study guide has been written with the goal of helping you to navigate through the chapters of the text, explore key concepts and information, synthesize this information into an easily recalled form, and put information into practical use. As you use the study guide, keep your text handy, along with pencils, markers, and pens. It is helpful to many students to keep notes, work with fellow students, and be consistent in working with the study guide. Many students find it helpful to use the study guide prior to the instructor's discussion of the chapter material. The following features of this Study Guide are designed to help you master chapter content in *Child Development*

Learning Objectives

The learning objectives represent the most important information in the chapter. Use these as a quick study tool: Before your test, read each learning objective and make sure you have learned that information.

True or False Key Content Questions

Use these to test your knowledge of important chapter content. Note the areas you're weakest on and study these again.

Fill In The Blank Key Terms

Use these to test yourself before a quiz or exam by reviewing the list to determine which key terms you still don't understand or remember. At a minimum you should be able to recall the terms and their definitions. Ideally you should be able to utilize these terms and definitions in short answer and essay questions if challenged to do so.

Matching Key People Questions

This feature reinforces your knowledge of major chapter concepts as it asks you to match the key people to the idea or concept with which they are associated.

Multiple Choice Knowledge Questions

Each chapter contains a selection of multiple-choice questions that cover the main content of the chapter. They help prepare you to take a multiple-choice exam, as well as reviewing the entire chapters' content one last time.

Critical Thinking Questions

Use these rigorous questions to test your comprehension of key concepts. It tests the boundaries of your understanding. Suggested answers appear in bulleted form in the Answer Key.

Application Questions

These will help you to bring the text to life and make it more meaningful for you personally.

Cognitive Map Exercises

This fill-in the blank feature reinforces what you have learned earlier in the chapter and is a really good revision tool. Complete them and keep them to hand when needing to test your overall grasp of a chapter.

Review Priorities

Frankly rate yourself and your understanding of the chapter and use this to help you in your revision and study plan for the course.

Answer Key

Located at the end of each chapter, this provides answers to the above mentioned exercises.

Some Final Thoughts . . .

This *Study Guide* will enhance your ability to learn and remember knowledge about *Child Development.* However, effective studying involves more than the specific things you do to learn the material; it includes developing good general study habits, plans, and strategies.. . . *about active learning*: Research has shown that study activities do not really help unless you use them in a very active way. If you agree with us, I hope that all of the activities in this *Study Guide* will be useful both as ready-made suggestions for study and as models for activities that you invent on your own to help you achieve your own course goals and objectives.

Now, let's talk about effective ways to study. You may already know some of these ideas, but oftentimes they can bear repeating. Other ideas may be new to you, so you may want to give them a try. Remember that we are all unique, so some strategies work better for some people than for others--try out a suggestion for a fair period of time (only you can decide what "fair" is), and if it works, great--if it doesn't try something else. Read the next section, written by Anita Rosenfield of DeVry Institute of Technology, Southern California, for some more in-depth tips and suggestions on how to succeed in this and other courses.

Happy Learning! *Wayne Benenson*

Being An Excellent Student

by Anita Rosenfield DeVry Institute of Technology, Southern California

Most students who are in college want to be good students, and most students have some particular goal in mind, which is probably why they chose the particular college or university they are attending. As you chose your college or university, and perhaps even an area of major interest or concentration, you had certain goals in mind, which likely included doing well in school, earning good grades, and graduating.

Unfortunately, many students do not do as well in college as they had hoped and expected. Let's examine some of the reasons for this disappointing outcome to see how to avoid them and to learn, instead, how to be a good student and guide your behavior to improve your chances of achieving your goals.

A common definition of education is that it is "how people learn stuff." For most of our history, educators have focused on the "stuff." Teachers were required to be masters of their respective academic fields. Even today, some states have requirements that speak only to the need to be qualified in the subject matter one teaches, not in the teaching methods themselves.

In the 1960s, we became more interested in the "people" part of the definition, which was evidenced by moving to strategies like open classrooms and free universities. The idea was that, given the opportunity to do so, people will naturally learn. Although these experiments were dismal failures, they taught us something.

The key to the definition of education is the word *how*. Today, thanks to a wealth of research on the principles that guide the phenomenon of learning, and on the nature of learning and memory, we know much more about how learning occurs and how we can make it better. By using these principles, we can become better students.

Formulating the Plan

Anything worth having is worth planning for. Whether you hope to learn to teach, to fly, to write for profit, or to change diapers correctly, you have in mind a goal. An everyday question from the first days in elementary school is, "What do you want to be when you grow up?" The answer to this question is one way of formulating a goal. Now that you are a college student, many people will expect you to know what you want to do for a profession or career. Yet you may not have the foggiest notion, or you might have an idea that is still slightly foggy. That is OK. What is clear, however, is that you want to succeed in your college courses. This is a relatively long-range goal, and as such can serve a purpose in keeping you on track.

But our day-to-day behavior is often hard to connect to our long-range goals. We need short-term goals to keep us organized and to be sure that the flow of our activities is in the direction we want to be going. To accomplish our long-range goals, we need to focus on three types of short-term goals. First, we need goals for the day; second, we need goals for the week; and third, we need goals for the semester or term. Let's look at each of these separately.

Goals for Today

It is helpful to keep a daily checklist, diary, or schedule as a reminder of what must be done each day. Check off the things as you accomplish them. A pocket calendar is particularly helpful for this task.

Goals for the Week

Students who are successful in college also schedule their time weekly. Sometime during the course of registration, you made up a schedule showing your classes for the whole week. If you have a job, you must allow time for that, too. Also, many college or university students have family obligations that need to be considered as well. Finally, everyone needs some time for relaxing, eating, sleeping, and playing (even in graduate school we were advised that we needed to find some time to have fun in order to keep our balance). With all these things in mind, it is no wonder many students find little time to study.

But good students do all these things, too, yet they study. Do they have more time? No, we all have the same amount of time. But successful students schedule their time carefully. So, make up a weekly schedule and block off time for all these necessary events: classes, work, relaxation, eating, sleeping, playing, family, and studying. Students who actually schedule their time and keep to their schedules are amazed at how much time they find they have!

As you make up your weekly schedule, you may find your study time in a large block. If this is true, please remember to take a short break every twenty to thirty minutes. This is called distributed practice and is far more efficient than studying for hours on end. After the first twenty or thirty minutes, most of us become much less efficient anyway. When you take that break, reward yourself somehow; then get back to your studying. Something I always tell my students is never to try to read a whole chapter in one sitting. In fact, when I am preparing for a new class, or have changed texts in a class I have been teaching, I take that advice myself!

Goals for the Semester

At the beginning of each semester, we find ourselves immersed in many new courses. Often, you will be confronted by several new professors with whom you have never worked before. It is difficult to sort out the expectations and demands of these several courses. However, it is important to organize the information that will be needed for completing all of the course requirements in order to be successful in the courses.

If you can, obtain a large wall calendar, and mark on it all the dates of tests, exams, and term paper due dates, being sure to write on the calendar the course for which each date applies. Now, estimate how long it will take you to make final preparations for those exams, and mark those dates as warning or alert dates. Look over the dates on which papers are due, and see if they are bunched together. If your college is typical, they will probably be close. You can help yourself to avoid the last-minute all-nighters if you simply determine a spread of due dates for yourself, and mark those on the calendar too. As you do this step, please be sure to avoid any days that have personal significance for you, such as birthdays, anniversaries, and so on. This calendar gives you an overview of major dates in your semester.

If you have followed this carefully, you now have a large semester calendar plastered on your wall, a weekly schedule of major life events, classes, and study times taped over your desk, and a daily checklist of must-do items in your pocket or purse. **So, your scheduling is on its way. Let's look now at other important strategies.**

Attending Classes

Many students believe that, since they are in college, they can decide whether to go to class at all. This is true. Some students also believe that attendance in class is not important to their grade. This is not true! Some colleges or universities have attendance requirements, so that if students miss a given number of classes it will either lower their grade a full letter grade, or the instructor may drop the student from the course; some instructors have in-class activities that count toward students' grades, so if students are not in class, they do not get credit for participating. Even without such strategies, students who do not attend class sessions almost always do more poorly on the tests and exams. Perhaps they were absent when a crucial item was discussed, or when the instructor lectured over the material this examination requires. Remember, that more often than not, instructors will include information in their lectures that is not in your textbook, and that information (whether from class lecture, videos shown in class, guest lectures, and so on) is fair game for tests. Moreover, if you are not there, the instructor cannot get to know you, and therefore cannot give you the benefit of the doubt on your answers. It should come as no surprise that in study after research study, the data clearly show that those students who attend class regularly receive the highest grades and actually learn more, too! So, the first rule of being an effective student is to attend classes. Besides, how else can you get your money's worth?

But okay, now that you've determined you will go to every class, what will you do?

Benefiting from Lectures

Sometimes students think that if they come to class and "pay attention," they will remember what the instructor talked about; they think that if they take notes, they will miss much of what the instructor says. But sitting and paying attention is difficult. For one thing, most people can think much faster than they can speak. While the instructor lectures at 80 words per minute, the student thinks at about 350 words per minute! If the student is using this extra "thinking capacity" to focus on what the instructor is saying, it is fine. This rarely lasts more than five minutes at a time, however. Most of the time, this extra "thinking capacity" is used in daydreaming!

Daydreaming can be helpful in resolving our emotional problems, planning the course of our lives, and avoiding work. Often, it is motivated by the desire to avoid work. For whatever motive, however, daydreaming is not compatible with attending a lecture. Human beings simply cannot attend to more than one stimulus at one time. And you have to admit, your daydreams can be ever so much more interesting than your professor's lectures.

Attending lectures is best done while. Use plenty of paper, and leave blank lines at regular intervals, or leave wide side margins. You will use these spaces later (they are not wasted!). If the instructor permits it, be brave and interrupt with questions if you do not understand what is being said. One thing I try to stress to my students is that I may know what I am talking about, but it may be unclear to them--and if it's unclear to one student, it may well be unclear to other students. So, for the sake of the other students who didn't understand what I was talking about, each student should take on the responsibility of asking me to clarify what I said, or to expand in a way that will help them understand. Remember that lectures have a way of progressing and building on earlier information. It is important to understand each point, or later points will be lost. (But please, DO NOT ask the person sitting next to you what the professor said--it disrupts the class, disturbs your neighbor, and you are likely NOT to get an accurate response!)

When you take notes, write out the major points, and try to just make simple notes on the supporting minor points. If you miss something, and you cannot ask a question about it, approach the instructor immediately afterward, when it is likely to still be fresh in both your minds. DO NOT try to write down every word, and DO try to use abbreviations or symbols, or, you could do what I did--learn shorthand! (Or, make up your own.)

Often my students will ask if they may tape record my lectures. Personally, I have no objection to having students do this. In fact, I did this my first term back in college but found it was terribly tedious trying to transcribe the lecture. The students for whom this may be particularly helpful are those who have visual, auditory, or motor impairments. However, do not ever tape record a lecture without first asking for and obtaining the professor's permission.

Within one or two hours after the lecture, on the same day, go back over your notes, and do two things. First, fill in the rest of the minor points. This often amounts to completing the sentence or other element. Second, write brief summaries and any questions that you now have in the blank spaces (lines or margins) you left earlier (clever of you to leave those spaces!). These few minutes spent reviewing and organizing your notes will pay off in greatly improved memory. The questions you have you can ask in class, or during the instructor's office hours, and reap two benefits. First, you will get the answers. Second, you will demonstrate that you are a serious student, and that will impress your instructor.

One other thing about going to class. While this is not always true, I have found that typically my best students sit in front. And most students seem to have a need to have "their seat," while a few students have a need to move around, sitting in one seat one day and a different seat the next. It wasn't until my graduate school days that I realized why I needed "my seat"--as a student, we are being overwhelmed with new information, a stressful experience; we need some structure we can count on to reduce that stress. So, if you are one of those who likes to wander, be considerate of your classmates' needs for stress reduction.

By the way, to get the most out of the lectures, do complete the assigned reading BEFORE the class begins so you are familiar with the material. This will help you keep up with what the instructor is talking about, will reduce the amount of information you do not understand, but may also bring up important questions for you to ask in class if the instructor does not talk about them.

Reading For Learning

We all know how to read. You are proving it by reading these words. Hopefully, you are also realizing some ideas as a result of reading. If you are only reading words, please WAKE UP! STOP DAYDREAMING!

We can read a variety of things: newspapers, movie reviews, novels, magazines, and textbooks. Textbooks are unlike all the others, and must be read with a strategy all their own.

There are many reading and studying strategies, and all of them work to an extent. Perhaps you learned one or more in the course of going to high school. Perhaps you even took a how-to-study course when you entered college. If so, you probably learned one or two of these systems. If you have one you like, that works for you, keep it. If you are interested in learning a new one, read on.

The PQ4R Method

One of the most successful and most widely used methods of studying written material was the SQ3R method, first developed at The Ohio State University. Researchers had noted that students who were more successful were more active readers. More recently, this method has been updated to the PQ4R Method, which adds an additional step. This method teaches you the same skills that have made many thousands of students successful. If you use this method when you read and study, you will be more successful, too. I have outlined the steps below and the text describes this method in Chapter 13.

The P stands for PREVIEW. After you have read the overview or chapter outline, and the list of learning objectives, you should survey the chapter in the text. This is also called skimming. Look at the headings and subheadings, and get the gist of the major points in this chapter. Check off each point in the outline of this Study Guide as you pass it in the pages of the text.

The Q stands for QUESTION. Reading is greatly enhanced if you are searching for the answers to questions. For this text, the Student Study Guide provides learning objectives that can serve as questions. For other texts, make up questions for yourself, based on the chapter overview or on your own survey of the chapter. Be sure that you have at least one question for each major unit in the chapter; you will be less efficient at studying those units for which you do not have questions.

The first of the four Rs is for READ. As you read, look for the answers to the questions you posed, or to the study or learning objectives furnished for you. When you find material that answers these questions, put a mark (X) or a "post-it" note in the margin next to that material. This will help now, since you are actively involved, and later, when you review. It is a good idea to wait to underline or highlight lines of text until after you have read the entire chapter at least once, so you will know what is and what is not most important. (In fact, while some "authorities" suggest you underline or highlight no more than 10% of what you are reading, I find that when most of us begin to underline or highlight, we wind up doing it to most of the chapter--I suggest not doing it at all because it becomes too passive, which counteracts your attempts to read "actively.")

The second R stands for REFLECT. As you are reading, stop every so often and reflect on the material to increase its meaningfulness. This includes analyzing the material, thinking about how to apply it to your own life, interpreting the information, and connecting it with information you already have in your long-term memory.

The third R is for RECITE. One of the oldest classroom techniques in the world (Aristotle used it) is recitation. In the classroom version, the teacher asks the questions and the students answer them. Unless you can get your teacher to study with you regularly, you'll have to play both roles. Periodically stop in your reading and say aloud (if possible) what the author is telling you. Try to put it in your own words, but be sure to use technical terms as you learn them. If you are not in a situation where you can recite out loud, do it in writing. Just thinking it is not enough. When should you pause to recite? A good rule of thumb is that each time you come to the end of a major subheading, you should recite. One professor encourages his students to recite at least one sentence at the end of each paragraph, and two or three or more sentences at the end of each subunit (when you come to a new heading).

People who do not use recitation usually forget half of what they read in one hour, and another half of the half they remembered by the end of the day. People who use recitation often remember from 75 to 90 percent of what they studied. This technique pays off. By the way, if anyone questions why you are talking to yourself, tell them that a psychologist recommended it.

The fourth R is for REVIEW. You should review a chapter soon after you have studied it (using the PQ and first 3Rs). You should review it again the day or evening before a test. It is not usually helpful to cram the night before a test, and particularly not the day of the test! That type of studying does not produce good memory, and is likely to make you more anxious during the test itself.

Taking Tests

One of the things students fear most is failure. Failure signifies that things are not going well, and alerts us to the possibility that we may not achieve our goals. Unfortunately, many students see tests and exams as opportunities to fail. They prepare by becoming anxious and fearful, and trying to cram as much as possible right before the exam. These students rarely do well on the exam. They often fail, thus accomplishing just what they feared.

Taking tests requires strategy and planning. First, it is helpful to know what type of tests you will have. Your instructor probably told you during the first class meeting, or it may be in the class syllabus or course outline. If you do not know, ask.

If you are going to be taking essay exams, the best way to prepare is by writing essays. Before you do this, it is a good idea to find out what types of questions the instructor asks, and what is expected in a response. Again, it is helpful to ask the instructor for this material. Perhaps you can even see some examples of essay questions from previous years--some instructors at some colleges have copies of their exams on file in the department office or in the library. By finding out what is expected, you can formulate a model against which you can evaluate your answers.

Now, using the learning objectives, or some essay questions you wrote, actually sit down and write out the answers. I have prepared at least two essay questions for each chapter in this text. HINT: If you usually feel more anxious during a test, it may help you to practice writing your essays in the room in which the test will be given. Simply find a time when the room is vacant, and make yourself at home.

If your instructor gives multiple-choice tests, then you should practice taking multiple-choice tests. For each chapter, either use questions provided in the Student Study Guide, or make up your own. You may find it helpful to work out an arrangement to pool questions with other students, thereby reducing the amount of work you have to do, and developing a network of friends. Or, you may ask your professor if he or she would entertain the idea of having students write some of the exam questions--some of my professors did that in my undergraduate classes, and it is something I sometimes have my students do.

Whichever way you do it, the important thing is to prepare for tests and exams. Preparation is about 95 percent of the secret to getting a good grade. (Yes, there is some actual luck or chance involved in test scores, as even your instructor will admit!) Preparation is not only a good study and review technique, but also helps to reduce anxiety.

Dealing With Test Anxiety

Anxiety can be a helpful response when it occurs at low levels. In 1908, Yerkes and Dodson showed that the amount of anxiety that could benefit performance was a function of the difficulty and complexity of the task. As the difficulty of the task rose, anxiety became less helpful and more likely to interfere with performance.

If you have ever been so anxious in a test situation that you were unable to do well, even though you knew the information, you have test anxiety. If you get your exams back, and are surprised that you marked wrong answers when you knew the correct answers, or if you can only remember the correct answers after you leave the examination room, you too may have test anxiety.

Strategy Number One: Effective Study

Use study habits that promote learning and make the best use of time. Strategies, such as scheduling your time and using the PQ4R system, reduce anxiety by increasing confidence. As you come to realize that you know the material, your confidence rises and anxiety retreats.

Strategy Number Two: Relaxation

Each of us develops a unique pattern of relaxation. Some people relax by going to a specific place, either in person or mentally. Others relax by playing music, by being with friends, by using autogenic relaxation phrases, or by meditating. Whatever you do, be aware of it, and try to practice relaxation techniques. If you are good at relaxing, try thinking about those situations that make you anxious, and relax while you think of them. To do this, allow yourself to think only briefly (fifteen to thirty seconds at a time) of the situation that makes you anxious, and then relax again. After a number of such pairings, you will find that thinking about that situation no longer makes you anxious. At this point, you may be surprised to find that the situation itself also no longer produces anxiety. You may find that it is helpful to think about these anxiety-provoking situations in a sequence from those that produce very little anxiety to those that are more anxiety-evoking. Such a list, from low to high anxiety, might look something like this:

1. Your instructor announces that there will be a test in four weeks.
2. Your instructor reminds you of the test next week.
3. As you study, you see on the course outline the word *test*, and remember next week's test.
4. One of your friends asks you if you want to study together for the test, which is the day after tomorrow.
5. You choose not to go out with your friends because of the test tomorrow.
6. As you get up in the morning, you remember that today is the day of the test.
7. You are walking down the hall toward the classroom, thinking about what questions might be on the test.
8. The instructor enters the classroom, carrying a sheaf of papers in hand.
9. The instructor distributes the papers, and you see the word *test* or *exam* at the top.
10. After reading the first five questions, you have not been able to think of the answer to any of them.

If you work at it gradually and consistently, pairing these types of thoughts (briefly) with relaxation and remembering to let go and relax after each one, this will dispel test anxiety and make test taking a more productive and successful experience.

Strategy Number Three: Thinking Clearly

Most students who have test anxiety think in unclear and unproductive ways. They say to themselves things like: "I can't get these answers correct . . . I don't know this stuff . . . I don't know anything at all . . . I'm going to fail this test . . . I'm probably going to flunk out of school . . . I'm just a dumb nerd." These thoughts share two unfortunate characteristics: they are negative and they are absolute. They should be replaced. When we tell ourselves negative and absolute thoughts, we find it impossible to focus on the test material. The result is that we miss questions even when we know the answers. Our thinking prevents us from doing well.

A good strategy for replacing these negative and absolute thoughts is to practice thinking positive and honest thoughts, such as: "I may not know all the answers, but I know some of them . . . I don't know the answer to that right now, so I will go on to the next one and come back to that . . . I don't have to get them all right . . . I studied hard and carefully, and I can get some of them correct . . . I am a serious student, and have some abilities . . . I am prepared for this test, and know many of the answers . . . This test is important, but it is not going to determine the course of my entire life and if I don't do well, it doesn't mean I'm a horrible person or a dummy."

By thinking clearly, honestly, and positively, we quiet the flood of anxiety and focus on the task at hand. Students who use this technique invariably do better on the tests. It takes practice to think clearly, but it is worth the effort. After a while, you will find that it becomes natural and does not take any noticeable effort. And as anxiety is reduced, more energy is available for studying and for doing well on examinations. The eventual outcome is more enjoyment with learning, better learning, more success in college, and the achievement of your goals.

Strategy Number Four: Guided Imagery

Something I often do with my students before a test is to have them relax (see strategy Two), close their eyes, and visualize themselves walking into a tall building. They go into the elevator in the building and take it to the top floor, which is fifty-six stories up. They walk out of the elevator, and go to the stairwell, then climb to the top of the building. There is no railing on the top of the building. I direct them to walk over to the very edge of the building and put their toes at the very edge, then look down. I ask them to think about how they are feeling as they are looking down onto the street from the top of this building. I then tell them to back up, have the realization that they can fly--just spread out their arms and they can fly. Then they are directed back to the edge of the building, knowing that they can fly. They put their toes on the edge, look down, then spread their arms and fly, eventually flying down to land safely on the ground below. Next I have them visualize themselves in the classroom; on the desk before them is their test. They look at the test and see themselves reading the questions, saying "I know that answer. Yes, I remember learning that." They visualize themselves being successful, answering all the questions correctly, feeling good about themselves. Then I have them visualize getting their tests back, with a big "A" on the test.

Some students are much better able to visualize than others. You can try combining strategy two with this strategy to help you improve your visualization, since it can be an effective success strategy.

Strategy Number Five: Do the Easy Ones First

One technique I learned while studying for the GRE (Graduate Record Exam) was to read each question and answer the ones I knew, then go back to the harder ones. Two things to watch out for on this: first, be sure you get the answers in the right place--sometimes when we skip a question or two, we wind up marking the wrong space, so check that your answer to question 10 is in space 10; second, you may find you're stumped by the first several questions--don't let that throw you, just keep going because there is bound to be one you jump on and say, "Yes! I know that one." Answer the easy ones first, then go back to the others after you've built up your confidence seeing you DO know "stuff." Then, always go back over the whole test to be sure you answered every question (the exception here is if you have a professor who takes more than one point off for wrong answers--in that case, it's better not to answer than to answer wrong, but I don't know anyone who does that).

Strategy Number Six: State Dependent Learning

Research has found that we remember information best when we are in the same "state" we were in when we first learned the information. So, for example, you might remember a certain song when prompted by a specific stimulus (seeing someone who reminds you of your "first true love"); or, we will remember things we learned when we were particularly happy if we are again in that mood. This goes for physical contexts as well--so that we have an advantage if we take an exam in the same room where we learned the information in the first place. But it also goes to physical context in terms of our bodies--if you drink coffee or caffeine-laden sodas when you study, try to do the same before your exam. On the other hand, if you don't consume caffeine when you study, by all means, DO NOT suddenly have a cup of coffee before your exam. Because of the power of this phenomenon, you may want to create a particular mental context for yourself when you study so that you can put yourself into the same mental context when you take your exams.

Strategy Number Seven: Take a Break

If you find yourself getting stressed out during the test, take a break. Put your pencil down, breath deeply, you may even want to put your head down on the desk (please, do not fall asleep!). Use the relaxation techniques or the guided imagery strategy; visualize yourself looking at the test and suddenly realizing that you DO know the answers to at least most of the questions. Then go back to taking the test.

Remember, that with all of these test taking strategies, if you don't do the first one, none of the others will help! Passing the course requires that you actively study the material.

Memory Techniques

No matter how much you read, it won't help you if you don't remember *what* you read. The most critical factor in remembering is being able to apply what you have learned. Of course, some things such as people's names, or certain dates, or statistical information are not easily applied to your life, so you'll have to use other techniques. But first, let's talk about the "easy way."

Apply It To Your Life

If you can take the material you are learning and use it in your everyday life, you will remember it without any problem. Connect it with what you already know, either from life experience or other courses you have taken. Sometimes what you are learning fits nicely with what you already knew; sometimes it will contradict what you learned before. This is an opportunity to look at how the new information fits in with the old--were there new research findings? Or, is it merely a difference of opinion? Make these associations--don't keep the information for any class neatly compartmentalized--if you do, you'll have a hard time trying to find it when you need it.

Teach It to Someone Else!

When we start teaching something to someone else, we find we HAVE TO learn it, and by trying to explain the material to another person, we examine it and think about it differently. So, take the material you are learning in this class (or any class) and teach it to someone else. When they ask you questions, you can look them up and find the answers, or think them out together, or ask someone else. As you explain these concepts to someone else (your children, your friends, or even your dog), you will suddenly see them in a totally different light.

Mnemonic Techniques

Some things are just really difficult to apply to your own life. Dates, names, places, statistics, and such may not have a great deal of meaning for you. In that event, use the tricks that memory specialists use--mnemonics. There are many different types. For example, one famous mnemonic is an acronym for remembering the Great Lakes: HOMES=Huron, Ontario, Michigan, Erie, and Superior; or the colors of the rainbow is a man's name: ROY G. BIV=Red, Orange, Yellow, Green, Blue, Indigo, and Violet (if not for this "man," I'd never remember indigo!) You can make up your own acronyms by taking the first initial of any term, person, etc. It's easiest, though, if it's something that makes sense to you.

Another mnemonic technique is called the "method of loci," and I've been told it's one that medical students use to remember body parts. You list the things you need to remember, then visualize yourself walking around a familiar place (like your living room), putting one item on a particular piece of furniture. Then, when you need to remember that item, you go through your "living room" to see where it is.

One other mnemonic technique is the story method. Take the information you need to remember and put it into a story.

Be an "Information Dropper"

This is similar to the suggestion to teach, but less formal. Ask your friends to "indulge" you by listening to what you learned in your Life Span Development class (or any other class). Then *tell* them what you are learning. You may, in fact, find that you have managed to help one of your friends by sharing this information!

Rote Memory

If you can remember back to grade school, when you learned to multiply, somehow the only way that seems to happen is by repeating the multiplication tables over and over and over again. Personally, I think this is about the worst way to learn most anything, but for some things (like multiplication tables) it works. The Flashcards that are included in each chapter of this Study Guide are a way to help you learn through repeating the material you don't know until you are able to answer the questions posed without looking at the reverse side of the cards. Hopefully you will then go further, and apply the information to other areas of your life.

Most Important

Remember this: professors don't actually "teach" their students, rather, they facilitate learning so students end up teaching themselves. While we try really hard to motivate our students, keep them interested, and present information in a way that helps students to understand, the ultimate responsibility for learning rests with the student. Some students have learned *despite* their professors, others don't learn even with the very best of professors. So, keep your goals in mind, study hard, ask questions, and aim for success!

Further Resources

Making the Grade Student CD-ROM

Packaged for FREE, this user-friendly CD-ROM gives you an opportunity to test your comprehension of the course material in a manner which is most comfortable and beneficial to you. Included are practice tests for each chapter that cover topics in the child development course and an Internet primer.

On-Line Learning Center http://www.mhhe.com/santrockcd9

An expansive resource for students, this site includes:

- Self-assessment quizzes for each chapter
- Study tools, including crossword puzzles
- Links to relevant web sites
- PowerPoint Presentations
- Child Development Image Gallery

Multimedia Courseware for Child Development

Charlotte J. Patterson

This video based 2 CD ROM set covers classic and contemporary experiments in Child Development. Respected researcher Charlotte J. Patterson selected the video and wrote modules that can be assigned to students. The modules also include suggestions for additional projects as well as a testing component. (0-07-234475-X)

For those of you with "Print Disabilities" including blindness, visual impairment, learning disabilities or other physical disabilities, please check out the Recording for the Blind and Dyslexic website at www.rfbd.org/ or call customer service at (800) 221-4792. This educational library has 77,000 taped titles including textbooks, and reference and professional materials for people who cannot read standard print because of a disability.

We Want to Hear from You!

Help us to improve the quality of future supplements. Take a moment to visit our website and share your thoughts as you complete our supplements evaluation form. Your feedback will greatly help us in the future. The form is located at <u>http://www.mhhe.com/developmental</u>

APA Style

For information on APA writing style and guidelines, please refer your students to the American Psychological Association's web site at http://www.apa.org, or link to this site by visiting Santrock's *Child Development* On-Line Learning Center at http://www.mhhe.com/santrockcd9

Using the Internet in Child Development

There are numerous possibilities or ways to use the Internet in Child Development courses. In fact, the shear vastness of available information is often overwhelming for both instructors and students alike. Most of you have some idea about how to search for information available on the Internet, but you need to have the critical thinking skills necessary to discern whether the information you are locating is valid and useful. The following five criteria may be helpful in assisting you with analyzing the appropriateness of information available on the Internet.

1. **Accuracy**
2. **Authority**
3. **Objectivity**
4. **Currency**
5. **Coverage**

You can often struggle with search strategies or become easily frustrated if you cannot locate the type of information you want. There are several excellent tutorials available online which can assist in this process and most libraries have resources designed to help students create more sophisticated searching methodologies. The following sites may provide some assistance:

Tutorial for beginning users:
http://www.lib.berkeley.edu/TeachingLib/Guides/Internet/FindInfo.html

Created by the library staff at Berkeley this is an excellent place for both instructors and students to learn more about using the Internet. The tutorial is divided into two sections with the first providing information about how to access the Internet and use Netscape. The second part of the tutorial discusses how to search for information and includes a comparative chart of the best five search engines, explanations of meta-search tools, and convenient handouts which can be used for class exercises. Also available in the handouts section are Power Point slides and instructor's notes.

Guide to Meta-search engines:

http://www.indiana.edu/~librcsd/search/meta.html

This is a useful description of 13 meta-search engines with links to each and can aid both instructors and students in searching for Internet resources.

SECTION 1: THE NATURE OF CHILD DEVELOPMENT
CHAPTER 1: INTRODUCTION

A. LEARNING OBJECTIVES

Why Study Children?

1. Explain why it is important to study children and child development.

Child Development-Yesterday and Today

2. Explain how philosophies of the original sin view, John Locke's tabula rasa view and Jean-Jacques Rousseau's innate goodness view apply to the understanding of child development.
3. How do the concerns of health, families, education, culture, and ethnicity influence children's development?
4. How does governmental social policy influence children's development?

The Nature of Development

5. Describe the interaction of biological, cognitive, and socioemotional processes on the patterns of change throughout the lifespan.
6. Identify the positions of nature/nurture, continuous/discontinuous, and early/late experiences.

B. TRUE OR FALSE KEY CONTENT QUESTIONS

Why Study Children?

1. T F One reason why it is important to study children and child development is to understand how children change as they grow up and the forces that contribute to this change.

Child Development—Yesterday and Today

2. T F Demographic trends indicate an increasing ethnic diversity in the United States.
3. T F Before the 18th Century childhood was seen as an inconvenient "waiting" period during which adults suffered the incompetencies of the young.
4. T F During the past century, the study of child development evolved from a philosophical and psychological perspective to a direct observation and experimentation perspective.
5. T F The ultimate responsibility for the health and well-being of our children rests with physicians.
6. T F Despite its size, the culture of a country influences the identity, learning and social behavior of its members.

The Nature of Development

7. T F Biological, cognitive, and creative processes are interwoven as a child develops.
8. T F The nature/nurture controversy is a debate about whether development is primarily influenced by maturation or by experience.
9. T F The continuity of development view is that development involves gradual, cumulative change.
10. T F The discontinuity of development view is that development involves distinct stages in the life span.

11. T F The early-later experience issue focuses on when experiences determine a child's development.

12. T F Most developmentalists recognize the wisdom of taking extreme positions on what influences development.

Careers in Child Development

13. T F Careers in child development are diverse but usually do not require extensive education.

C. FILL IN THE BLANK KEY TERMS

1. Sociocultural contexts of development encompass the three concepts of contexts, culture, and ________.

2. Historical, economic, social, and cultural legacies all influence the _________ of an individual's development.

3. A sense of membership in an ethnic group, based on shared language, religion, customs, values, history and race is called __________.

4. Sex refers to the _________ dimension of being male or female, whereas _________ refers to the sociocultural aspect of being female or male.

5. Children were treated as miniature adults with no special status prior to ______ .

6. Development is the product of biological, cognitive, and _______ processes.

7. The five major periods of child development include _________, infancy, early childhood, middle and late childhood, and adolescence.

8. _________ is the sequence of changes that result from the genetic blueprint.

9. Those who contend that development is a gradual process emphasize the _________ of development, whereas proponents of ________assert that development entails a series of distinct stages.

10. The __________experience doctrine argues that infant experience is the key determinant of development.

D. MATCHING KEY PEOPLE QUESTIONS

___ 1. The president of *Children's Defense Fund* who advocates actively on the behalf of children.

___ 2. The individual who proposed an enlightened view of the nature of children and their rearing.

___ 3. The African-American who became president of the American Psychological Association.

___ 4. The developmental researcher who devised the photographic dome to study children unobtrusively.

___ 5. Researcher who observed the environmental and behavioral influence on children's behavior.

___ 6. Swiss psychologist famous for identifying cognitive stages from infancy through adolescence.

___ 7. This psychiatrist stressed that a child's experience with parents in the first five years of life is important determinants in later personality development.

___ 8. French psychologist who studied attention and memory in the early 1900s.

A. Kenneth Clark

B. John Watson

C. Sigmund Freud

D. Alfred Binet

E. Jean-Jacques Rousseau

F. Marian Wright Edelman

G. Jean Piaget

H. Arnold Gesell

I. Jerome Kagan

J. John Locke

K. Philippe Aries

E. MULTIPLE CHOICE KNOWLEDGE QUESTIONS

1. The goal of crosscultural research is to determine

    a. how socioeconomic status affect child development.

    b. the universal aspects of child development.

    c. how a culture changes across time.

    d. how human beings grow and develop.

2. Philippe Aries's review of art and publications during the Middle Ages led him to conclude that

    a. infancy was accepted as a distinctive period of life by Europeans as early as the Middle Ages.

    b. childhood was not recognized as a distinctive period by Europeans prior to the 1600s.

    c. adolescence was the focus of much early literature and art throughout the world.

    d. early literature recognized several distinct developmental periods.

3. The current view of childhood assumes that

    a. children are similar to adults in most ways.

    b. children are best treated as young adults.

    c. childhood is basically a "waiting period."

    d. childhood is a unique period of growth and change.

4. According to Marian Wright Edelman, the social policy of the United States shows that

    a. our beliefs and policies both reflect "family values."

    b. our beliefs and our policies have little to do with "family values."

    c. our beliefs, but not our policies reflect "family values."

    d. our policies, but not our beliefs reflect "family values."

5. Proponents of the nurture view would argue that

   a. the environment a person is raised in determines his or her longevity

   b. genetics determines all behavior.

   c. how long an individual's parents lived is the best predictor of his or her longevity.

   d. genetics and the environment an individual is raised in combine to determine longevity.

6. If the results of a study of cognitive development indicated that the change from concrete thinking to abstract thinking occur abruptly, which of the following views has been supported?

   a. continuity

   b. stability

   c. discontinuity

   d dialectical

7. The question, "Will the shy child who never speaks turn into a quiet, shy adult or will the child become a sociable, talkative person?" is concerned with which developmental issue?

   a. maturation and experience

   b. continuity and discontinuity

   c. early and later experience

   d. nature and nurture

8. Most psychologists believe that development is due

   a. largely to nature

   b. largely to nurture.

   c. to nature and nurture acting separately.

   d. to an interaction of nature and nurture.

9. The most commonly shared element among careers in child development is

   a. working with disturbed youth

   b. training beyond the undergraduate level

   c. teaching children.

   d. doing research both to prepare for a career and to continue as a professional in the field.

10. Parenting is an important profession, yet many parents have significant shortcomings in that they

   a. do not value having children grow into socially mature individuals.

   b. are unsure about how they can help their children develop well.

   c. depend too much on the advice of experts.

   d. put their own goals ahead of the needs of their children.

F. CRITICAL THINKING QUESTIONS

1. Explain why it is important to study children and child development?

2. Define culture. How does cultural development influence a group of people?

3. Compare and contrast the early experience doctrine with the later experience doctrine of child development. Which doctrine would you advocate? Why?

4. How do prevention programs and competency training increase a child's resilience?

G. APPLICATION QUESTIONS

Explain these themes of child growth and development as they apply to one or more of the following question(s) below:

- *the nature/nurture controversy*
- *the continuity/discontinuity controversy*
- *the early/late experience controversy*

1. What psychological or social traits characterize the "ideal" person you would like to marry?

2. What psychological or social traits characterize the "ideal" child?

3. What psychological or social traits characterize would you like to see all adults achieve in order to have a successful culture/civilization?

H. COGNITIVE MAPS

INTRODUCTION

Why Study Children?

- Children are society's future
- Gain understanding of self and others
- Prepare for career and/or parenting
- Influence Education/schools to be more effective

Child Development – Today and Yesterday

Historical Views of Childhood

- Children viewed as miniature adults

KEY PERSON
(1)____________________
- Original sin view
- Tabula rose view

KEY PERSON
(2)____________________
- Innate

(3)____________________
Jean-Jacques Rousseau

The Modern Study of Child Development

- Maturational Theory, Observation strategies

KEY PERSON
(4)____________________
- Questionnaires

KEY PERSON
(5)____________________
- Evolutionary Theory, journals

Charles Darwin
- Psychosexual stages, unconscious mind

KEY PERSON
(6)____________________
- (7)__________________ Theory

John Watson
- Genetic (8)__________________

James Mark Baldwin
- Cognitive development stages

KEY PERSON
(9)____________________
- Summarizes the field of developmental psychology

KEY PERSON
(10)____________________

Today's Children: Some Contemporary Concerns

- Health and well being
- Families and parenting
- Education
- Context, culture/cross cultural studies, and ethnicity/ethnic identity

KEY PERSON
(11)____________________

Social Policy and Children's Development

- Social Policy

KEY PERSON
(12)____________________
Resilient Children

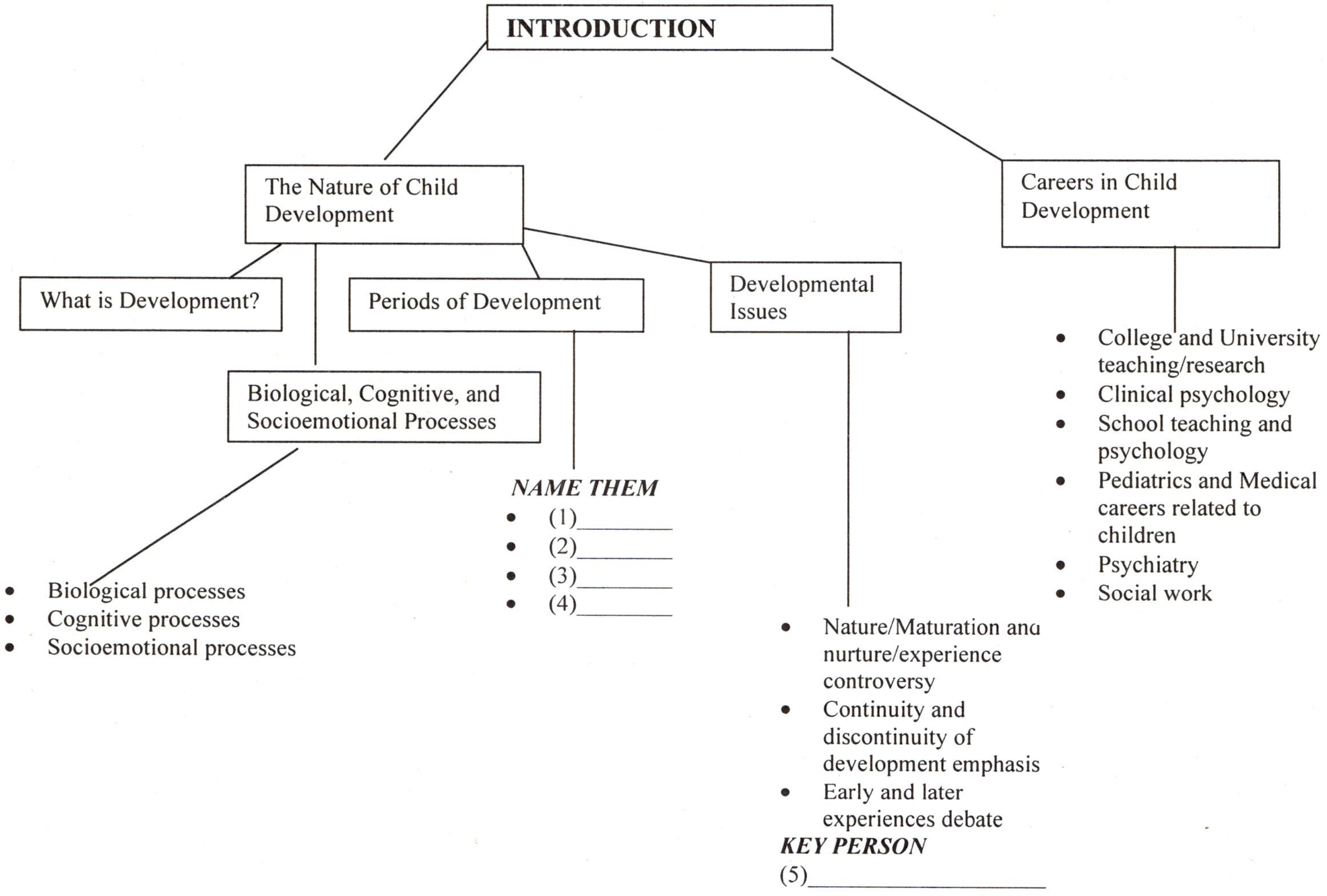
INTRODUCTION
The Nature of Child Development
Careers in Child Development
What is Development?
Periods of Development
Developmental Issues
Biological, Cognitive, and Socioemotional Processes
• Biological processes
• Cognitive processes
• Socioemotional processes
NAME THEM
• (1)________
• (2)________
• (3)________
• (4)________
• Nature/Maturation and nurture/experience controversy
• Continuity and discontinuity of development emphasis
• Early and later experiences debate
KEY PERSON
(5)____________________
• College and University teaching/research
• Clinical psychology
• School teaching and psychology
• Pediatrics and Medical careers related to children
• Psychiatry
• Social work

I. REVIEW PRIORITIES

Assess your present understanding of the material in this chapter by rating yourself for each heading using the following scale:

1 – I thoroughly understand material and its context to other sections.

2 – I understand most of the material and have a basic grasp of the context to other sections.

3 – I have a shaky understanding of the material and a poor grasp of the context.

4 – I have an inadequate understanding of the material.

Why Study Children? ____

Child Development-Yesterday and Today

- Historical Views of Childhood ____
- The Modern Study of Child Development ____
- Today's Children: Some Contemporary Concerns ____
- Social Policy and Children's Development ____

The Nature of Development

- Biological, Cognitive, and Socioemotional processes ____
- Periods of Development ____
- Developmental Issues ____

Careers in Child Development ____

ANSWER KEY

B. TRUE OR FALSE KEY CONTENT QUESTIONS

1. T
2. T
3. T
4. T
5. F
6. T
7. F
8. T
9. T
10. T
11. T
12. F
13. F

C. FILL IN THE BLANK KEY TERMS

1. ethnicity
2. cultural context
3. ethnic identity
4. gender; biological
5. 1600
6. socioemotional
7. prenatal period
8. maturation
9. continuity; discontinuity
10. early

D. MATCHING KEY PEOPLE QUESTIONS

1. F
2. E
3. A
4. H
5. B
6. G
7. C
8. D

E. MULTIPLE CHOICE KNOWLEDGE QUESTIONS

1. b
2. b
3. d
4. c
5. a
6. c
7. c
8. d
9. b
10. b

F. CRITICAL THINKING QUESTIONS

1.

- Responsibility for children is a collective responsibility
- Childhood lays an important foundation for the adult years'
- Childhood has distinct periods where children master skills
- Children need to be protected from the excesses of the adult world

2.

- Culture refers to the behavior patterns, beliefs, and other products of a particular group of people that are passed on from generation to generation.
- Cultural products are the result of the interaction between people and their environment
- A cultural group can be large (e.g., the United States) or small (e.g., African tribe)
- A cultural group influences the social behavior of its members

3.

- The early experience doctrine suggests that prime learning and cognitive development occur in the first few years of life. If the infant does not experience warm, nurturing care during these years later development will be diminished.
- The later experience doctrine suggests that entire life-span development is more important than a rigid identification to one period. Later sensitive care-giving is just as important as earlier sensitive care-giving.

4.

- The literature on resiliency indicates that a combination of individual, family and extrafamilial factors improve resiliency in children. Successful prevention programs promote specific skill-building in children. Improving a child's competence in problem-solving, assertiveness, self-control, and decision-making can help reduce aggressive behavior and improve social interaction.

H. COGNITIVE MAPS

A.

1. Philippe Aries
2. John Locke
3. goodness view
4. Arnold Gesell
5. G. Stanley Hall
6. Sigmund Freud
7. Behaviorist
8. epistemology
9. Jean Piaget
10. Robert Cairns
11. Ligdern Kagiteibasi
12. Marian Wright Edelman

B.

1. Prenatal period
2. Infancy
3. Early childhood
4. Middle and late childhood
5. Jerome Kagan

CHAPTER 2: THE SCIENCE OF CHILD DEVELOPMENT

A. LEARNING OBJECTIVES

Why Research on Child Development is Important

1. Why is it important to be objective when examining research on child development?

Theories of Child Development

2. Define theory, hypothesis, and the scientific method.

Research Methods

3. Compare and contrast research conducted in a laboratory with naturalistic observation.

Research Challenges

4. Why is it important to be cautious about studies reported in the media?
5. Name some ethical concerns when conducting child development research.
6. Why is it important to have multiple studies about child development topics?

B. TRUE OR FALSE KEY CONTENT QUESTIONS

Why Research on Child Development is Important

1. T F Science is defined not by how it investigates, but by what it investigates.
2. T F Scientific research is objective, systematic, and testable.

Theories of Child Development

3. T F Sigmund Freud's personality structure is characterized by id, ego, and shame.
4. T F Erik Erikson's is based on eight stages of psychosocial development that confronts individuals with a crisis that must be addressed.
5. T F Jean Piaget's four-stage cognitive development theory asserts that mental development is a continuous creation of increasingly complex forms.
6. T F Lev Vygotsky's contribution to cognitive theory claims that cognitive skill development is separate from language development and sociocultural activities.
7. T F An unconditioned response (UR) is a learned response, which is nonautomatic.
8. T F Phobias are irrational fears.
9. T F B. F. Skinner's operant conditioning is based on how consequences influence behavior.
10. T F Social cognitive theorists believe that children acquire behaviors, thoughts, and feelings through observing others' behavior.
11. T F Imprinting refers to the unique characteristic of an individual's fingerprints.
12. T F Ecological theory supports the view that multiple environments such as family peer, and school give a more complete picture of an individual's development.

Research Methods

13. T F Of the theories discussed in the first part of the chapter, psychoanalytic theory is least likely to advocate the use of case studies.

14. T F The goal of correlational research is to describe how strongly two events are related or associated.

15. T F The goal of experimental research is to determine the cause of behavior through carefully controlled experiments.

16. T F Longitudinal research involves studying the same individuals over a long period of time, usually several years or more.

17. T F The abstract is the results of the data that appears at the end of a research journal article.

Research Challenges

18. T F The code of ethics adopted by the American Psychological Association (APA) protects researchers from legal harassment from participants.

19. T F It is difficult to over generalize using a small clinical sample size.

20. T F It is permissible to make claims about group needs based on individual research.

C. FILL IN THE BLANK KEY TERMS

1. According to Freud, individuals go through five stages of ____________development.
2. Resolving each of the previous psychosocial ___________ in a positive way results in satisfaction with life and defines the eight stages of Erickson's theory. If one or more of the previous crisis has been resolved in a negative way, __________ may result.
3. Jean Piaget says that children __________ their own cognitive worlds.
4. A _________ is an automatic stimulus-response connection.

5. Phobias can be produced by the process of _________ conditioning, and eliminated by the process of ___________ conditioning.

6. Behaviorists say that a consequence that increases the probability of a response is called ______, and a consequence that decreases the probability of a response is called _____.

7. The social learning approach has underscored the importance of _______ processes, and the role of ________in controlling their own behavior.

8. The ethological view emphasizes the biological basis of behavior and careful _________in natural settings.

9. An in-depth look at an individual, a _________, provides historical information about a person's emotional concerns or difficulties, childhood experiences, and family relations.

10. Cross-cultural research helps us determine to what extent aspects of development are _______ across cultures, or __________ to a particular culture.

11. _________ strategies allow investigators to predict a second variable given information about a first variable.

12. The advantage of the _______ strategy over the correlational strategy is that it can demonstrate a __________ relationship between two variables.

13. In an experiment, researchers manipulate the ________ variable, and measure the its effect on the _________ variable.

14. __________ assignment to conditions assures that experimental groups do not differ in any systematic way.

15. If researchers want to employ children in their research, they must obtain _________ from both the parents or legal guardians, and explain what the children themselves will ______.

16. Media presentations may be misleading because the ___________ conclusions cannot be drawn from correlational research.

D. MATCHING KEY PEOPLE QUESTIONS

___ 1. The psychoanalysist who asserted that repression, caused by unconscious and threatening impulses, is the most powerful defense mechanism.

___ 2. The individual who argued that more children from ethnic minority backgrounds needs to be included in research.

___ 3. The originator of an environmental, contextual theory of development that includes five environmental systems.

___ 4. One of the two individuals whose behavioral theory emphasizes the roles of behavior, cognition, and environment in development.

___ 5. A psychoanalytic theorist who proposed that development entails eight psychosocial stages.

___ 6. The Russian physiologist who developed the concept and procedure of classical conditioning.

___ 7. The individual who proposed life course theory.

___ 8. The proponent of a cognitive theory of development that entails four qualitatively different stages.

A. Erik Erikson

B. Keith Stanovich

C. Sigmund Freud

D. Urie Bronfenbrenner

E. Lev Vygotsky

F. Konrad Lorenz

G. Jean Piaget

H. Ivan Pavlov

I. Glen Elder, Jr.

J. B. F. Skinner

K. Albert Bandura

L. Sandra Graham

E. MULTIPLE CHOICE KNOWLEDGE QUESTIONS

1. Developing a study schedule is a function of the

   a. id.

   b. ego.

   c. superego.

   d. ego-ideal.

2. Erik Erikson's theory emphasized

   a. repeated resolutions of unconscious conflicts about sexual energy.

   b. success in confronting specific conflicts at particular ages in life.

   c. changes in children's thinking as they matured.

   d. the influence of sensitive periods in the various stages of biological maturation.

3. When four-year-old Amadeus hears a concerto on the radio, he begins to move his hands up and down in a motion that resembles a person playing the piano. Amadeus's behavior examplifies Piaget's

   a. sensorimotor stage.

   b. preoperational stage.

   c. concrete thinking stage.

   d. formal operational stage.

4. One of the strong points of behavior theory is its

   a. belief that cognitive processes are irrelevant for understanding development.

   b. emphasis on the relationship between environmental stimuli and children's behavior.

   c. emphasis on reducing children's behavior to fine-grained elements.

   d. emphasis on the role of information processing as a mediator between behavior and environment.

5. If you want to increase the number of times your spouse does the dishes, B. F. Skinner would tell you to

   a. yell at your spouse when he or she does not do the dishes.

   b. kiss your spouse when he or she does the dishes.

   c. leave the sink full of dishes until your spouse does them.

   d. ask your spouse nicely to do the dishes.

6. The frequent finding that adults who abuse their children typically come from families in which they themselves were abused supports which theory of child development?

   a. Freudian psychoanalytic theory

   b. information processing theory

   c. ecological theory

   d. social learning theory

7. Barbara insists that to assure bonding she must be conscious and have an opportunity to see and hold her baby immediately after its delivery. Which of the following theories would agree with Barbara?

   a. ethological theory

   b. humanistic theory

   c. psychoanalytic theory

   d. learning theory

8. A major strength of ecological theory is its framework for explaining

   a. environmental influences on development.

   b. biological influences on development.

   c. cognitive development.

   d. affective processes in development.

9. How is a questionnaire study different from one that uses interviews?

   a. Questionnaires usually involve in-depth probing into the details of a person's life.

   b. Interviews may be carried out over the phone, while questionnaires are always completed with the researcher present.

   c. Questionnaires ask respondents to indicate their answers on paper instead of answering orally.

   d. Interviews are the preferred method for cross-cultural research.

10. Florence Denmark recommends reducing sexism in developmental research by

   a. not drawing conclusions from correlational strategies.

   b. selecting participants in a way that allows for appropriate generalizations.

   c. requiring participants to sign informed consent sheets.

   d. publishing exclusively in professional journals.

F. CRITICAL THINKING QUESTIONS

1. What are the strengths and weaknesses of these theories: psychoanalytic, cognitive, behavioral/social learning, ethological, and ecological.

2. Compare and contrast research conducted in the laboratory with naturalistic observation.

3. Why do researchers use random assignment in experimental research?

4. Explain how gender bias may have influenced research on female achievement in math.

G. APPLICATION QUESTIONS

The continuum of approaches in disciplining children spans from authoritarian to permissive. Alternatives between these extremes are often controversial. Research suggests that children who have the opportunity for choice and self-direction in the preschool years are better able to make wise choices as adolescents.

1. Describe what effective discipline means to you?

2. Which of the theories reviewed in this chapter support your beliefs?

H. COGNITIVE MAPS

THE SCIENCE OF CHILD DEVELOPMENT

Why Research on Child Development is Important

- Information from personal experiences isn't always (1)_______
- Research evaluates the (2)_________ of information

The Scientific Research Approach

PLEASE LIST:

(3)____________________

(4)____________________

(5)____________________

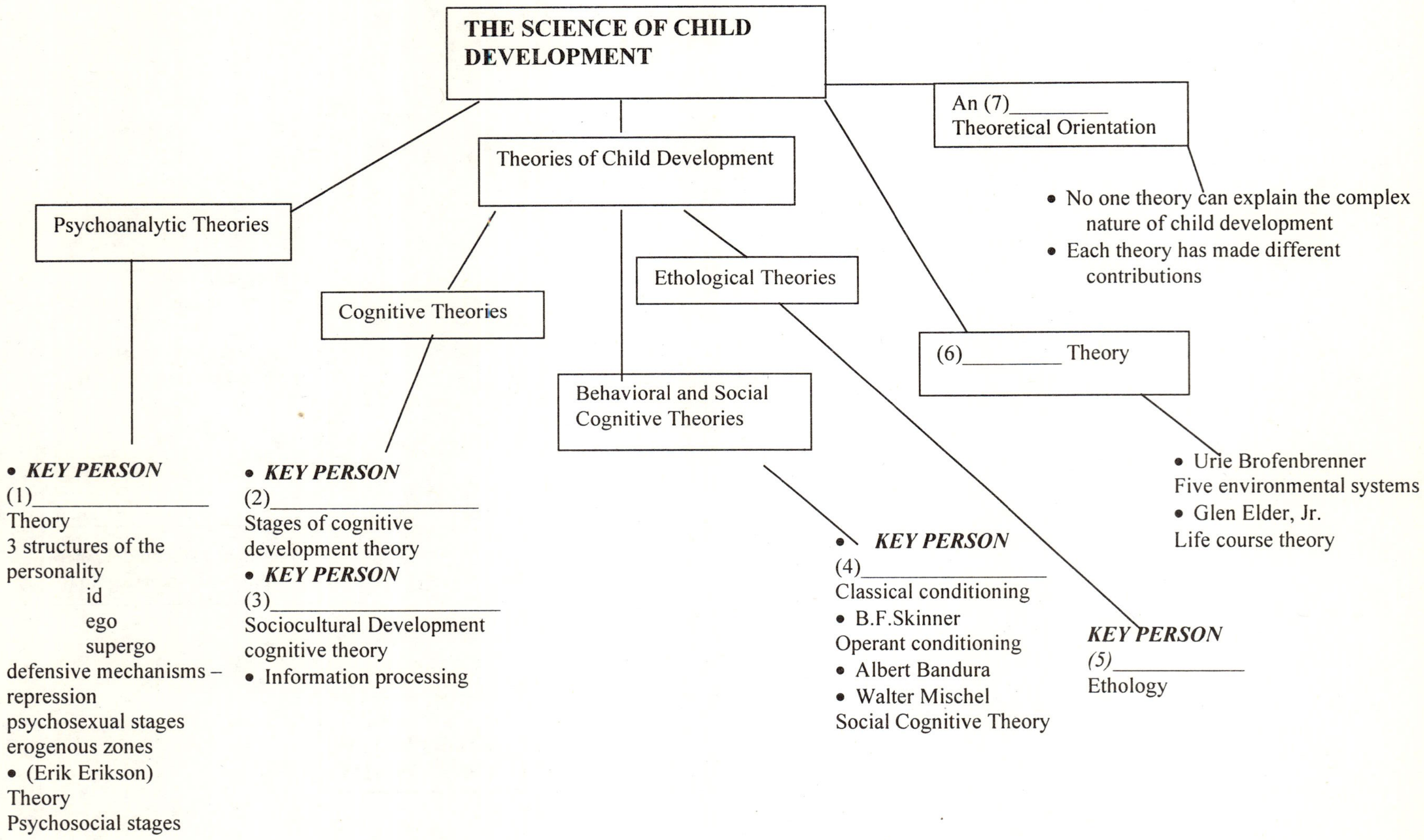
THE SCIENCE OF CHILD DEVELOPMENT
Psychoanalytic Theories
Theories of Child Development
Cognitive Theories
Ethological Theories
Behavioral and Social Cognitive Theories
An (7)________ Theoretical Orientation
• No one theory can explain the complex nature of child development
• Each theory has made different contributions
(6)________ Theory
• Urie Brofenbrenner
Five environmental systems
• Glen Elder, Jr.
Life course theory
• KEY PERSON
(1)________________
Theory
3 structures of the personality
id
ego
supergo
defensive mechanisms – repression
psychosexual stages
erogenous zones
• (Erik Erikson)
Theory
Psychosocial stages
• KEY PERSON
(2)__________________
Stages of cognitive development theory
• KEY PERSON
(3)____________________
Sociocultural Development cognitive theory
• Information processing
• KEY PERSON
(4)________________
Classical conditioning
• B.F.Skinner
Operant conditioning
• Albert Bandura
• Walter Mischel
Social Cognitive Theory
KEY PERSON
(5)___________
Ethology

THE SCIENCE OF CHILD DEVELOPMENT

Research Methods

Observation

- Highly _(1)_________
- Laboratory and naturalistic observations

Interviews and Questionnaires

- Interviews are usually face-to-face
- Questionnaires/surveys usually in (2)_______ form
- Limitation is that individuals give (3)_______ answers rather than the (4)________

Standardized Tests

- Measures (5)_________/-(6)____________

Case Studies

- In depth look at an individual
- Limitation is the in-depth portrayal of an individual cannot be generalized

Correlational Research

- Describes the relation between (7)_____or (8)_______ characteristics
- Correlation does not equal (9)___________

Experimental Research

- Determines cause and effect
- Dependable variable
- Independent variable
- Random assignment

Time Span of Research

- 2 approaches:
(10)_______________
(11)_______________

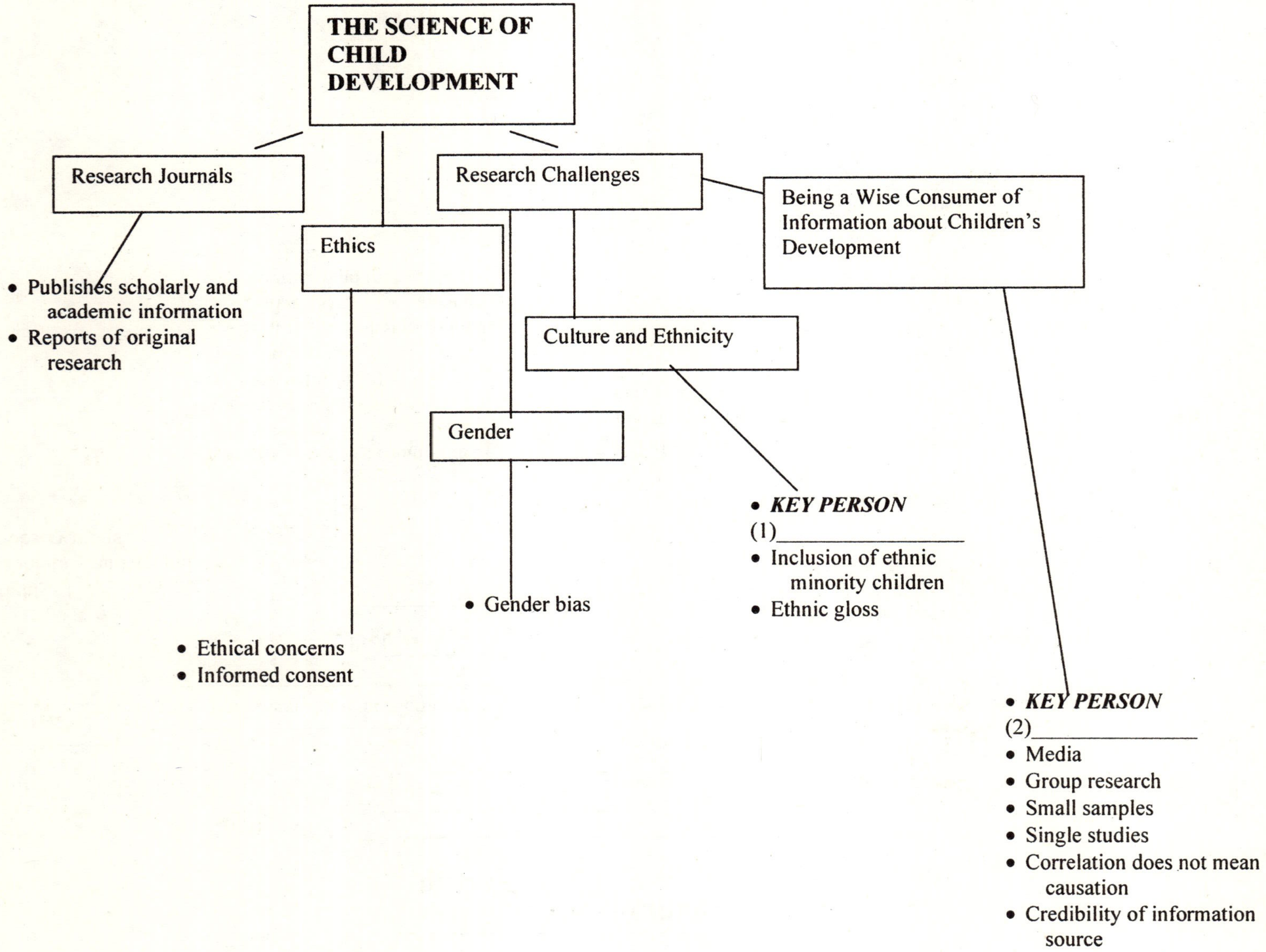

THE SCIENCE OF CHILD DEVELOPMENT
Research Journals
Publishes scholarly and academic information
Reports of original research
Ethics
Ethical concerns
Informed consent
Research Challenges
Gender
Gender bias
Culture and Ethnicity
KEY PERSON
(1)________________
Inclusion of ethnic minority children
Ethnic gloss
Being a Wise Consumer of Information about Children's Development
KEY PERSON
(2)______________
Media
Group research
Small samples
Single studies
Correlation does not mean causation
Credibility of information source

I. REVIEW PRIORITIES

Assess your present understanding of the material in this chapter by rating yourself for each heading using the following scale:

1 – I thoroughly understand material and its context to other sections

2 –I understand most of the material and have a basic grasp of the context to other sections

3 –I have a shaky understanding of the material and a poor grasp of the context

4 –I have an inadequate understanding of the material

Why Research on Child Development is Important _____

The Scientific Research Approach

- Theories of Child Development _____
- Psychoanalytic Theories _____
- Cognitive Theories _____
- Behavioral and Social Cognitive Theories _____
- Ethological Theories _____
- Ecological Theories _____
- Eclectic Theories _____

Research Methods

- Observation _____
- Interviews and Questionnaires _____
- Standardized Tests _____
- Case Studies _____

- Correlational Research _____
- Experimental Research _____
- Time Span Research _____

Research Challenges

- Ethics _____
- Gender _____
- Culture and Ethnicity _____
- Being a Wise Consumer _____

ANSWER KEY

B. TRUE OR FALSE KEY CONTENT QUESTIONS

1. F
2. T
3. F
4. T
5. T
6. F
7. F
8. T
9. T
10. T
11. F
12. T
13. F
14. T
15. T
16. T
17. F
18. F
19. F
20. F

C. FILL IN THE BLANK KEY TERMS

1. psychosexual
2. crises; despair
3. construct
4. reflex
5. classical; counter
6. reinforcement; punishment
7. cognitive; individuals
8. observation
9. case study
10. universal; specific
11. Correlational
12. experimental; causal
13. independent; dependent
14. Random
15. consent; experience
16. causal

D. MATCHING KEY PEOPLE QUESTIONS

1. C
2. L
3. D
4. K
5. A
6. H
7. I
8. G

E. MULTIPLE CHOICE KNOWLEDGE QUESTIONS

1. B
2. B
3. B
4. B
5. B
6. D
7. A
8. A
9. C
10. B

F. CRITICAL THINKING QUESTIONS

1.

	Strengths	Weaknesses
psychoanalytic	early, unconscious experiences emphasis	cognition hardly emphasized
cognitive & environment emphasis	interaction, adaptation,	little emphasis on information processing
behavioral/social learning	environment viewed as cause of behavior	little emphasis on cognition
ethological	biology viewed as cause of behavior	little emphasis on cognition
ecological	environmental systems & sociohistorical emphasis	little emphasis on cognition & biology

2.

- Laboratory studies allow researchers more control over the behavior of participants. This allows for more systematic observation. However, laboratory studies are criticized as being artificial. Naturalistic observation happens in real world settings, such as classrooms, homes, museums, malls, etc. It is very difficult to control for extraneous variables in such settings. Also, the unpredictability of interactions cannot be isolated.

3.

- Random assignment involves putting participants with similar attributes (age, family background, intelligence, socioeconomic factors, etc.) in experimental and control groups by chance alone. Random assignment greatly reduces the probability that the two groups will differ. This allows researchers to have more confidence about interpreting the effect or intervention given to the experimental group.

4.

- Effort needs to be made to make research equitable for both males and females
- In the past, research was often biased against females

H. COGNITIVE MAPS

A.

1. objective
2. accuracy
3. Scientific method
4. Theory
5. Hypothesis

B.

1. Sigmund Freud
2. Jean Piaget
3. Lev Vgotsky
4. Ivan Pavlov
5. Konrad Lorenz
6. Ecological
7. Eclectic

C.

1. systematic
2. print
3. desirable
4. truth
5. outcome
6. performance
7. two
8. more
9. causation
10. Cross-sectional approach
11. Longitudinal approach

D.

1. Sandra Graham
2. Keith Stanovich

SECTION 2: BIOLOGICAL PROCESSES, PHYSICAL DEVELOPMENT AND PERCEPTUAL DEVELOPMENT

CHAPTER 3: BIOLOGICAL BEGINNINGS

A. LEARNING OBJECTIVES

Evolutionary Perspective

1. Define and give examples of natural selection.
2. Define and give examples of adaptive behavior.

Heredity and Reproduction

3. Explain how *in vitro* fertilization is a remedy for infertility.
4. Describe the method to determine abnormalities for *amniocentesis*, *ultrasound sonography*, and the *chorionic villus* test.

Genetic Principles and Methods

5. State the dominant-recessive principle.

Heredity-Environment Interaction

6. Define and distinguish between fraternal twins and identical twins.

B. *TRUE OR FALSE KEY CONTENT QUESTIONS*

Evolutionary Perspective

1. T F Natural selection favors individuals that are best adapted to survive and reproduce.
2. T F Evolutionary psychology emphasizes the importance of adaptation, reproduction, and "survival of the fittest" in explaining behavior.

Heredity and Reproduction

3. T F The nucleus of each human cell contains 42 chromosomes, which come in 21 pairs, one from each parent.
4. T F Mitosis is the process by which cells divide into gamates for cell growth and repair.
5. T F Reproduction begins when a female gamete (ovum) is fertilized by a male gamete (sperm) to produce a zygote.
6. T F Zygote intrafallopian transfer is a process in which an egg and a sperm are combined in a laboratory dish.
7. T F Researchers have found that adopted children and adolescents often show more psychological and school-related problems than non-adopted children.
8. T F In the United States over 100,000 infants, about 3 percent, are born each year with a genetic disorder or malformation.
9. T F The Human Genome Project is the construction of a map of each human gene.
10. T F Chorionic villa sampling is a prenatal test during the last trimester to detect for birth defects.

Genetic Principles and Methods

11. T F If one gene of a pair is dominant and one is recessive the dominant gene overrides a recessive gene.
12. T F Canalization describes the study of hereditary influence on development.

13. T F Fraternal twins develop from a single fertilized egg that splits into two genetically replicas.

14. T F In 1971, the U.S. Supreme Court ruled that IQ tests are discriminatory and cannot be administered as a condition of employment.

Heredity-Environment Interaction

15. T F Niche-picking refers to finding a niche or setting suited to one's compatibility, such as attractive adolescents seeking out attractive peers.

16. T F Nonshared environmental experiences is likely to be the reason one sibling's personality is different from another's.

C. FILL IN THE BLANK KEY TERMS

1. Darwin reasoned that the individuals who survived were best ___________ to their environments, and passed their _________ on to the next generation.
2. ____________ are human reproductive cells that are created in the testes of males and the ovaries of females.
3. The union of an ovum and a sperm cell produces a _____________ through the process of reproduction.
4. Compared to non-adopted children, adopted children experience ____________ problems.
5. A genetic disorder resulting in a problem with red blood cell formation is called sickle-cell _________.
6. ____________ syndrome results from an extra X chromosome in males.
7. ____________ syndrome can cause retardation in women, and is due to the absence of an X chromosome.
8. ____________ syndrome presumably is related to excessive male aggression.
9. Although two brown-eyed parents can have a blue-eyed child, two blue-eyed parents cannot have a brown-eyed child. This outcome means that the gene for brown eyes is __________ and the gene for blue eyes is _____________.

10. _________ refers to an individual's actual heredity constitution, whereas __________ refers to the observable and measurable characteristics of an individual.

D. MATCHING KEY PEOPLE QUESTIONS

___ 1. A behavior geneticist who believes that parental genotypes influence the environments that they provide for their offspring.

___ 2. The individual who proposed the principle of natural selection.

___ 3. The individual who argues that intelligence is largely determined by heredity.

___ 4. The individual who directs the Minnesota Study of Twins Reared Apart Project.

___ 5. An evolutionary psychologist who believes that behavior needs input from psychological mechanisms.

___ 6. A behavior geneticist who believes that shared environments account for little of the variation in children's interests and personality.

___ 7. Author of the book *The Nature Assumption*, which asserts that an individual's genetic imprint is more important to development than the influence of parents and peers.

___ 8. A Russian American who asserts that the human species is selected for learn ability, which allows us to be flexible and adaptable.

A. Thomas Bouchard

B. Judith Harris

C. Charles Darwin

D. Robert Plomin

E. David Buss

F. Arthur Jensen

G. Theodore Dobzhansky

H. Sandra Scarr

I. William Greenough

J. Jerome Kagan

K. T. Berry Brazelton

E. MULTIPLE CHOICE KNOWLEDGE QUESTIONS

1. If heredity is an important determinant of a specific behavior, what prediction can we make about expression of the behavior in identical twins reared apart compared to its expression in fraternal twins reared apart?

   a. Fraternal twins will express the behavior more similarly than identical twins.

   b. There will be little similarity in the expression of the behavior in either set of twins.

   c. Identical twins will express the behavior more similarly than fraternal twins.

   d. The behavior will be expressed as similarly by identical twins as it is by fraternal twins.

2. The process of cell division in which each pair of chromosomes separates and joins a daughter cell is called

   a. reproduction.

   b. mitosis.

   c. meiosis.

   d. gametization.

2. *In vitro* fertilization is a possible solution to infertility that involves

   a having sperm and egg unite outside of a woman's body.

   b implanting a fertilized egg into a substitute mother's womb.

   c enhancing the possibility of conception by taking fertility drugs.

   d incubating a zygote outside of a woman's body.

4. A physician orders that an amniocentesis be performed to determine whether a woman's fetus is genetically normal. This procedure will involve

    a. taking a blood sample from the mother.

    b. drawing a sample of the fluid that surrounds a baby in the womb.

    c. taking a sample of the placenta between the eighth and eleventh week of pregnancy.

    d. taking a blood sample from the fetus.

5. Assume that the gene for green hair is dominant, whereas the gene for blue hair is recessive. Which of the following statements is most accurate?

    a. Parents with green hair can have a child with blue hair.

    b. Parents with blue hair can have a child with green hair.

    c. Parents with blue hair cannot have a child with blue hair.

    d. Parents with green hair cannot have a child with green hair.

6. A person's genetic heritage is his or her __________, whereas the expression of the genetic heritage is his or her _____________.

    a. genotype; phenotype

    b. dominant character; recessive character

    c. phenotype; genotype

    d. recessive character; dominant character

7. In an adoption study, a psychologist compares the behavior of

    a. identical fraternal twins.

    b. family members and randomly selected others.

    c. fraternal twins with each other.

    d. children living with adoptive parents and children living with biological parents.

8. Children who are highly active, easily distractable, and move very fast frequently elicit adult attempts to quiet them down, punishment for lack of concentration, and angry warnings to slow down. This describes an example of a/an ___________/environment interaction.

a. passive genotype

b. active genotype

c. niche-picking genotype

d. evocative genotype

9. All three of the Brodsky children grew up in the same house, went to the same school, and observed their parents' dedication to charitable work. These expectations constitute the children's

a. shared environmental influences.

b. non-shared environmental influences.

c. niche-picking experiences.

d. heritability.

10. The key difference between evolutionary and cultural change is that evolutionary change alters __________, whereas cultural change alters ___________.

a. reproduction; environment

b. heredity; environment

c. environment; behavior

d. development; learning

F. CRITICAL THINKING QUESTIONS

1. What are some psychological consequences for families receiving fertility treatments?

2. Explain why genotypes drive experience.

3. Why does Arthur Jensen favor nature over nurture as an explanation of intelligence?

G. APPLICATION QUESTIONS

Although the initial number of neurons (nerve cells) a child possesses is genetically determined, it is just the beginning of more neurons and synapses (connections) that are produced after birth. At this time, the environmental factors become critically important.

1. How does interaction with the infant by the parent(s) strengthen the synapses?

2. What might happen to brain development to a child raised in a stressful, unpredictable, or violent environment?

H. COGNITIVE MAPS

BIOLOGICAL BEGINNINGS

The Evolutionary Perspective

Natural Selection & Adaptive Behavior

KEY PERSON

- (1)________________
- Species that are best adapted to survive
- Behavior that promotes the organisms survival

Evolutionary Psychology

KEY PERSON

- (2)________________
- Adaptation, reproduction, and "survival of the fittest"
- Bidirectional/Interactions

BIOLOGICAL BEGINNINGS

Heredity and Reproduction

What are Genes?

- Chromosomes
- DNA
- Genes
- Mitosis

Reproduction

- Meiosis
- Gene transmission by (1)____________
- Zygote formed through (2)____________
- Infertility

Adoption

- Adjustment difficulties
- Age of children

Abnormalities in Genes and Chromosomes

- Defects – phyenylketonuria (PKU), down syndrome, sickle-cell anemia, klinefelter syndrome, fragile Xsyndrome, and XYY syndrome
- Genetic counseling

Tests to determine abnormalities –
(3)___________, ultrasound
(4)__________, chorionic (5)_____ ________, and maternal blood test

BIOLOGICAL BEGINNINGS

Genetic Principles, Methods And Influences

Genetic Principles

- Dominant recessive genes principle
- Polygenic Inheritance

KEY PERSON

- Sandra (1)______
- Reaction range
- Genotype
- Phenotype
- Canalization

Methods Used by Behavior Geneticists

KEY PERSON

- Thomas (2)_________
- Twin Study- identical twins, fraternal twins
- Adoption Study

Heredity's Influence on Development

- Arthur Jensen
- Intelligence is influenced by heredity
- Richard Hernstein and Charles Murray

– intelligence and class structure

BIOLOGICAL BEGINNINGS

Heredity Environment Interaction

Genotype-Environment Correlations

Sandra Scharr

- Passive Genotype environment correlations
- Evocative Genotype – Environment Correlations
- Active (niche-picking) genotype-environment correlations

Shared and Nonshared Environmental Influences

KEY PERSON

Robert (1)________

- Environmental experiences contribute to sibling differences

Conclusions about Heredity-Environment Interaction

KEY PEOPLE

Gilbert (2)_________

William (3)_________

- Extensive interaction of heredity and environment
- Full genetic expression develops throughout the lifespan
- The mixture of genes we inherit and our unique environments are complex

Judith Harris

- Controversial book- *The Nurture Assumption*

I. REVIEW PRIORITIES

Assess your present understanding of the material in this chapter by rating yourself for each heading using the following scale:

1 – I thoroughly understand material and its context to other sections

2 – I understand most of the material and have a basic grasp of the context to other sections

3 – I have a shaky understanding of the material and a poor grasp of the context

4 – I have an inadequate understanding of the material

Evolutionary Perspective

- Natural Selection and Adaptive Behavior ____
- Evolutionary Psychology ____

Heredity and Reproduction

- What Are Genes ____
- Reproduction ____
- Adaptation ____
- Abnormalities in Genes and Chromosomes ____

Genetic Principles and Methods

- Some Genetic Principles ____
- Methods Used By Behavior Geneticists ____
- Heredity's Influence on Development ____

Heredity-Environment Interaction

- Heredity-Environment Correlations ____
- Shared and Non-shared Environmental Influences ____
- Conclusions About Heredity-Environment Interaction ____

ANSWER KEY

B. TRUE OR FALSE KEY CONTENT QUESTIONS

1. T
2. T
3. F
4. F
5. T
6. F
7. T
8. T
9. T
10. F
11. T
12. F
13. F
14. T
15. T
16. T

C. FILL IN THE BLANK KEY TERMS

1. adapted; genes
2. Gametes
3. zygote
4. more
5. anemia
6. Klinefelter
7. Turner
8. XYY
9. dominant; recessive
10. Genotype; phenotype

D. MATCHING KEY PEOPLE QUESTIONS

1. H
2. C
3. F
4. A
5. E
6. D
7. B
8. G

E. MULTIPLE CHOICE KNOWLEDGE QUESTIONS

1. c
2. c
3. a
4. b
5. a
6. a
7. d
8. d
9. a
10. b

F. CRITICAL THINKING QUESTIONS

1.
   - The increasing use of fertility drugs is producing greater numbers of multiple births. Multiple births increases the likelihood that the babies will have life-threatening problems, such as low birth weight. These medical risks also mean higher costs, which may not be paid by insurance companies. However, families begun by using reproductive technologies showed no differences on children's socioemotional development than families begun from natural conception.

2.
   - Genotypes are an individual's inherited environment that is related to genetic propensities. For example, a cooperative, attentive child evokes more instructional response from adults than an uncooperative, belligerent child. This is an example of evocative-genotype environmental correlation. In another example, attractive adolescents seek out attractive adolescent peers. This is an example of active-genotype environmental correlation.

3.
   - Arthur Jensen compared identical twins reared together with those reared apart to show that genetic factors are more important than environmental factors. However, scholars have criticized Jensen's findings because his use of standardized tests is a weak indicator of intelligence. A second criticism of Jensen's study was the lack of controls on potential environmental influences.

H. COGNITIVE MAPS

A.

1. Charles Darwin
2. David Buss

B.

1. gametes
3. fertilization
4. amniocentesis
5. sonography
6. villi sampling

C

1. Scharr
2. Bouchard

D.

1. Plomin
2. Gottlieb
3. Greenough

CHAPTER 4: PRENATAL DEVELOPMENT AND BIRTH

A. LEARNING OBJECTIVES

Prenatal Development

1. List maternal conditions that affect prenatal development.
2. Define teratogen.
3. Describe the effects of alcohol, smoking, and drugs on fetal development and later life.

Birth

4. Describe the three stages of birth: the first stage, the second stage, and the afterbirth.
5. Compare and contrast the Apgar Scale with the Brazelton Neonatal Assessment Scale

Postpartum Period

6. Summarize the physical adjustments women make during postpartum.
7. Define bonding. Why is bonding between an infant and parent(s) directly after birth so crucial?

B. TRUE OR FALSE KEY CONTENT QUESTIONS

Prenatal Development

1. T F Prenatal development is divided into three periods: germinal, embryonic, and fetal.
2. T F The placenta is a life-support system connecting arteries and vein to the baby.
3. T F The blastocyst is the outer layer of cells that develops during the embryonic period.
4. T F Organogenesis is the process of organ formation occurring during the first two months of prenatal development.
5. T F During the fetal period life-support systems develop and organ systems form.
6. T F The danger of structural defects caused by teratogens is greatest early in embryonic development.
7. T F Because the fetus depends entirely on its mother for nutrition, it is important for the pregnant woman to have good nutritional habits.
8. T F According to Christine Dunkel-Schetter, there is a strong link between stress during pregnancy and having a high birthweight baby.
9. T F Fetal alcohol syndrome can produce abnormalities in the babies of mothers who drank alcohol heavily during pregnancy.
10. T F Cigarette smoking by pregnant women leads to preterm births and lower birthweights.
11. T F Most expectant mothers make infant feeding decisions (bottle or breast) prior to the sixth month of pregnancy.

Birth

12. T F A doula, usually a woman, is part of the birthing team who provides continuous physical, emotional support for the mother before, during and after childbirth.
13. T F At the time of birth, the baby is covered with anoxia, a protective skin grease.
14. T F An epidural block is an anesthesia that numbs the woman's body from the waist down.
15. T F A cesarean section is a delivery of the baby through the abdomen.

16. T F A preterm infant is one born prior to 40 weeks between conception and delivery.

17. T F A low birthweight infant weights less than 6 ½ pounds.

18. T F The Apgar Scale assesses the health of a newborn by evaluating the infant's size, smell, and cry.

Postpartum Period

19. T F The postpartum is the period after childbirth, lasting approximately six months, when the woman's body adjusts to the process of childbearing.

20. T F The father also goes through a postpartum adjustment.

C. FILL IN THE BLANK KEY TERMS

1. __________ takes place when one sperm from the male unites with an _________ from the female.
2. The ___________ periods of prenatal development include the germinal period, the embryonic period, and the fetal period.
3. After three months, the fetus is ___________ inches long and weighs ___________ ounce, and gender can be identified.
4. Abortion became legal in the United States in _______ , and can be used to terminate unwanted pregnancies legally during the first _________ months.
5. An agent that can cause a birth defect is called a _________.
6. Various _________ diseases and conditions such as rubella, syphilis, genital herpes, and AIDS can produce birth defects.
7. The usual source of the mother's infection is either use of ___________ drugs or heterosexual contact with intravenous drug users.
8. As women get older, they are ________ likely to conceive.
9. Maternal consumption of drugs, such as tranquilizers, alcohol, tobacco, marijuana, heroin, and cocaine, affects ________ development.

10. Even moderate drinking may __________ infant's level of attention and alertness.

11. Cigarette smoking has been associated with __________ prematurity rates and lower birth weights. ________ problems are also more common in the offspring of smokers.

12. During the first and longest stage, uterine contractions __________ in frequency and intensity, and also become more regular.

13. A very long delivery can result in _________ , an impaired supply of ___________ to the infant.

14. Although surgical removal of an infant from the uterus, a ___________ section, is safer than a breech delivery, it does entail other complications.

15. One concern is that drugs can cross the ___________ barrier and affect the infant.

16. The Lamaze method of childbirth, a widely used form of prepared childbirth, focuses on breathing and ____________ . This method has increased the involvement of _______ in the entire process of childbirth.

17. Babies born before 38 weeks after conception are now referred to as _________ babies, whereas babies who weigh less than ________ pounds at birth are referred to as low-birthweight babies.

18. The ___________ Neonatal Behavioral Assessment Scale assesses the infant's reflexes, neurological function, and reactions to people. A very low score on the Brazelton may indicate _________ damage.

19. Other physical changes include ___________ , the return of the uterus to its prepregnant size, and rapid changes in _________ production.

20. ____________ is a controversial concept that implies that there is a ___________ period in the development of a close emotional attachment between mother and the infant.

D. MATCHING KEY PEOPLE QUESTIONS

___ 1. A French obstetrician who advocated a procedure referred to as "birth without violence."

___ 2. A researcher who has examined the role of touch and massage in development.

___ 3. An obstetrician who developed natural childbirth through breathing and relaxation techniques.

___ 4 Developer of a scale to assess the health of newborns at one and five minutes after birth.

___ 5 Developer of a scale to assess the health of newborns within 24–36 hours after birth.

A. Virginia Apgar

B. Tiffany Field

C. Ferdinand Lamaze

D. T. Berry Brazelton

E. Ann Streissguth

F. Grantley Dick-Read

G. Arlene Eisenberg

E. MULTIPLE CHOICE KNOWLEDGE QUESTIONS

1. How does the placenta/umbilical cord life-support system prevent harmful bacteria from invading a fetus?

   a. Bacteria are too large to pass through the placenta's walls.

   b. The placenta generates antibodies that attack and destroy bacteria.

   c. Bacteria become trapped in the maze of blood vessels of the umbilical cord.

   d. No one understands how the placenta keep bacteria out.

2. The fetal period is best described as a time when

   a. major organ systems emerge from the less differentiated endoderm and mesoderm.

   b. support systems that sustain the fetus become fully formed and functioning.

   c. fine details are added to systems that emerged during the embryonic period.

   d. teratogens are most likely to impair development.

3. Which of the following phrases defines a teratogen?

   a. a life support system that protects the fetus

   b. an agent that stimulates the formation of organs

   c. an abnormality in infants of alcoholics mothers

   d. an environmental factor that produces birth defects

4. Which of the following statements about the relationship between age and pregnancy outcomes is most accurate?

   a. Adolescent mothers are most likely to have retarded children.

   b. More women become pregnant through artificial insemination in their thirties and their forties than do women in their twenties.

   c. Mothers over age 30 are most likely to have retarded babies.

   d. Adolescent mothers suffer the lowest infant mortality rates of any age group.

5. Which of the following statements about a mother's emotional state and prenatal development is most accurate?

   a. The emotional state of a mother influences prenatal development and birth.

   b. The emotional state of a mother influences birth but not prenatal development.

   c. The emotional state of a mother influences prenatal development but not birth.

   d. The emotional state of a mother has no influence on either prenatal development or birth.

6. Which of the following statements about fetal alcohol syndrome is most accurate?

   a. The infant is often physically deformed and below average in intelligence.

   b. It commonly results in miscarriages.

   c. It causes ectopic pregnancies

   d. Babies suffering from this syndrome are often born before term and with low birth weights.

7. Mrs. Peters is bearing down hard with each contraction. She is in the _________ stage of labor.

   a. first

   b. second

   c. third

   d. final

8. What is the reason for administering analgesics to a woman during labor?

   a. to minimize the risk of cesarean sections

   b. to speed delivery

   c. to facilitate natural childbirth

   d. to lessen the pain for the mother

9. In contrast to the Brazelton scale, the Apgar Scale primarily assesses a newborn's

   a. psychological status.

   b. reflexes.

   c. physiological health.

   d. responsivity to people.

10. Which of the following terms refers to a physical change that occurs to women after childbirth?

   a. decompression

   b. menstruation

   c. involution

   d. natural selection

F. CRITICAL THINKING QUESTIONS

1. Explain how a mother's emotions and experience of stress can influence prenatal development, birth, and the newborn.

2. Why does a breech position complicate the delivery of a baby?

3. How does massage help improve the developmental outcomes of "at-risk" infants?

G. APPLICATION QUESTIONS

Changes in a child's family situation can cause stress. The adjustment to a mother's pregnancy and the arrival of a new sibling can cause strain on a young child.

1. What suggestions would you make to help a child deal with a birth in the family?

H. COGNITIVE MAPS

PRENATAL DEVELOPMENT AND BIRTH

Prenatal Development

Its Course

- germinal period
  - blastocyst
  - trophoplast
  - implantation
- embryonic period
  - endoderm
  - ectoderm
  - mesoderm
  - placenta
  - umbilical cord
  - amnion
  - organogenesis
- fetal period

Miscarriage and Abortion

- medical issues
- psychological issues
- ethical issues
- social issues

Teratology and Hazards

- teratogen
- maternal factors
  - diseases
    - rubella
    - syphilis
    - genital herpes
    - AIDS
  - condition
    - age
    - nutrition
    - emotional state and stress
  - drugs – Ann (1)__________ ***KEY PERSON***
    - alcohol
      - fetal alcohol syndrome
    - nicotine
    - caffeine
    - marijuana
    - cocaine
    - heroin
- paternal factors
  - exposure to lead, radiation, pesticides, and petrochemicals
  - Vitamin C deficiency
  - cocaine
  - smoking

PRENATAL DEVELOPMENT AND BIRTH

The Birth Process

- Stages of birth
  - First Stage – until the cervix dilates 4 centimeters
  - Second Stage – until the baby's complete emergence
  - Third Stage – Afterbirth
- Fetus/Newborn Transition
  - Stress and adaptation
  - Anoxia
- Childbirth and attendants
- Methods of delivery
  - Medicated – Three kinds of drugs
    - (1)___________
    - (2)___________
    - (3)___________
  - Natural Childbirth
    Grantley Dick-Read
  - Prepared Childbirth
    KEY PERSON
    (4)______________
  - Cesarean delivery
    breech position

Birth

Preterm Infants and Age/Weight Considerations

- Preterm infant
  - conceptual age
  - illness
  - stimulation – Tiffany Field
  - individualized developmental plan
- Low-birthweight infants
  - developmental problems
  - social factors

Measures of Neonatal Health

- Apgar Scale
- Brazelton Neonatal Behavioral Assessment Scale

KEY PERSON

(5)_______________________

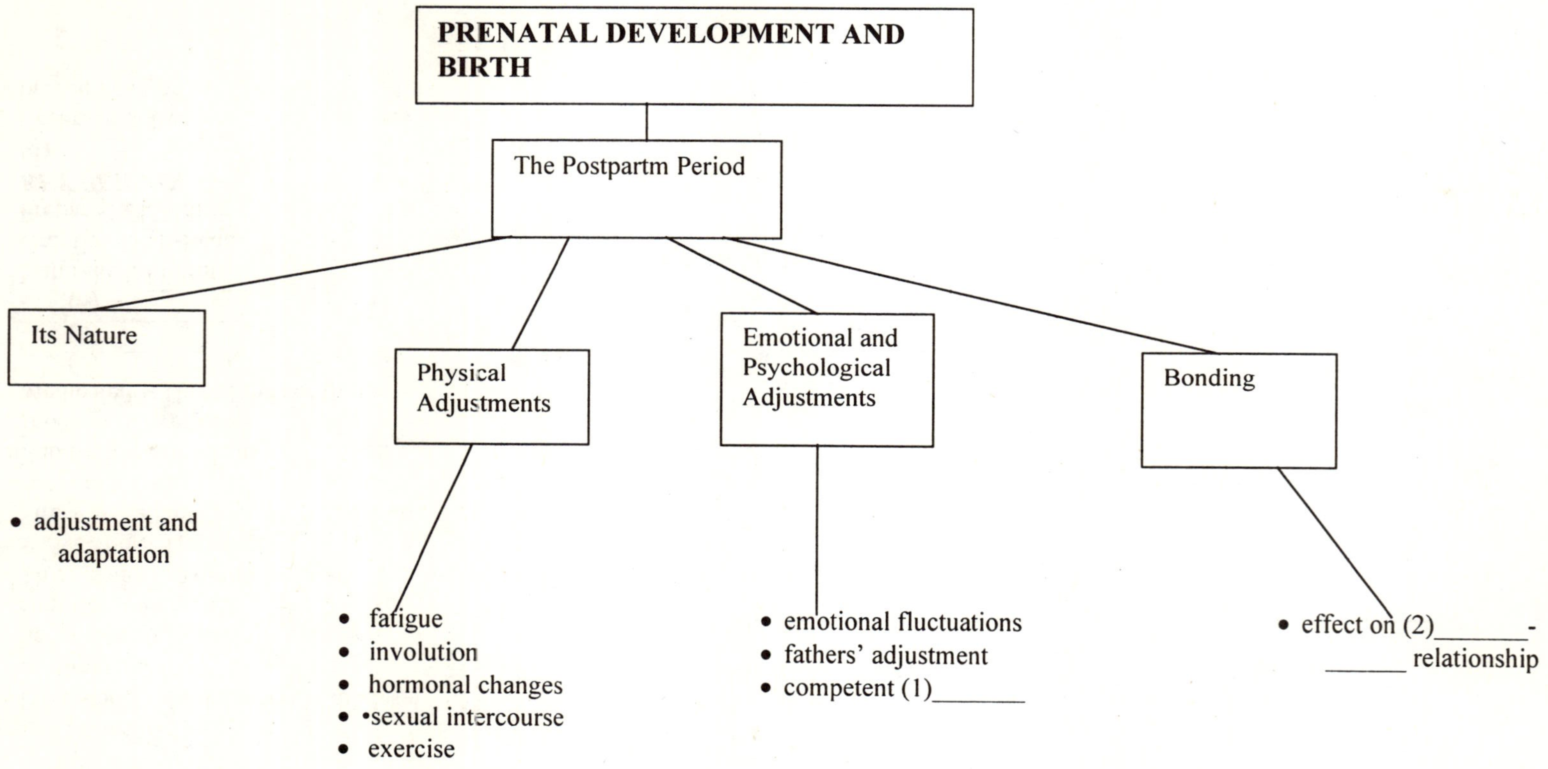
PRENATAL DEVELOPMENT AND BIRTH
The Postpartm Period
Its Nature
Physical Adjustments
Emotional and Psychological Adjustments
Bonding
• adjustment and adaptation
• fatigue
• involution
• hormonal changes
• •sexual intercourse
• exercise
• emotional fluctuations
• fathers' adjustment
• competent (1)_______
• effect on (2)_______-_______ relationship

I. REVIEW PRIORITIES

Assess your present understanding of the material in this chapter by rating yourself for each heading using the following scale:

1 – I thoroughly understand material and its context to other sections

2 – I understand most of the material and have a basic grasp of the context to other sections

3 – I have a shaky understanding of the material and a poor grasp of the context

4 – I have an inadequate understanding of the material

Prenatal Development

- Its Course _____
- Miscarriage and Abortion _____
- Teratology and Hazards _____

Birth

- The Birth Process _____
- Preterm Infants and Age-Weight Considerations _____
- Measures of Neonatal Health _____

Postpartum Period

- Its Nature _____
- Physical Adjustments _____
- Emotional and Psychological Adjustments _____

ANSWER KEY

B. TRUE OR FALSE KEY CONTENT QUESTIONS

1. T
2. F
3. F
4. T
5. F
6. T
7. T
8. F
9. T
10. T
11. T
12. T
13. F
14. T
15. T
16. F
17. F
18. F
19. F
20. T

C. FILL IN THE BLANK KEY TERMS

1. Fertilization; ovum
2. three
3. 3; 1
4. 1973; six
5. teratogen
6. maternal
7. intravenous
8. less
9. prenatal
10. lower
11. higher; Respiratory
12. increase
13. anoxia; oxygen
14. cesarean
15. placental
16. relaxation; fathers
17. preterm; 5.5
18. Brazelton; brain
19. involution; hormone
20. Bonding; critical

D. MATCHING KEY PEOPLE QUESTIONS

1. C
2. B
3. F
4. A
5. D

E. MULTIPLE CHOICE KNOWLEDGE QUESTIONS

1. a
2. c
3. d
4. c
5. a
6. a
7. b
8. d
9. c
10. c

F. Critical Thinking Questions

1.
   - The mother's emotional state can influence the birth process. A stressed-out mother might have irregular contractions and a more difficult labor. This may cause irregularities in the baby's oxygen supply or slower adjustment after birth.
   - Maternal anxiety may result in a hyperactive and irritable infant. The newborn may also have more feeding and sleeping problems. In the Dunkel-Schetter study women under stress are four times more likely to deliver premature babies than low-stress pregnant women.
   - Researchers have found that women who have an optimistic outlook believe they have more control over the outcome of their pregnancy.

2.
   - Normally, the baby's head comes through the vagina first during delivery. However, when the baby's buttocks is the first part to emerge from the vagina, the baby is in a breech position.
   - This position where the head does not come through first can cause respiratory problems. A cesarean delivery, also called caesarian section, is usually performed if the baby is in a breech position.

3.
   - Touch and massage can improve the growth, health and well-being of infants and children. Dr. Tiffany Field's research has demonstrated the benefits of massage in reducing labor pain. Infants who received massage therapy had lower stress, improved sociability and better gastrointestinal and metabolic efficiency. Massaged infants were also more active and alert. Their hospital stays were six days shorter than nonmassaged babies.

H. COGNITIVE MAPS

A

1. Streissguth

B

1. Analgesia
2. Anesthesia
3. Oxytocies
4. Ferdinand Lamaze
5. T. Berry Brazelton

C

1. parenting
2. parental-infant

CHAPTER 5: PHYSICAL DEVELOPMENT IN INFANCY

A. LEARNING OBJECTIVES

Physical Development and Growth in Infancy

1. Define and contrast *cephalocaudal pattern* and *proximodistal pattern*.
2. Define and contrast neurons, *dentrite*, *axon,* and *myelin sheath*.

Motor Development

3. Define and contrast *gross motor skills* and *fine motor skills*.

Sensory and Perceptual Development

4. Define and contrast *sensation* and *perception*.
5. Define *intermodal perception*. Why is it controversial?

B. *TRUE OR FALSE KEY CONTENT QUESTIONS*

Physical Development and Growth in Infancy

1. T F The sequence in which the greatest physical growth occurs from bottom to top (legs, trunk, head) is called the cephalocaudal pattern.
2. T F The sequence in which the greatest growth starts at the center of the body and moves toward the extremities is called the proximodistal pattern.
3. T F In the first months of life human brain cells are created at a rate of 250,000 per minute.
4. T F The cerebral cortex plays a critical role in brain functioning, such as perception, thinking, and language.
5. T F Neuroscientists believe that the brain's flexibility and resilience are developed through repeated experience.
6. T F Most adults spend a fourth of their night in REM sleep; most infants spend a third of their night in REM sleep.
7. T F Sudden infant death syndrome (SIDS) occurs when an infant stops breathing, usually during daytime naps.
8. T F From birth to one year of age, infants triple their weight and increase their length by 50 percent.
9. T F The growing consensus is that bottle-feeding is better for the baby's health during the first six months of life.
10. T F Toilet training is expected to be attained by about three years of age in North America.

Motor Development

11. T F The sucking reflex enables newborns to get nourishment before they have associated a nipple with food.
12. T F The rooting reflex occurs when something touches the infant's palms.
13. T F The Moro reflex is the infant's response to a loud noise or sudden movement.

14. T F The American Academy of Pediatricians recommends structured exercise classes for babies to increase coordination and gross motor development.

15. T F Infants have to see their own hands when reaching for an object.

16. T F Developmental biodynamics emphasizes that perception and action go together when new skills are learned.

Sensory and Perceptual Development

17. T F Sensation is the interpretation of what is sensed.

18. T F The constructivist view advocated by Piaget suggests that an infant constructs a perception of the world from sensory input and experiences.

19. T F Newborns can see and distinguish colors.

20. T F Infants as young as three months have depth perception.

21. T F Hearing can occur several weeks before birth in the fetus.

22. T F Infants as young as three months can connect visual and auditory stimuli.

C. FILL IN THE BLANK KEY TERMS

1. T. Barry Brazelton observed that infants often suck their __________, or other objects, and that this behavior may continue for some time.
2. The ____________ principle indicates that the pattern of growth proceeds from the head downward.
3. The ____________ principle indicates that the pattern of growth proceeds from the center of the body outward.
4. Although infant growth ____________ during the second year, infants have achieved about ______ percent of their adult weight and nearly ______ percent of their adult height by the end of the second year.
5. Walking and moving one's arms exemplify ________ motor skills, whereas picking up a rattle exemplifies a ______ motor skill.
6. REM sleep is a stage that is correlated with __________.

7. A special concern about infant sleep is _______ , which occurs when an infant stops breathing during sleep and dies.

8. There is a __________ about feeding babies on demand or on a regular schedule.

9. North American parents expect their children to be toilet trained by __ years old.

10. _________ occurs when information contacts sensory receptors in the eyes, ears, mouth, nose, and on the skin.

11. ___________ is the interpretation of what is sensed.

12. Fantz discovered that infants prefer to look at patterns rather than colors, and the ability to perceive visual patterns is __________.

13. Immediately after birth, newborns can hear; however, their sensory thresholds are _________ than those of adults.

14. Although male infants react to the pain of circumcision by crying and fussing, they cope well with this procedure by __________ deeply.

15. Six-day-old infants preferred the smell of their mother's ________ pad.

16. ____________ perception is the ability to relate and integrate information about two or more sensory modalities.

D. MATCHING KEY PEOPLE QUESTIONS

___ 1 A behaviorist who argued that infants should be fed on a schedule rather than on demand.

___ 2. An experimenter who used the looking chamber to determine the visual preferences of infants.

___ 3. A developmental psychologist who stresses the importance of cognition and early experience in development.

___ 4 A developmental theorist who is a major proponent of the constructivist view of intermodal perception.

___ 5 A psychologist who argued that individuals perceive in order to move and move in order to perceive.

___ 6. Researchers who used the visual cliff to study infant perception.

___ 7. A pediatrician who observed infants to determine the incidence of their sucking when they were nursing and how their sucking changed over time.

___ 8. A researcher who found that infants do not have to see their hands when reaching for an object.

___ 9. A researcher who studied how newborns cope with stress by observing their reactions during circumcision.

___10. An author who believes that the importance of early experience in development has been exaggerated.

A Megan Gunnar

B. Esther Thelen

C. T. Berry Brazelton

D. John Breur

E. Robert Fantz

F. Eleanor Gibson & Richard Walk

G. Elizabeth Spelke

H. Rachel Clifton

I. John Watson

J. Jean Piaget

K. William James

E. MULTIPLE CHOICE KNOWLEDGE QUESTIONS

1. Which statement best characterizes infant reflexes?

   a. Infants once needed reflexes but no longer do.

   b. Reflexes are genetically coded survival mechanisms for all infants.

   c. Modern infants rely more on learning than on reflexes.

   d. All reflexes disappear by the end of infancy.

2. Which principles explain why an embryo's hands develop before its fingers, and why the head develops before the body?

   a. cephalocaudal, cephalocaudal

   b. cephalocaudal, proximodistal

   c. proximodistal, cephalocaudal

   d. proximodistal, proximodistal

3. Which of the following statements most accurately describes height and weight changes during infancy?

   a. Both increase more rapidly during the second year than during the first year.

   b. Girls increase in height and weight faster than do boys during infancy.

   c. The sexes grow at the same rate during infancy.

   d. Both height and weight increase more rapidly during the first year than during the second year.

4. Developmentalists have hypothesized that the large amount of REM sleep in infants

   a. is a dream state related to infant fears.

   b. is a symbolic return to the womb.

   c. is cause by the need to eat or eliminate.

   d. is a form of self-stimulation.

5. Juan was a low-birthweight infant, whereas John was a premature infant. Which of the following statements applies to them?

   a. Neither is vulnerable to SIDS.

   b. Juan is less vulnerable to SIDS than John.

   c. Juan is more vulnerable to SIDS than John.

   d. Both are vulnerable to SIDS.

6. Jill's parents followed John Watson's advice about feeding, and Jack's parents followed today's trend. Which schedule did they use, respectively?

   a. scheduled feeding; demand feeding
   b. demand feeding; scheduled feeding
   c. bottle-feeding; breast-feeding
   d. breast-feeding; bottle-feeding

7. When infants were placed on one side of the visual cliff, they refused to go to their mothers who were coaxing them from the other side. This result was cited as evidence for which of the following?

   a. depth perception
   b. failure of visual acuity
   c. inability to hear at a distance
   d. inability to crawl

8. What evidence indicates that a fetus can hear?

   a. A fetus moves when a loud noise occurs.
   b. Newborns prefer their mother's voice to a stranger's voices.
   c. Hearing is more sensitive and better developed among newborns who have been experimentally stimulated before birth.
   d. Newborns prefer to hear stories that were read to them just before they were born.

9. When an infant turns its head at the sound of footsteps in the hall and then smiles when it sees Mom come into the room, the infant is using

   a. depth perception.
   b. intermodal perception.
   c. auditory perception.
   d. visual perception.

10. Which dietary element will health-conscious parents omit from their baby's diets if they do not study infants' dietary needs?

    a. protein

    b. carbohydrates

    c. fat

    d. sugar

F. CRITICAL THINKING QUESTIONS

1. Explain why infants spend so much time in REM sleep.

2 Discuss the pros and cons of breast-feeding versus bottle-feeding.

3. What is appropriate exercise for infants?

G. APPLICATION QUESTIONS

Erik Erikson identified eight stages of human development that guide temperment and drive. Each stage presents a tension or crisis between opposing extremes that the individual needs to resolve on the road to maturity. The second stage, *autonomy vs. shame*, characterizes the preschool youngster. Youngsters work at defining themselves as separate from adults. They learn to define themselves as individuals. They feel shame when they do not develop emotional autonomy. Individual shame is caused by misunderstandings when adults do not understand what is happening when children assert themselves.

1. Adults sometimes think their job is to eliminate naughtiness in children. This may cause a child, testing his/her independence, to believe he/she is being bad. Has this ever happened to you? How did you resolve the issue?

2. Giving children choices meets their need for independence and helps them learn cooperation. Cite examples of tasks and responsibilities young children can handle to make them feel grown up by making meaningful contributions.

H. COGNITIVE MAPS

PHYSICAL GROWTH AND DEVELOPMENT IN INFANCY

Cephalocaudial and Proximodistal Patterns

- (1)__________ pattern – growth from the top to the bottom
- (2)__________ pattern – growth from the center of the body to the extremities

Height and Weight

- average North American newborn is 20 inches long and weighs 7 ½ lbs.
- first birthday – infants have tripled their birthweight and height is 1 ½ times their birth length
- age two – average weight is 26-32 lbs., about 1/5th their adult weight –

The Brain

- Neuron

cell (3)__________
cell (4)__________
cell (5)__________

- cerebral cortex has four lobes

NAME THEM

(6)__________ lobe
(7)__________ lobe
(8)__________ lobe
(9)__________ lobe

- cerebral cortex has two hemispheres, left and right - lateralization
- Early experiences help form neural connections

Mark Rosenzweig
Mark Johnson

- Overstimulation can be harmful

Infant States

- states of consciousness
- REM sleep (rapid eye movement)
- SIDS – sudden infant death syndrome

Nutrition

- adequate nutrition
- demand versus scheduled feeding
- breast versus bottle-feeding
- malnutrition marasmus

Ernesto Pollitt

Toilet Training

- usually by (10)__-years-old
- relaxed, supportive environment

MOTOR DEVELOPMENT

Reflexes

- sucking reflex

KEY PERSON

- (1) _ ________ __________
- rooting reflex
- moro reflex
- grasping reflex

Gross and Fine Motor Skills

- Gross Motor Skills

1 month – lift (2)____
3-4 months – (3)___ ____
6 months – (4)___
8 months – (5)___
12 months – (6)___

- Fine Motor Skills

2 months – holds rattle
4 months – carries object to mouth
6 months – grabs, reaches for
10 months – pincer grasp
12-18 months – scribbles
18-24 months – zips and unzips, turn doorknob
eye-hand coordination
Rachel Clifton

Developmental Biodynamics

Rachel Clifton

KEY PERSON

Esther (7)_______

- perception and action

SENSORY AND PERCEPTUAL DEVELOPMENT

What Are Sensation and Perception?

- sensation- information interacts with sensory receptors
- perception – interpretation of what is sensed

Theories of Perceptual Development

- constructivist view

KEY PERSON

- Jean (1)_______
- ecological view
- Eleanor and James J. Gibson
- affordances

Visual Perception

- visual acuity and col

William James

- visual preferences

KEY PERSON

Robert (2)______

- perception of faces
- perceptual constancy

size constancy

shape constancy

- depth perception

Richard Walk

- visual expectations

Elizabeth Spelke

Other Senses

- hearing
- touch and pain
- Megan Gunnar
- smell
- taste

Intermodal Perception

- ecological view versus the (3)_________ view
- nature and nurture contributions

Perceptual-Motor Coupling and Unification

- development of perception and action is mutual and reciprocal

(4)____
____

I. REVIEW PRIORITIES

Assess your present understanding of the material in this chapter by rating yourself for each heading using the following scale:

1 – I thoroughly understand material and its context to other sections

2 – I understand most of the material and have a basic grasp of the context to other sections

3 – I have a shaky understanding of the material and a poor grasp of the context

4 – I have an inadequate understanding of the material

Physical Development and Growth in Infancy

- Cephalocaudal & Proximodistal sequence _____
- Height & Weight _____
- The Brain _____
- Nutrition _____
- Toilet Training _____

Motor Development

- Reflexes _____
- Gross & Fine Motor Skills _____
- Developmental Biodynamics _____

Sensory and Perceptual Development

- What Are Sensation & Perception _____
- Theories of Perceptual Development _____
- Visual Perception _____
- Other Senses _____

- Intermodal perception _____
- Perceptual-Motor Coupling & Unification _____

ANSWER KEY

B. TRUE OR FALSE KEY CONTENT QUESTIONS

1. F
2. T
3. T
4. T
5. T
6. F
7. F
8. T
9. F
10. T
11. T
12. F
13. T
14. F
15. F
16. T
17. F
18. T
19. T
20. F
21. T
22. T

C. FILL IN THE BLANK KEY TERMS

1. fingers
2. cephalocaudal
3. proximodistal
4. slows; 20; 20
5. gross; fine
6. dreaming
7. SIDS
8. controversy
9. 3
10. Sensation
11. Perception
12. innate
13. higher
14. sleeping
15. breast
16. Intermodal

D. MATCHING KEY PEOPLE QUESTIONS

1. I
2. E
3. G
4. J
5. B
6. F
7. C
8. H
9. A
10. D

E. MULTIPLE CHOICE KNOWLEDGE QUESTIONS

1. b
2. c
3. d
4. d
5. d
6. a
7. a
8. d
9. b
10. c

F. CRITICAL THINKING QUESTIONS

1.

- The amount of Rapid Eye Movement (REM) sleep changes over the life span. Approximately 50 percent of an infant's sleep is REM sleep. Most adults spend only 20 percent of the night in REM sleep and elderly adults drop to less than 15 percent. Since infants sleep approximately 16 hours per day, the large amount of REM sleep may provide stimulation necessary for brain development.

2.

- Breast-feeding provides human milk that is clean and digestible and helps immunize the newborn from disease. Breast-fed babies gain weight more rapidly. However, only half of mothers nurse newborns. Mothers who work outside the home find it difficult to breast-feed infants. Also, there is no evidence that bottle-fed infants suffer physiological or psychological harm. Many parents, especially working mothers, breast feed during the first few months (often using a pump to extract breast milk that can be stored for a later feeding) of the newborn's life and bottle-feed thereafter.

3.

- Although toddlers are quite active, pediatricians do not recommend structured exercise. It is easy to go beyond the infant's physical limitations without knowing it and cause dislocations.
- Exercise for infants is not aerobic. They cannot adequately stretch their bodies at this age.
- It is better to engage infants in passive exercise that encourage such appropriate physical development as pushing, pulling, crawling, etc.

H. COGNITIVE MAPS

A.

1. Cephalocaudial
2. Proximodistal
3. production
4. migration
5. elaboration
6. Frontal
7. Occipital
8. Temporal
9. Parietal
10. 3

B

1. T. Berry Brazelton
2. head
3. roll over
4. sit
5. crawl
6. walk
7. Thelen

C

1. Piaget
2. Fantz
3. Constructivist
4. Bennett Bertenthal

CHAPTER 6: PHYSICAL DEVELOPMENT IN CHILDHOOD AND PUBERTY

A. LEARNING OBJECTIVES

Physical Development in Early Childhood

1. Explain why children lose their "top-heavy" look during their preschool years.
2. How do researches learn about hand preference of infants and toddlers?

Physical Development in Middle and Late Childhood

3. Why should elementary school children be involved in active rather than passive activities?

Health and Illness

4. Describe caregiver behavior that promotes children's health. Describe caregiver behaviors that hinder children's health.
5. Why is poverty a special concern to children's health?
6. What is the cause of obesity?
7. Define *set point*. How does exercise lower it?

Puberty and Adolescence

8. Define and contrast *estradiol* and *testosterone*.
9. Describe the differences of *sexual scripts* and sexual expectations between adolescent boys and girls.
10. Define and contrast *anorexia nervosa* and *bulimia*.

B. *TRUE OR FALSE KEY CONTENT QUESTIONS*

Physical Development in Early Childhood

1. T F The average child grows over 2 1/2 inches in height and gains 5–7 pounds a year during early childhood.
2. T F Myelination is the insulation of fat over the nerve cells that dampens the speed of information traveling through the nervous system.
3. T F Children double their strength capacity during middle and late childhood.

Physical Development in Middle and Late Childhood

4. T F Boys are usually better at gross motor skills and girls are better at fine motor skills during middle and late childhood.
5. T F An average preschool child requires 2,400 calories per day.

Health and Illness

6. T F Running, swimming, cycling, and hiking are recommended exercises for children.
7. T F About one quarter of all illness and deaths among children are associated with inadequate hygiene.
8. T F A child is obese if he/she is 10 percent over the expected weight for height.
9. T F Cancer is the second leading cause of death in children 5–14 years old.
10. T F Leukemia is the most common form of childhood cancer.
11. T F One death of every three in the world is the death of a child under five.

Puberty and Adolescence

12. T F On the average, puberty begins and peaks two years earlier for girls than boys.

13. T F Early-maturing boys are more likely to smoke, drink, be depressed, have older friends, and request earlier independence.

14. T F The number of adolescent females reporting having intercourse has increased more rapidly than the proportion of males.

15. T F The rate of homosexuality has increased during the 20th Century.

16. T F Only 100,000 adolescent females become pregnant each year.

17. T F Many adolescents underestimate their risk of getting an STD or AIDS.

18. T F Alcohol is the most widely used drug by adolescents.

19. T F The rate of adolescent suicides, which doubled in the last 30 years, dramatically increases at about age 18.

20. T F Successful intervention/prevention programs include: Early identification, individual attention, and community-wide intervention.

C. FILL IN THE BLANK KEY TERMS

1. The ___________ of growth begun in the second year continues in early childhood.
2. The hormone that controls growth is secreted by the ____________ gland at the base of the brain.
3. The process of _____________ covers nerve cells with fat, and ____________ the speed of information transmission in the brain.
4. Children also develop their ______________ motor skills such as grasping and block stacking.
5. During middle and late childhood, children need more/less food than they did in early childhood.
6. One's __________ , or easily maintained body weight, can be lowered only by exercise.
7. During adolescence, girls experience ___________, their first menstrual period.
8. During puberty, levels of ____________ increase dramatically for boys, but not girls, whereas levels of ____________ increase dramatically for girls, but not for boys.

9. For boys the pubertal growth spurt begins at about age _______ years, whereas it begins at _______ years for girls.

10. During adolescence, teens are preoccupied with their bodies, and their body _________.

11. Most research confirms that, at least during adolescence, it is better to be a(n) _________ -maturing boy than a _______ -maturing boy.

12. Early/Late maturation for girls is a mixed blessing because they experience more popularity and more problems in school.

13. Stereotyped patterns for sexual behavior are deemed sexual _____________ .

14. Sexually transmitted diseases include ___________ , which is caused by bacteria and is characterized by painful ___________.

15. Herpes simplex virus II causes ________ in the genital area, and can cause __________ damage in infants exposed to the virus during birth.

16. AIDS destroys the body's ____________ system.

17. The rate of adolescent pregnancy in the United States is __________ than other industrialized countries.

18. ____________ is the most commonly abused drug by adolescents.

19. The suicide rate begins to rise rapidly at about ______ years old.

20. Adolescent eating disorders include anorexia nervosa and ___________ .

D. MATCHING KEY PEOPLE QUESTIONS

___ 1. Successful left-handed individuals.

___ 2. A program designed to improve children's cardiovascular health.

___ 3. A national polling organization that surveys adolescent sexual behavior.

___ 4 A researcher who analyzed the types of foods that lead to obesity in children.

___ 5 A psychologist who studies the U.S. adolescent pregnancy rate.

___ 6. A psychologist who views sexuality as a normal aspect of adolescent development.

___ 7. Researchers who monitored drug use by American secondary students.

___ 8. An adolescent health expert who developed a life skills education curriculum.

A Lloyd Johnston, Patrick O'Malley, & Gerald Bachman

B. Alan Guttmacher Institute

C. David Hamburg

D. Leonardo Da Vinci, Benjamin Franklin, & Pablo Picasso

E. Judy Rodin

F. Heart Smart

G. Shirley Feldman

H. P. Lindsay Chase-Lansdale

I. Daniel Yankelovich

J. Joy Dryfoos

E. MULTIPLE CHOICE KNOWLEDGE QUESTIONS

1. Myelination improves the efficiency of the central nervous system the way that

   a. talking to an infant speeds his ability to produce a first word.

   b. reducing the distance between two children playing catch reduces the time it takes for a baseball to travel from one child to the other.

   c. the ingestion of certain chemicals (e.g., steroids) can improve overall muscle development.

   d. the insulation around an electrical extension cord improves the efficiency.

2. Which of the following would be considered a fine motor skill?

   a. bouncing a ball

   b. walking a straight line

   c. stacking blocks

   d. throwing a ball overhand

3. Which behavior of newborns predicts hand preference later in life?

   a. direction of eye gaze

   b. direction of head turning

   c. consistent use of one hand to grab things

   d. tendency to roll to the right or left

4. Which pattern best portrays changes in gross and fine motor skills in middle and late childhood?

   a. Girls out-perform boys in gross motor skills.

   b. Boys out-perform girls in gross motor skills.

   c. There are no sex differences in the development of gross and fine motor skills.

   d. Boys out-perform girls in fine motor skills.

5. Which of the following countries has the lowest child mortality rate?

   a. United States

   b. Sweden

   c. Afghanistan

   d. Japan

6. What is the most effective way for parents to promote good fitness habits in their children?

   a. Encourage children to play competitive sports.

   b. Involve the entire family in a vigorous exercise program.

   c. Limit the time spent watching television.

   d. Create a substantial challenge for children, such as training for a marathon.

7. The most noticeable changes in body growth for females include all of the following *except*

a. height spurt.

b. tendencies towards obesity.

c. breast growth.

d. menarche.

8. Andrea rationalizes her sexual behavior with her boyfriend by saying that she is in love with him. Her belief is part of her

a. sexual contract.

b. personal fable.

c. sexual orientation.

d. sexual script.

9. According to Kinsey, the percentage of adolescent males who are homosexual is

a. 10 percent

b. 8 percent

c. 4 percent

d. 2 percent

10. Infants born to adolescent mothers are more likely to have

a. neurological problems.

b. low birthweight.

c. childhood illness.

d. All of the above are correct.

11. Which is *not* a recommendation for dealing with a suicidal adolescent?

   a. Ask if the person has a plan for killing himself.

   b. Heed warning signs and take them seriously.

   c. Assure the person everything is under control.

   d. Help the person find appropriate counseling.

12. In order to be classified as a "very high-risk youth," 15-year-old Wayne would have to

   a. commit a serious crime.

   b. be a heavy drug user.

   c. be sexually active, but not using contraceptives.

   d. All of the answers are correct.

F. CRITICAL THINKING QUESTIONS

1. What are the positive and negative consequences for children's participation in sports?

2. Describe the gender differences in adolescents' perceptions of their bodies.

3. What are the differences in sexual scripts between adolescent males and females?

G. APPLICATION QUESTIONS

Erik Erikson identified eight stages of human development that guide temperment and drive. Each stage presents a tension or crisis between opposing extremes that the individual needs to resolve on the road to maturity. The fourth stage, *industry vs. inferiority*, characterizes childhood during the middle and late (elementary school) years. During the end of the childhood period children direct their energy toward mastering knowledge and intellectual skills. Teachers have a special responsibility during this period to nurture children towards accomplishments. The danger during this period is the development of a sense of inferiority—of being incompetent and unproductive.

1. Can you recall being embarrassed, in the upper elementary grades, by not feeling competent in an academic subject. Which subject? How did you resolve it? Did your teacher help or hinder the process?

The fifth stage, *identity vs. identity confusion*, characterizes the adolescent years. At this time, individuals are faced with finding out who they are and where they are going in life. Adolescents are confronted by many new roles and expectations, especially in relation to work and romantic relationships. If the adolescent explores different possible paths in a healthy manner, then a positive identity will be achieved. If the adolescent does not fully explore the varied roles of adulthood identity confusion takes over.

2. Describe issues you have had with parents or teachers as you asserted your own, unique identity. In retrospect, how would you react differently today with adults who held authority over you about negotiating your emerging identity? Where are you in the birth order of your family? Is it easier or harder for older siblings to make this transition? Is it easier or harder for younger siblings to make this transition?

H. COGNITIVE MAPS

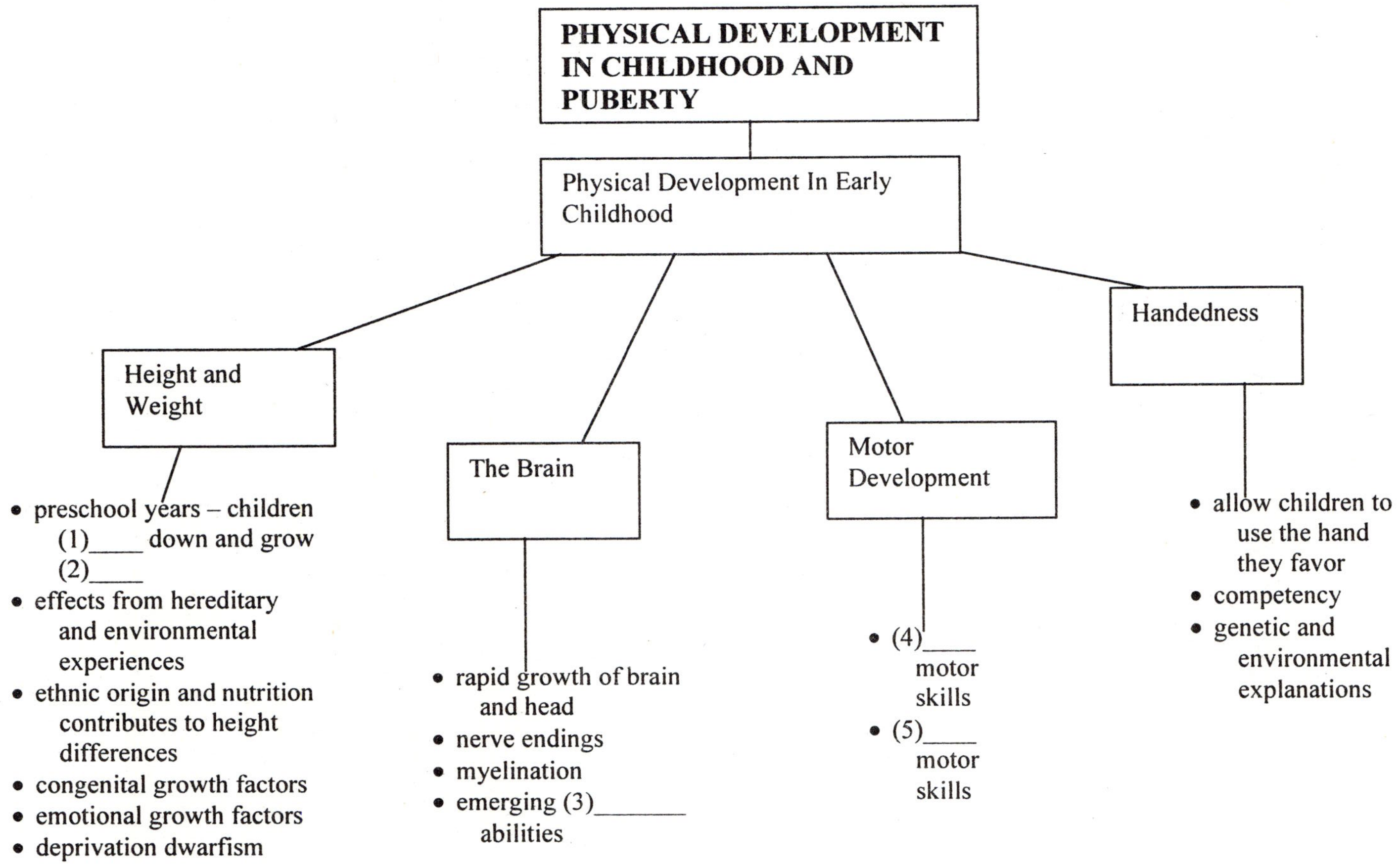
PHYSICAL DEVELOPMENT IN CHILDHOOD AND PUBERTY
Physical Development In Early Childhood
Height and Weight
• preschool years – children (1)____ down and grow (2)____
• effects from hereditary and environmental experiences
• ethnic origin and nutrition contributes to height differences
• congenital growth factors
• emotional growth factors
• deprivation dwarfism
The Brain
• rapid growth of brain and head
• nerve endings
• myelination
• emerging (3)_______ abilities
Motor Development
• (4)____ motor skills
• (5)____ motor skills
Handedness
• allow children to use the hand they favor
• competency
• genetic and environmental explanations

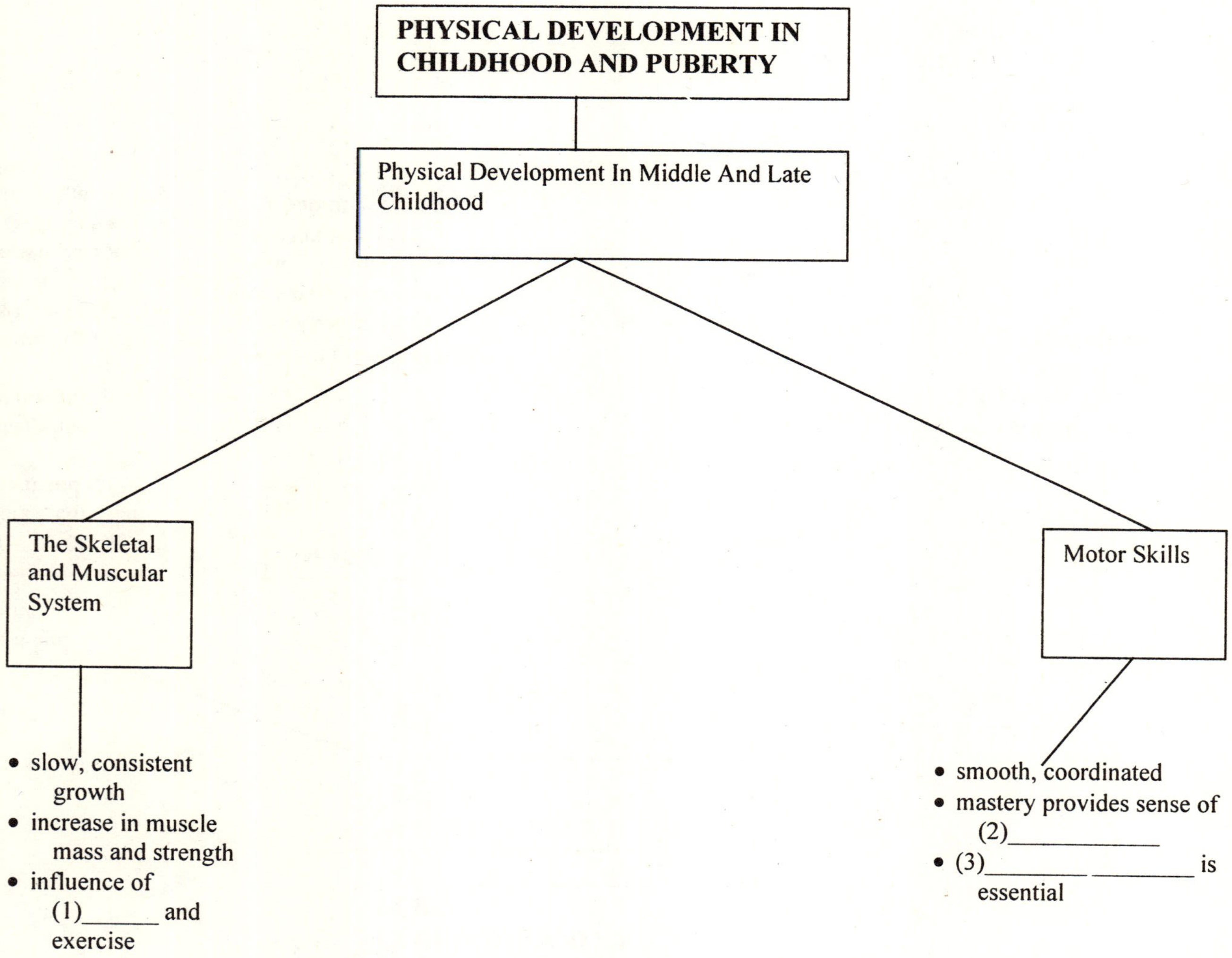
PHYSICAL DEVELOPMENT IN CHILDHOOD AND PUBERTY
Physical Development In Middle And Late Childhood
The Skeletal and Muscular System
• slow, consistent growth
• increase in muscle mass and strength
• influence of (1)______ and exercise
Motor Skills
• smooth, coordinated
• mastery provides sense of (2)____________
• (3)________ ________ is essential

PHYSICAL DEVELOPMENT IN CHILDHOOD AND PUBERTY

- Health And Illness
  - A Developmental Perspective on Children's Health
    - (1)____, cognitive, and social development
    - preventive measures taken by adults
    - outdoor play environments
    - health education programs
  - Nutrition
    - basal (2)________ rate (BMR)
    - increase energy needs
    - problems of poor nutrition
    - balanced diet
  - Exercise
    - adults model health practices
    - school physical education classes
    - viewing television
    - sports – positive and negative consequences
  - Young Children's Illness and Health in the United States
    - vaccines
    - fatal illnesses of childhood
    - passive smoking
    - low income families
  - The State of Illness and Health in the World's Children
    - diarrhea – oral rehydration therapy (ORT)
    - measles, tetanus, whooping cough - immunization
    - acute respiratory infection
    - undernutrition
    - timing of births
    - hygiene
  - Obesity, Cancer, and Cardiovascular Disease
    - obesity
    - causes
    - consequences
    - treatment
    - Judy Rodin
    - • cancer
    - types in children
    - (3)_________ most common
    - cardiovascular disease
    - effort to improve cardiovascular health

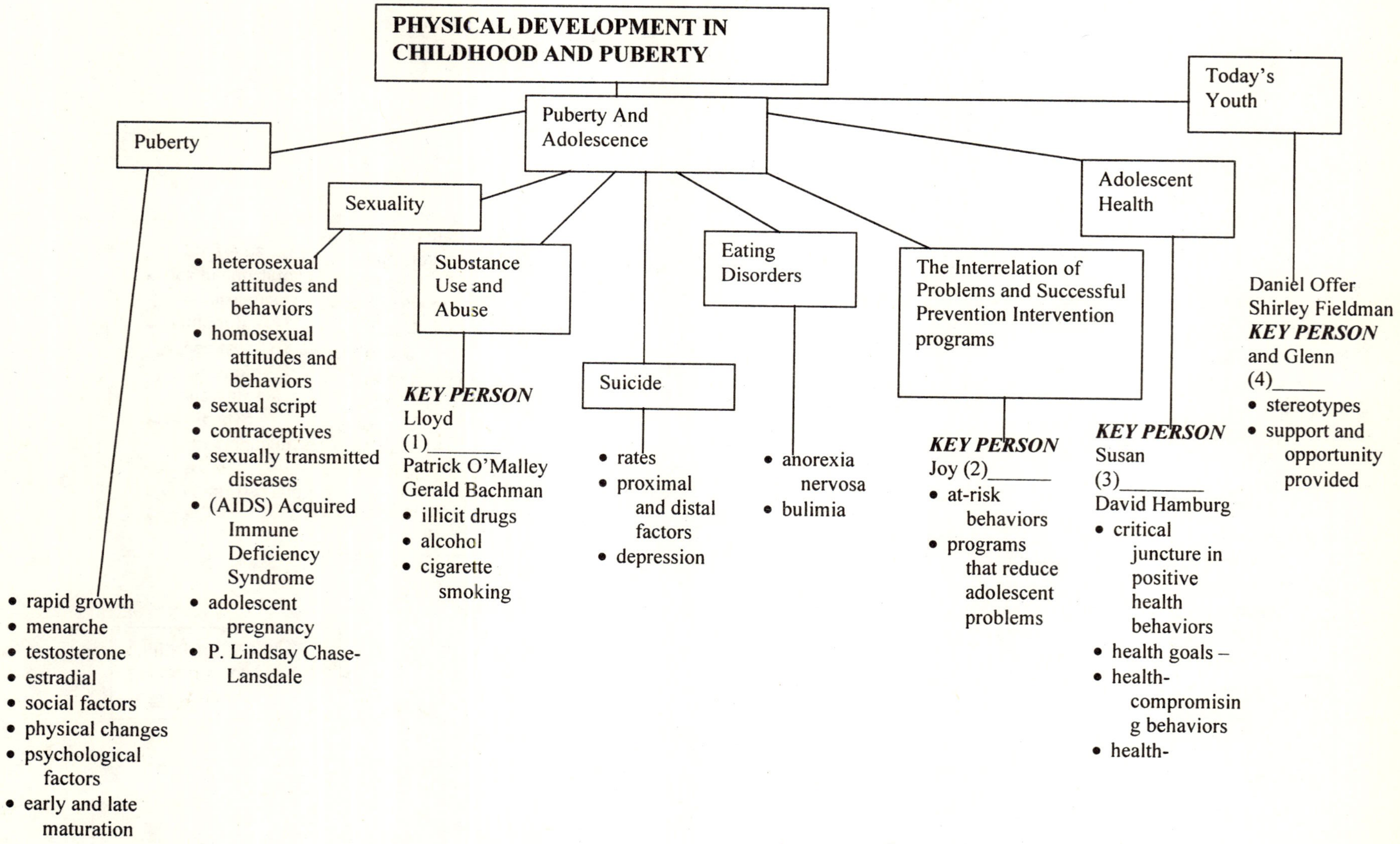

PHYSICAL DEVELOPMENT IN CHILDHOOD AND PUBERTY
Puberty And Adolescence
Today's Youth
Puberty
• rapid growth
• menarche
• testosterone
• estradial
• social factors
• physical changes
• psychological factors
• early and late maturation
Sexuality
• heterosexual attitudes and behaviors
• homosexual attitudes and behaviors
• sexual script
• contraceptives
• sexually transmitted diseases
• (AIDS) Acquired Immune Deficiency Syndrome
• adolescent pregnancy
• P. Lindsay Chase-Lansdale
Substance Use and Abuse
KEY PERSON
Lloyd
(1)______
Patrick O'Malley
Gerald Bachman
• illicit drugs
• alcohol
• cigarette smoking
Suicide
• rates
• proximal and distal factors
• depression
Eating Disorders
• anorexia nervosa
• bulimia
The Interrelation of Problems and Successful Prevention Intervention programs
KEY PERSON
Joy (2)______
• at-risk behaviors
• programs that reduce adolescent problems
Adolescent Health
KEY PERSON
Susan
(3)________
David Hamburg
• critical juncture in positive health behaviors
• health goals –
• health-compromising behaviors
• health-
Daniel Offer
Shirley Fieldman
KEY PERSON
and Glenn
(4)______
• stereotypes
• support and opportunity provided

I. REVIEW PRIORITIES

Assess your present understanding of the material in this chapter by rating yourself for each heading using the following scale:

1 – I thoroughly understand material and its context to other sections

2 – I understand most of the material and have a basic grasp of the context to other sections

3 – I have a shaky understanding of the material and a poor grasp of the context

4 – I have an inadequate understanding of the material

Physical Development in Early Childhood

- Height & Weight _____
- The Brain _____
- Motor Development _____
- Handedness _____

Physical Development in Middle and Late Childhood

- Skeletal & Muscular Systems _____
- Motor Skills _____

Health and Illness

- A Developmental Perspective on Children's Health _____
- Nutrition _____
- Exercise _____
- Illness & Health in the United States _____
- Illness & Health in the World's Children _____
- Obesity, Cancer & Cardiovascular Disease _____

Puberty and Adolescence

- Puberty ______
- Sexuality ______
- Substance Abuse & Abuse ______
- Suicide ______
- Eating Disorders ______
- Prevention & Intervention Programs ______
- Adolescent Health ______

ANSWER KEY

B. TRUE OR FALSE KEY CONTENT QUESTIONS

1. T
2. F
3. T
4. T
5. F
6. T
7. F
8. F
9. T
10. T
11. T
12. T
13. F
14. T
15. F
16. F
17. T
18. T
19. F
20. T

C. FILL IN THE BLANK KEY TERMS

1. slowing
2. pituitary
3. myelination; increases
4. fine
5. more
6. set point
7. menarche
8. testosterone; estradiol
9. 11; 9
10. images
11. early; late

12. Early
13. scripts
14. chlamydia; urination
15. blisters; brain
16. immune
17. higher
18. Alcohol
19. 15
20. bulimia

D. MATCHING KEY PEOPLE QUESTIONS

1. D
2. F
3. B
4. E
5. H
6. G
7. A
8. C

E. MULTIPLE CHOICE KNOWLEDGE QUESTIONS

1. d
2. c
3. b
4. b
5. b
6. b
7. b
8. d
9. c
10. d
11. c
12. d

F. CRITICAL THINKING QUESTIONS

1.

- Children's participation in sports can provide exercise, physical skill development, and a setting to develop friendships. However, sports can also have a negative impact when adults stress unrealistic expectation to win. When ambitious parents or organizations push children to engage in long an arduous training to achieve success, a distorted (and exploitive) view of sports gets communicated to the child. Ideally, sports participation is an opportunity for a child to increase physical strength, develop motor coordination, and improve flexibility.

3.

- One universal aspect of adolescence is a preoccupation with their bodies and their body image. During puberty adolescents are acutely sensitive to the changes in their body image. Generally, adolescent girls are less happy with their body image than are boys. During late puberty body fat increases. This is certainly a tender spot for adolescent girls. Later- maturing girls are taller and thinner and, by tenth grade, were more satisfied with their body.

- During late puberty, body muscle mass increases. This would be viewed as desirable by adolescent boys. Longitudinal studies indicate that late-maturing boys develop a stronger sense of identity than early-maturing boys. Since they had a long lead time regarding their physical development, late-maturing boys had more time to focus on personal achievement and career aspirations.

4.

- A sexual script is a stereotyped pattern for how individuals should behave sexually. Differences in the way males and females are socialized contribute to confused role expectations in sorting out their sexual identity. Adolescent girls link sex with love–adolescent females more than adolescent males have intercourse with partners they love and would like to marry. Adolescent males understand the pressure of adolescent girls to have a boyfriend when they give the line, "If you really loved me, you'd have sex with me."

H. Cognitive maps

A.

1. slim
2. taller
3. cognitive
4. gross
5. fine

B

1. heredity
2. accomplishment
3. physical activity

C

1. motor
2. metabolism
3. Leukemia

D

1. Johnston
2. Dryfoos
3. Millstein
4. Elliott

SECTION 3: COGNITION AND LANGUAGE DEVELOPMENT

CHAPTER 7: COGNITIVE DEVELOPMENTAL APPROACHES

A. LEARNING OBJECTIVES

Piaget's Cognitive Developmental Theory

1. Define and contrast *assimilation* and *accommodation*. Give examples for infants and young children.

Piaget's Stages of Cognitive Development

2. Describe the characteristics of the sensorimotor stage.
3. Define *object permanence*.
4. Describe the characteristics of the preoperational stage.
5. Define and contrast *egocentrism* and *animism*.
6. Describe the characteristics of the concrete operation stage.
7. Explain *reversibility*.
8. Describe the characteristics of the formal operation stage.
9. Describe *idealism, imaginary audience,* and *personal fable*.

Exploring Piaget's Theory

10. Explain how neo-Piagetians have modified Piaget's theory.

Vygotsky's Theory of Cognitive Development

11. Define *zone of proximal development* (ZPD).

B. TRUE OR FALSE KEY CONTENT QUESTIONS

Piaget's Stages of Cognitive Development

1. T F Assimilation occurs when children adjust to new information.
2. T F Piaget's concept of grouping behavior into higher-order levels of thought is called organization
3. T F It is the similar way of understanding the world that makes one stage more advanced than another in Piaget's stages of cognitive development.
4. T F Simple reflexes are one characteristic of the sensorimotor stage.
5. T F Object permanence is one of the infant's most important accomplishments.
6. T F If infants are surprised at the disappearance of an object, it is assumed they believe it continues to exist.
7. T F Recent research on infant cognitive development suggests that infants' perceptual abilities happen later than Piaget first believed.
8. T F Operations are externalized actions that allow a child to do physically what before he or she did mentally.
9. T F An example of animism is a child saying, "The sidewalk made me fall down."
10. T F In the preoperational thought stage, the child lacks a sense of conservation and asks a ton of questions.
11. T F The preoperational child can easily classify numbers and objects.
12. T F In the concrete operational thought stage, a child can engage in reversible mental action on real concrete objects, like different shapes of clay.
13. T F The concrete operational child still has difficulty with seriation, the sequential ordering.
14. T F In the formal operation thought stage hypothetical-deductive reasoning is the means for problem-solving.

Exploring Piaget's Theory

15. T F Adolescents think about ideal characteristics of themselves, others, and the world.

16. T F One criticism of Piaget's theory concerns developmental synchrony, that is, various aspect of a stage emerge continuously.

Vygotsky's Theory of Cognitive Development

17. T F The lower limit zone of proximal development (ZPG) are tasks a child can accomplish with the assistance of a more skilled person.

18. T F Scaffolding means changing the level of support by using a more skilled person for help.

19. T F Vygotsky believed that young children use language for self-regulation such as inner speech or private speech.

20. T F Vygotsky believed that self-talk reflects immaturity.

C. FILL IN THE BLANK KEY TERMS

1. Jean Piaget contends that children __________ their own cognitive worlds.
2. The sensorimotor period corresponds to the period of __________ that ranges from birth to about _____ years of age.
3. The understanding that objects do not cease to exist when out of perceptual contact is called object _________ .
4. The ________ period lasts from 2 to 7 years of age.
5. The inability to distinguish between one's own perspective and the perspective of another is called ________ .
6. The view that inanimate objects are alive or that plants and similar forms have human qualities is called _________ .
7. When liquid is dumped from a tall beaker to a short one, a child who has/has not mastered conservation will say that the shorter beaker has more/less water in it than the taller beaker.

8. __________ operational thinking appears at about age 7 or 8, and entails operations, mental actions that are __________ .

9. The ability to __________ is an operation that allows one to divide things into different sets and subsets on the basis of __________ characteristics.

10. The fourth state of Piaget's theory of cognitive development, __________ operational thought, begins between the age of 11 to 15.

11. Formal operational thought is more __________ than children's thought.

12. The two features of adolescent egocentrism include the imaginary __________ and the personal fable.

13. One criticism of Piaget's approach is that children are <u>more/less</u> cognitively competent and adults are <u>more/less</u> cognitively competent than Piaget supposed.

14. Lev Vygotsky indicates that tasks that are too __________ for children to handle alone, but can be done with assistance of someone more skilled fall into the zone of proximal development, or __________ .

15. The zone of proximal development is just one aspect of Vygotsky's theory about how social and cultural factors influence __________ development.

D. MATCHING KEY PEOPLE QUESTIONS

___ 1 A psychologist who developed the conceptual framework of cognitive development.

___ 2 Researcher who believes that personal fable and imaginary audience help define an adolescent's sense of uniqueness.

___ 3 A psychologist who believes that attention is an important explanation for conservation, and that conservation appears earlier than Piaget thought.

___ 4 A developmental psychologist who argues that guided participation, especially in cultural activities, are important aspects of children's development.

___ 5 A researcher who documents how infants can separate an object from their backgrounds.

___ 6 A psychologist who wrote of the wide variation of performance in adolescent cognition.

A. Jean Piaget

B. Rochel Gelman

C. Renee Baillargeon

D. Marshall Haith

E. David Elkind

F. Daniel Keating

G. Gisela Labouvie-Vief

H. John Flavell

I. Lev Vygotsky

J. Barbara Rogoff

E. MULTIPLE CHOICE KNOWLEDGE QUESTIONS

1. Organization and ______ enable a child to effectively interact with the environment.

    a. accommodation

    b. adaptation

    c. assimilation

    d. schema

2. If Linda tries to incorporate new features of the environment into her thinking by modifying existing schemes, she is using

    a. organization.

    b. adaptation.

    c. assimilation.

    d. accommodation.

3. Carrol is playing with a toy when it accidentally becomes hidden by a cloth. A blank look comes over Carrol's face, and he picks up another toy. This child's behavior is likely to occur in the

    a. sensorimotor stage.

    b. preoperational stage.

    c. intuitive stage.

    d. concrete operational stage.

4. Nancy's handkerchief was blown away by the wind. She was heard to say, "The wind is mean and wants to steal my hanky." This is evidence of __________ thought.

   a. egocentric

   b. symbolic

   c. intuitive

   d. animistic

5. One way to solve the conservation of weight problem is to understand that the long, thin lump of clay can be returned to its former shape. This is an example of the concept of

   a. mental identity.

   b. reversibility.

   c. hypothesis testing.

   d. contrary-to-fact reasoning.

6. Concrete operations allow the child to

   a. mentally construct hypotheses and theories.

   b. Imagine the necessary steps in solving a problem.

   c. Coordinate several characteristics rather than focus on a single property of an object.

   d. Imagine and analyze the thoughts of others compared to the thoughts of himself.

7. The formal-operational thinker is

   a. more tied to reality than the preoperational or concrete-operational child who uses a sort of pseudo-logic.

   b. exceptionally insightful about the practical aspects of life.

   c. demanding of a literally true answer to most problems.

   d. capable of abstraction.

8. Kim, an adolescent, is walking down the hallway of her school and is certain that everyone is watching her. This is an example of

   a. a personal fable.

   b. an adolescent paranoia.

   c. an imaginary audience.

   d. all of the above are correct.

9. Piaget's theory has been criticized on the basis that

   a. the concepts are not very interesting.

   b. children do not seem to behave the way he described.

   c. the idea of development following a series of stages has not been well supported by the evidence.

   d. assimilation and accommodation do not work the way he described.

10. Margo is teaching Tom to play a new composition for the piano. Initially Margo must provide each explanation, many hints, and several demonstrations. As Tom practices, Margo's instruction is reduced. Gradually Tom learns to perform the composition well all by himself. This is an example of Lev Vygotsky's concept of

    a. assimilation.

    b. wisdom.

    c. apprenticeship training.

    d. zone of proximal development.

F. CRITICAL THINKING QUESTIONS

1. Imagine a conversation between a four year old and a 15 year old about how a rainbow appears and then disappears. Explain how their perceptions would differ using Piaget's stage theory.

2. Describe how neo-Piagetians would revise Piaget's original theory.

3. Piaget is considered a cognitive constructivist. Vygotsky is considered a social constructivist. Compare and contrast their theories as they apply to teaching and learning.

G. APPLICATION QUESTIONS

"Part of Piaget's study of children's thinking involved their understanding of the rules in games. He focused on the rules in the game of marbles. Younger children were not able to follow the rules but believed they were quite sacred and imposed by adults. [However], these children were unconcerned about following the rules. Older children felt free to change the rules by mutual consent but then felt bound by them. The way children deal with the rules of a game can help adults understand how children deal with societal rules and expectations." (Constructive Guidance and Discipline, Fields & Boesser, 1998)

1. Explain a situation from observation or memory of children playing a game. How do the rules vary by age?

2. An essential strategy in resolving disputes is the ability to see things from another view. Young children need adult help in learning this perspective taking. Vygotsky's theory explains that children can perform at higher levels with assistance than they can alone.

3. Case scenario: Dominique's pencil fell off his desk on to the floor. Felicia picked it up and claimed it was hers. If you were their teacher how would you apply Vygotsky's notion of ZPG to help teach perspective taking?

H. COGNITIVE MAPS

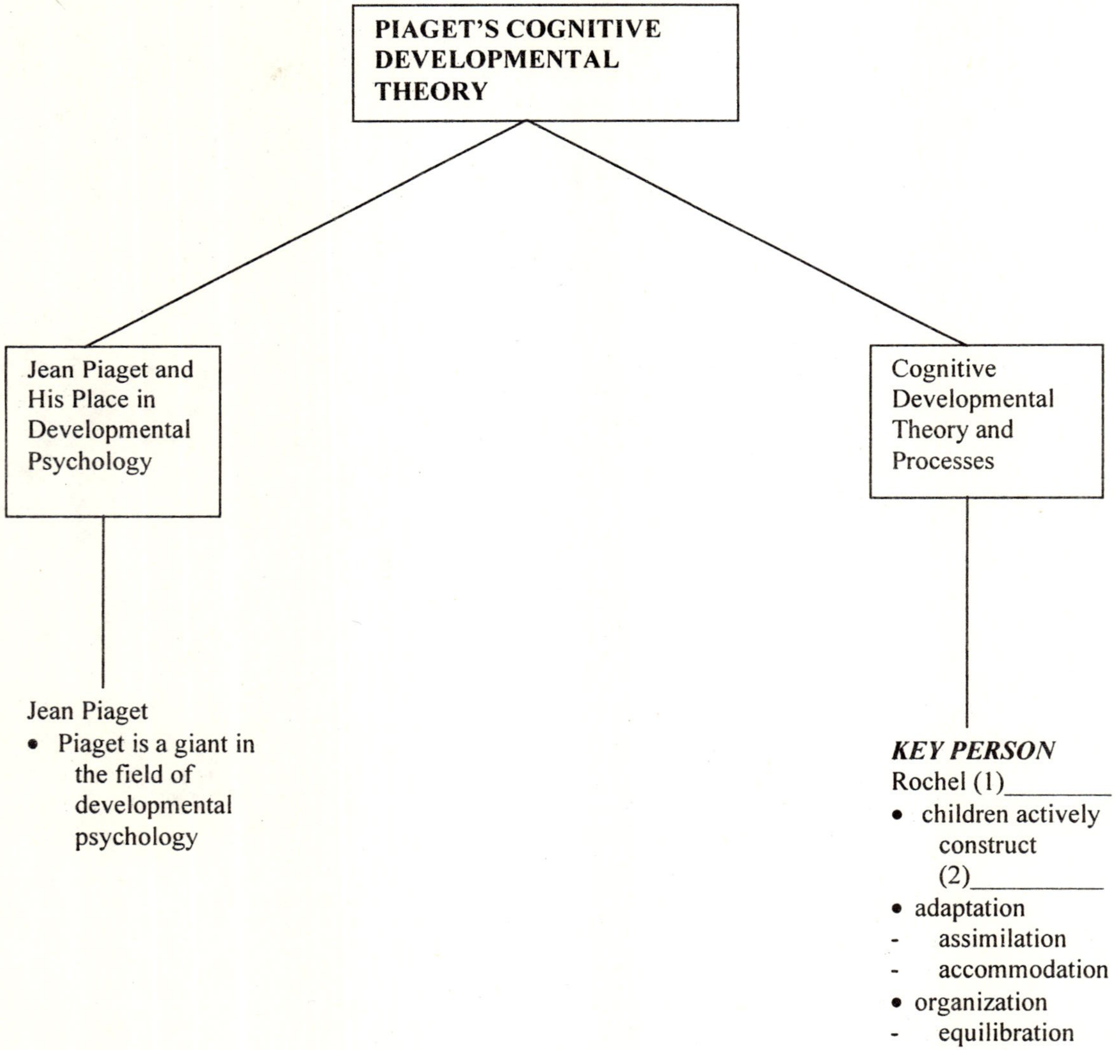
PIAGET'S COGNITIVE DEVELOPMENTAL THEORY
Jean Piaget and His Place in Developmental Psychology
Cognitive Developmental Theory and Processes
Jean Piaget
• Piaget is a giant in the field of developmental psychology
KEY PERSON
Rochel (1)________
• children actively construct (2)__________
• adaptation
- assimilation
- accommodation
• organization
- equilibration

PIAGET'S STAGES OF COGNITIVE DEVELOPMENT

Sensorimotor Thought

- birth – 2-years-old
- scheme
- six substages
  - simple reflexes
  - first habits and primary circular reaction
  - secondary circular reactions
  - coordination of secondary circular reactions
  - tertiary circular reactions, novelty and curiosity
  - internalization of schemes
- object permanence
  - Renee Baillargeon
  - AB error

Preoperational Thought

KEY PERSON
David (1)_______
- 2 - 7-years-old
- operations
- symbolic function substage
  - egocentrism

Barbel Inhelder
  - animism
- intuitive thought substage
  - centration
  - conservation

Concrete Operational Thought

- 7 to 11 years old
- horizontal (3)_________
- classification
- seriation
- transitivity

Formal Operational Thought

KEY PERSON
Daniel (2)________
- 11 to 15 years old
- hypothetical-deductive reasoning
- adolescent egocentrism
  - imaginary audience
  - personal fable

David Elkind

APPLYING AND EVALUATING PIAGET'S THEORY

Piaget and Education

- (1)___________ approach
- facilitate learning
- consider child's knowledge and level of thinking
- ongoing assessment
- promote intellectual health – avoid hurrying children
- provide classroom for exploration and discovery

Contributions and Criticisms

- contributions

KEY PEOPLE

Marshall (2)__________

John (3)_____________

- children's cognitive development field
- children are active thinkers
- observation skills

- criticisms
  - children's competence
  - stages
  - children reasoning at a higher level
  - cultural and educational influence
  - neo-Piagetians

LEV VYGOTSKY'S THEORY

Zone of Proximal Development

- ZPD – range of talks too difficult for children to master alone but with adult help or peers it can be learned

(1)__________

- adjusting guidance to fit the student's current level of dialogue

Language and Thought

- language plays a key role in cognition
- inner speech private speech
- language is socially based

Vygotsky and Education

- use zone of proximal development in teaching
- use scaffolding when children need help
- peers can be teachers
- monitor/encourage private speech
- assess ZPD
- use Vygotskian ideas in the classroom

Evaluating and Comparing Vygotsky's and Piaget's Theories

- Vygotsky's is (2)________ ______________ approach Barbara Rogoff
- Vygotsky and Piaget
  - constructivism
  - stages
  - key processes
  - role of language
  - views on education
  - teaching implications

I. REVIEW PRIORITIES

Assess your present understanding of the material in this chapter by rating yourself for each heading using the following scale:

1 – I thoroughly understand material and its context to other sections

2 – I understand most of the material and have a basic grasp of the context to other sections

3 – I have a shaky understanding of the material and a poor grasp of the context

4 –– I have an inadequate understanding of the material

Piaget's Cognitive Developmental Theory

- J. Piaget's Place in Developmental Psychology _____
- Cognitive Development Theory & Process _____

Piaget's Stages of Cognitive Development

- Sensorimotor Thought _____
- Preoperational Thought _____
- Concrete Operational Thought _____
- Formal Operational Thought _____

Exploring Piaget's Theory

- Piaget & Education _____
- Applying & Evaluating Piaget's Theory _____

Vygotsky's Theory of Cognitive Development

- The Zone of Proximal Development ____
- Scaffolding ____
- Language & Thought ____
- Vygotsky & Education ____
- Comparing Vygotsky & Piaget ____

ANSWER KEY

B. TRUE OR FALSE KEY CONTENT QUESTIONS

1. F
2. T
3. F
4. T
5. T
6. T
7. F
8. F
9. T
10. T
11. F
12. T
13. F
14. T
15. T
16. F
17. F
18. T
19. T
20. F

C. FILL IN THE BLANK KEY TERMS

1. construct
2. infancy; 2
3. object permanence
4. preoperational thought
5. egocentrism
6. animism
7. has not; less
8. Concrete; reversible
9. classify; several
10. formal
11. abstract
12. audience
13. more; less

14. difficult; scaffolding
15. cognitive

D. MATCHING KEY PEOPLE QUESTIONS

1. A
2. E
3. I
4. B
5. J
6. C
7. F

E. MULTIPLE CHOICE KNOWLEDGE QUESTIONS

1. b
2. d
3. a
4. d
5. b
6. c
7. d
8. c
9. b
10. d

F. CRITICAL THINKING QUESTIONS

1.

- The perception of the four year old is guided by preoperational thought. It is characterized by egotism and animism. The child's perception is intuitive, and he is unaware of how he knows. Accordingly, the rainbow comes because it is beautiful. It leaves when it is no longer beautiful.
- The perception of the 15 year old is guided by formal thought. It is characterized by abstract, idealistic, and logical thought. Adolescents are capable of hypothetical-deductive reasoning but develop a kind of egocentrism that involves an imaginary audience and personal fable about being unique and invulnerable. Accordingly, they will describe a rainbow coming from the combination of rain and sunlight. They might also speak of the myth of a pot of gold at the end of the rainbow.

2

- More emphasis given to information processing strategies such as attention and memory.
- More emphasis given to the speed at which children process information.
- More emphasis given to the type and complexity of tasks.
- More emphasis given to problem-solving, especially dividing tasks into smaller steps.

3

- Piaget believed that children learn best when they actively seek solutions for themselves. Therefore, the classroom should be turned into an environment of exploration and discovery. Children's intellectual growth would be promoted through peer interaction with naturalistic activities. Example: A math lesson is constructed around counting the number of days until Christmas.
- Vygotsky believed that education plays a central role in helping children develop necessary cultural tools. Like, Piaget, he believed that the teacher was more of a facilitator rather than a director. However, his views on the sociocultural development of children are more relevant and accessible, especially using the ZPD to improve children's literacy. Example: A reading lesson is reinforced using cross-aged tutors.

H. COGNITIVE MAPS

A

1. Gelman
2. knowledge

B

1. Elkind
2. Keating
3. décalage

C

1. constructivist
2. Haith
3. Flavell

D

1. Scaffolding
2. social constructivist

CHAPTER 8: INFORMATION PROCESSING

A. LEARNING OBJECTIVES

The Information Processing Approach

1. List and describe Siegler's three themes about what characterizes the information-processing approach (thinking, change mechanism, and self-modification).

Memory

2. Define memory. Describe Carolyn Rovee-Collier's research on infant memory.
3. Define *attention* and *selective attention,* and explain why attention must be flexible as well as selective.

Thinking

4. What are concepts? Explain why many children's concepts embody implicit theories about the world.
5. Describe the four steps in problem solving.

Metacognition

6. Explain how metacognitive strategies help students to think and problem solve.
7. Why are self-regulating learners high achievers and more responsible for their learning?

Domain Specific Academic Skills

8. What is the relationship between hand-on laboratory investigation and student's understanding of science?

B. *TRUE OR FALSE KEY CONTENT QUESTIONS*

1. T F The information-processing approach focuses on memory and thinking.
2. T F Encoding refers to how computers store and retrieve information.
3. T F Automaticity refers to the ability to process information with little or no effort.
4. T F Metacognition refers to self-awareness about cognition, that is, "knowing about knowing."
5. T F In terms of information-processing, attention refers to the formal posture of soldiers during individual or group presentation.
6. T F Young children tend to focus more on what is important rather than a task or situation.
7. T F Younger children are better at deploying attention than older children because they are more likely to construct a plan of action.
8. T F Dishabituation means a renewed interest in a stimulus.
9. T F Rehearsal is the conscious repetition of information over time that keeps the information in memory longer.
10. T F The theory "levels of processing" suggests that deeper processing produces better memory.
11. T F Self-reference is a way to elaborate information.
12. T F The keyword, strategy, avoids imagery in favor of word memorization.
13. T F Short term memory lasts about 30 seconds.
14. T F The faster six year olds repeated auditorially presented words, the shorter were their memory spans.
15. T F Procedural memory is the conscious recollection of information such as facts or events.
16. T F In areas where children are experts, their memory can exceed that of adults who are novices in that content area.
17. T F A schema is a script for an event.
18. T F Interference theory asserts that we forget not because we lose memories, but because other information gets in the way of what we are trying to remember.

19. T F The emotional blows of personal trauma can produce distortions of memory or repression to the unconscious mind.

20. T F Concepts are elements of the affect that demonstrate the complexity of emotions of common properties.

21. T F Working backwards in time helps establish subgoals for problem-solving.

22. T F Heuristics are strategies that guarantee an answer to a problem.

23. T F Critical thinking involves thinking productively and evaluating the evidence, but does not involve reflection.

24. T F High achieving students who set more specific learning goals are modeling self-regulatory strategies.

25. T F Metacognitive knowledge involves monitoring and reflecting on one's current thoughts.

C. FILL IN THE BLANK KEY TERMS

1. __________ refers to the retention of information over time.

2. Working memory is synonymous with _____________ -term memory that retains information for up to ____ seconds, and distinguished from ___________-term memory that is relatively permanent.

3. ___________ refer to concepts and knowledge about events that influence how an individual interprets new information.

4. The repeated presentation of a stimulus that causes reduced attention to that stimulus is called ___________, whereas the renewed interest in that stimulus is called __________.

5. Automaticity refers to the ability to process information with little or no __________.

6. Automaticity refers both to ___________ of processing and processing capacity.

7. Attention must be ____________ as well as selective.

8. The extended repetition of material after it has been presented is called ________.

9. The process of ____________ involves going beyond the information given to make information more memorable.

10. The keyword method uses ___________ images of key words to improve memory.

11. Knowledge about how the human mind works is called ___________ knowledge.

12. Henry Wellman proposed that children three years and older have a ___________ theory of how the mind works.

13. An attempt to find an appropriate way to attain a goal when barriers prevent its immediate attainment defines __________solving.

14. Observations by Andrew Meltzoff indicate that ______-month-old infants demonstrate deferred imitation.

15. __________ analysis is an approach to problem solving that begins with an examination of one's current situation and goal, and determining how to get from the current situation to the goal.

16. What distinguishes expert from novice problem solvers is how much time the experts spend on initial ___________.

17. Solving problems by relating them to previously encountered and better understood problems is called reasoning by ___________.

18. General problem solving skills are <u>more/less</u> important than specific problem solving skills in technological societies.

19. ___________ capacity is a limiting factor that helps explain why it takes so long for children to become competent readers.

20. The process of taking stock of what you are currently doing, what you will do next, and how effectively you are thinking defines the process of ____________ .

D. MATCHING KEY PEOPLE QUESTIONS

___ 1 Investigator who illustrated the importance of rehearsal and developmental change.

___ 2. Cognitive psychologist who identified two types of declarative memory: Episodic and semantic.

___ 3. A researcher who believes that memories are stored as verbal code or an image code.

___ 4. Proposed that children have a naïve theory of how the mind works.

___ 5. A researcher who studied infants' memories by hanging mobiles above their cribs.

___ 6. A developmentalist who observed deferred imitation by infants.

___ 7. A memory researcher who is skeptical about repressed memory of child abuse.

___ 8. Leading theorist who described three main characteristics of the information-processing approach.

A. Robert Siegler

B. Carilyn Rovee-Collier

C. John Flavell

D. Allan Paivo

E. Endel Tulving

F. Elizabeth Loftus

G. Judy Deloache

H. John Bransford

I. Max Wertheimer

J. Deanna Kuhn

K. Michael Pressley

L. Henry Wellman & Susan Gelman

M. Andrew Meltzoff

E. MULTIPLE CHOICE KNOWLEDGE QUESTIONS

1. The ___________ approach deals with how individuals analyze their many sources of information and the numerous steps used to make sense of this information.

   a. critical thinking

   b. information processing

   c. cognitive monitoring

   d. decisional

2. The directions for turning on the Nintendo game, Grandma's full name, and Marian's favorite flavor of ice-cream are

   a. stored in long-term memory.

   b. aspects of short-term memory.

   c. elements of sensory memory, as long as rehearsal occurs.

   d. examples of cognitive monitoring.

3. When asked what happens at a birthday party, Chrissy is clear that, "First you put on hats, then you play, then you sing Happy Birthday, and then you eat cake. Last you open." Chrissy is recounting a(n)

   a. schema.

   b. script.

   c. semantic network.

   d. heuristic.

4. Ten-year-old MaiLee lives in Hong Kong and quickly reads the local newspaper every day. Her seven-year-old brother takes much longer as he tries to say unfamiliar words out loud. In other words, compared to her brother, MaiLee exhibits greater

   a. automaticity.

   b. processing capacity.

   c. word processing.

   d. encoding.

5. A child's ability to focus on a parent's instructions even though baby brother is crying and the television is blaring is called

   a. encoding.

   b. attention.

   c. automaticity.

   d. memory.

6. You show a seven-year-old a grocery shopping list of 10 items and ask him to remember them when you go to the supermarket. You indicate that he can do this better if he organizes them into categories such as fruits, dairy products, and frozen foods. You are teaching the child to improve his memory via

   a. organization.

   b. attention.

   c. short-term-memory rehearsal.

   d. salience.

7. Twelve-year-old Laura decides to wait to tell her parents about her poor math grade after the dinner with her mother's boss. She knows that telling her them before dinner will disturb their ability to enjoy the dinner party. Here Laura is displaying her

   a. schemas about relationships with supervisors.

   b. semantic network about how parents behave.

   c. metacognitions about people.

   d. information processing strategies.

8. Programs about child-sexual abuse prevention often spend a great deal of time distinguishing between "good-touch" and "bad-touch." These programs are attempting to teach the child

   a. expertise.

   b. novice.

   c. concepts.

   d. metacognition.

9. The infant who is providing an example of deferred imitation is one who

   a. sticks out his tongue whenever he sees his mother stick out her tongue.

   b. appears to innately organize items into groups of two's.

   c. sees his mom wave goodbye to his dad and two hours later waves his hand "just like his mom did."

   d. continues to stare at his crib mobile even though it has just stopped spinning.

10. Both you and your professor have to deliver talks at two different high schools on "How Babies Learn to Talk." Your professor, an expert on language acquisition, is likely to spend most of her preparation time

    a. gathering information.

    b. rehearsing the completed speech.

    c. planning in her mind what she wants to communicate and how.

    d. sitting by the computer trying to organize facts.

11. All of the following are important elements of critical thinking *except*

    a. evaluating the similarities and differences between things.

    b. evaluating and understanding statements rather than just accepting them.

    c. applying "commonsense" and everyday knowledge to new problems.

    d. judging valid and invalid inferences from data.

12. The process of taking stock of what one is currently doing, what will be done next, and how effectively the mental activity is unfolding is referred to as

    a. psychological monitoring.

    b. abstraction.

    c. cognitive monitoring.

    d. thinking.

13. Much of the cognitive monitoring of young children comes from

   a. parents.

   b. television.

   c. the children themselves.

   d. peers.

14. What has been the general outcome of attempting to teach impulsive children to become more reflective in their classroom or test-taking behavior?

   a. Impulsive children rarely do as well as reflective children.

   b. The performance of both groups becomes about equal.

   c. Impulsive children soon surpass their reflective peers as a result of their high energy.

   d. While no immediate gain is usually seen, in the long-term, impulsive children gain from such training.

15. Which word is *not* typically associated with a repressed memory?

   a. anxiety-laden

   b. unconscious

   c. rehearsal

   d. psychoanalysis

F. CRITICAL THINKING QUESTIONS

1. A third grade teacher is concerned about one of her students' inability to understand how to subtract multiple digit numbers. On this particular day, two psychologists happen to be at her school. She asks them for assistance with her situation, unaware that one was trained in the information-processing approach and the other was trained in the cognitive development approach. Describe the advice she might get from each psychologist.

2. Memory is influenced by personal perspective. Consider how various customers or bystanders might remember the details of a bank robbery. Explain how memory is represented by network and schema. Finally, how is memory like a coat rack?

G. APPLICATION QUESTIONS

Memories can come from emotional sources as well as cognitive sources, simultaneously. For example, the stress from an interpersonal conflict often results in selective memory. Think of the last time you were involved in a dispute with someone significant in your life—a roommate, a boyfriend, a girlfriend, a parent, etc. Reflect on the following questions.

1. Was your interpretation of the people and events of the conflict different from their perception? Why?

2. How might both parties find common ground and separate the facts of the situation from the intent and intensity of the situation?

H. COGNITIVE MAPS

THE INFORMATION-PROCESSING APPROACH

Exploring the Information-Processing Approach

KEY PERSON

Robert (1)_______

- thinking
- change mechanisms
  - encoding
  - automaticity
  - strategy construction
  - generalization
- self modification
  - metacognition

Comparing the Information-Processing Approach with the Cognitive Developmental Approaches

- both identify cognitive capacities and limits
- information processing
  - processing limitations
  - strategies for overcoming limitations
  - knowledge about content
  - analysis of change
- Piaget's theory
  - cognitive stage
- Vygotsky's theory
  - social (2)__________ __ _______________

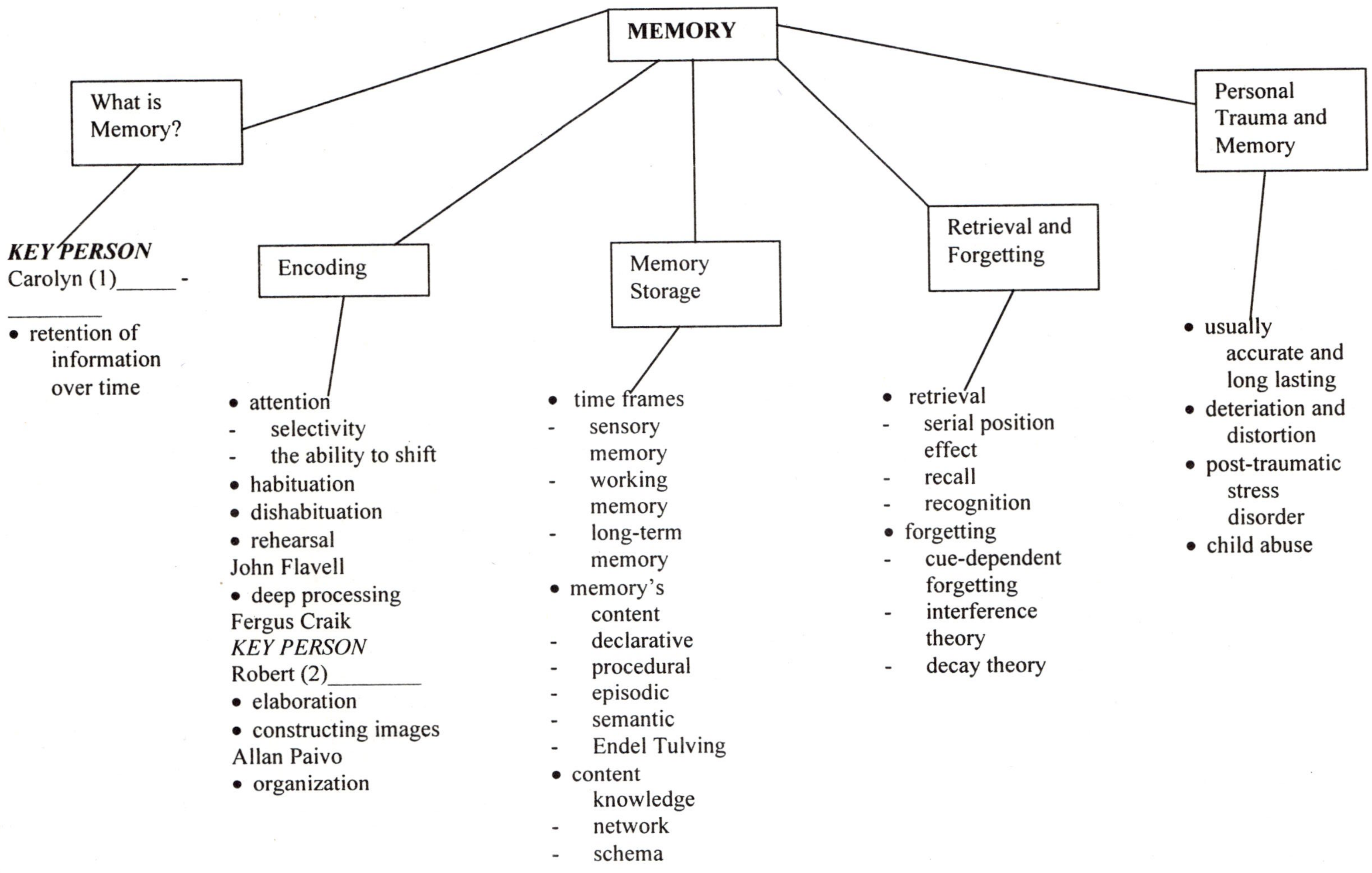
MEMORY
What is Memory?
KEY PERSON
Carolyn (1)_____ - ________
• retention of information over time
Encoding
• attention
- selectivity
- the ability to shift
• habituation
• dishabituation
• rehearsal
John Flavell
• deep processing
Fergus Craik
KEY PERSON
Robert (2)________
• elaboration
• constructing images
Allan Paivo
• organization
Memory Storage
• time frames
- sensory memory
- working memory
- long-term memory
• memory's content
- declarative
- procedural
- episodic
- semantic
- Endel Tulving
• content knowledge
- network
- schema
Retrieval and Forgetting
• retrieval
- serial position effect
- recall
- recognition
• forgetting
- cue-dependent forgetting
- interference theory
- decay theory
Personal Trauma and Memory
• usually accurate and long lasting
• deteriation and distortion
• post-traumatic stress disorder
• child abuse

THINKING

What Is Thinking?

- manipulating and (1)__________ information in memory

Forming Concepts

Henry Wellman
Susan Gelman

- theory of mind
- theory of living things
- theory of the physical world

Solving Problems

- find and frame problems
- develop problem solving strategies
  - subgoaling
  - algorithms
  - heuristics
  - means-end analysis
- evaluate solutions
- rethink and redefine problems and solutions over time
- wing rules to solve problems
- wing analogies to solve problems

Judy Deloache

- infant imitation

Andrew Meltzoff
Keith Moore

- problem-based learning

John Bransford

Critical Thinking

KEY PEOPLE

John (2)_______
Max (3)________
Jacqueline and Martin Brooks
Daniel Perkins
Sarah (4)_________
Deanne ()________

- thinking reflectively, productively, and evaluating the evidence
- open-mindedness
- intellectual curiosity
- planning and strategy
- intellectual carefulness
- "Fostering a Community of Learners"

Anne Brown
Joe Campione

- children teaching children
- reciprocal teaching
- on-line computer

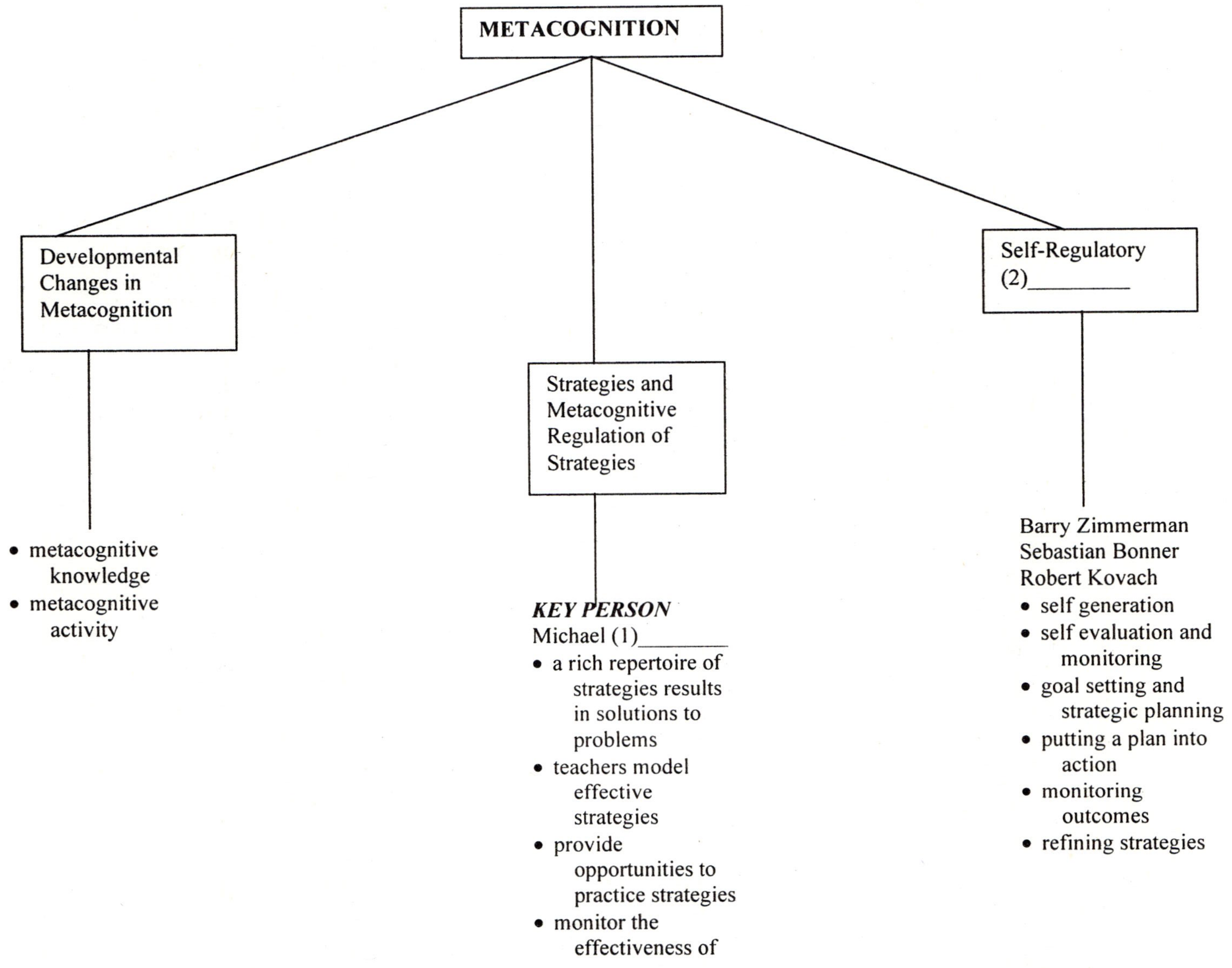
METACOGNITION
Developmental Changes in Metacognition
• metacognitive knowledge
• metacognitive activity
Strategies and Metacognitive Regulation of Strategies
KEY PERSON
Michael (1)________
• a rich repertoire of strategies results in solutions to problems
• teachers model effective strategies
• provide opportunities to practice strategies
• monitor the effectiveness of
Self-Regulatory (2)__________
Barry Zimmerman
Sebastian Bonner
Robert Kovach
• self generation
• self evaluation and monitoring
• goal setting and strategic planning
• putting a plan into action
• monitoring outcomes
• refining strategies

DOMAIN-SPECIFIC ACADEMIC SKILLS

Mathematical Thinking

- children understand many numerical concepts before (1)_____ grade
- controversy
  - cognitive or constructivist approach
  - practical or practice approach

Scientific Thinking

- constructivist approach

emphasis on discovery
  - hands-on, and collaboration
- discipline specific information

I. REVIEW PRIORITIES

Assess your present understanding of the material in this chapter by rating yourself for each heading using the following scale:

1 – I thoroughly understand material and its context to other sections

2 – I understand most of the material and have a basic grasp of the context to other sections

3 – I have a shaky understanding of the material and a poor grasp of the context

4 – I have an inadequate understanding of the material

The Information Processing Approach

- Exploring the Information-Processing Approach _____
- Comparing Information-Processing with Cognitive-Development _____

Memory

- What is Memory? _____
- Encoding _____
- Memory Storage _____
- Retrieval & Forgetting _____
- Personal Trauma & Memory _____

Thinking

- What is Thinking? _____
- Forming Concepts _____
- Solving Problems _____
- Critical Thinking _____

Metacognition

- Developmental Changes ______
- Strategies & Metacognitive Regulation of Strategies ______
- Self-Regulatory Learning ______

Domain Specific Academic Skills

- Mathematical Thinking ______
- Scientific Thinking ______

ANSWER KEY

B. TRUE OR FALSE KEY CONTENT QUESTIONS

1. T
2. F
3. T
4. T
5. F
6. F
7. F
8. T
9. T
10. T
11. T
12. F
13. T
14. F
15. F
16. T
17. F
18. T
19. T
20. F
21. T
22. F
23. F
24. T
25. T

C. FILL IN THE BLANK KEY TERMS

1. Memory
2. short; 30; long
3. Schemas
4. habituation; dishabituation
5. effort
6. age
7. flexible
8. rehearsal
9. elaboration
10. vivid
11. metacognitive
12. naive
13. problem
14. 9
15. means-end
16. planning
17. analogy
18. more
19. Memory
20. self-regulation

D. MATCHING KEY PEOPLE QUESTIONS

1. C
2. E
3. D
4. L
5. B
6. M
7. F
8. A

E. MULTIPLE CHOICE KNOWLEDGE QUESTIONS

1. b
2. a
3. b
4. a
5. b
6. a
7. c
8. c
9. c
10. c
11. c
12. c
13. a
14. a
15. c

F. CRITICAL THINKING QUESTIONS

1.

- Both psychologists would try to identify the student's mental capacity. The information-processing psychologist might focus more on process. An example would be to engage in problem-solving strategies to overcome the student's lack of understanding. This might include analysis of the content and the instructional procedures; how can the concept be broken down into smaller parts?
- The cognitive-development psychologist might focus more on cognitive products. Grounded in stage theory this psychologist would look at developmental expectations. Perhaps the student is cognitively between the preoperation stage and concrete operation stage. This student probably needs to work on classification skills before learning the mechanics of subtraction.

2.

- Memories can be organized graphically in a network design. Think of a spider's web. In the center is the core concept. From this generality, branches of associations can be formed. For example, weather can branch out to storm, which can branch out to lightning, which can branch out to electricity, etc. Weather can also branch out to weather report, which can branch out to television news, which can branch out to commercials, etc. The variety is endless and personally meaningful.
- Memories can also be organized around schematic scripts. This framework serves as a scaffolding by which new details can be added to reoccurring events or places. Thus, a fifth-grade student can perceive more resources a school provides than does a kindergarten student. Repetition and dealing with anomalies help process information into long-term memory. For example, a fire drill would be a new adventure or perhaps a distraction; for a fifth grader, it is a routine event.
- Both a memory and a coat rack hold only what is pertinent. Overloading each will cause it to collapse.

H. COGNITIVE MAPS

A.

1. Siegler
2. construction of knowledge

B.

1. Rovee-Collier
2. Lockhart

C

1. transforming
2. Dewey
3. Wertheimer
4. Tishman
5. Kuhn

D

1. Pressley
2. Learning

E.

1. 1st

CHAPTER 9: INTELLIGENCE

A. LEARNING OBJECTIVES

What is Intelligence?

1. Define intelligence. Why is it difficult to agree on a common definition?

Intelligence Tests

2. Compare and contrast the Stanford-Binet tests and the Wechsler Scales.
3. Compare and contrast Gardner's Multiple Intelligences and Sternberg's triarchic theory of intelligence.

Intelligence in Infancy and Development Transformations

4. What areas does the Gesell Scale assess? How does the developmental quotient relate to later IQ scores?
5. Characterize the nature of stability and change in childhood intelligence.

Controversies and Issues in Intelligence

6. Describe the heredity-environment controversy.
7. How do cultural and ethnic differences influence intelligence test scores?
8. Explain how IQ tests are used and misused.

The Extremes of Intelligence and Creativity

9. Define *mental retardation*.
10. Define *gifted*.
11. Define and contrast *creativity, convergent thinking,* and *divergent thinking*.

B. TRUE OR FALSE KEY CONTENT QUESTIONS

Intelligence Tests

1. T F The consistency of a performance is called reliability.
2. T F Validity measures the attribute it is suppose to measure.
3. T F A test that is valid is not necessarily reliable.
4. T F The term intelligence quotient (IQ) is an individual's chronological age divided by his/her mental age.
5. T F The Stanford-Binet test is given to individuals from birth to two years old.
6. T F The Weschsler Scales measure verbal, performance, and information characteristics.
7. T F Multiple Intelligences emphasizes eight frames of mind.
8. T F Robert Sternberg's Triarchic Theory argues that the basic unit of intelligence is a component to process information.

Intelligence in Infancy & Developmental Transformations

9. T F Due to later rapid cognitive growth there is no correlation between IQ scores of an eight year old and a 10 year old.
10. T F Advances in information-processing assessment conclude that infant tasks involving attention are closely related to later standardized intelligence tests in childhood.

Controversies and Issues in Intelligence

11. T F Environmental factors are more significant than genetic factors in the development of intelligence.
12. T F Culture-fair tests of intelligence require time limits.

The Extremes of Intelligence and Creativity

13. T F An individual who is mentally retarded has an IQ below 80.

14. T F An individual who is gifted has an IQ above 120 or higher.

15. T F An individual who is creative is likely to be a convergent thinker.

C. FILL IN THE BLANK KEY TERMS

1. Verbal ability, problem-solving, and learning from and adapting to everyday situations defines the concept of ____________ .
2. ___________ refers to how consistently an individual performs on a test.
3. The extent to which a test measures what it is supposed to measure is called ________.
4. Modern IQ tests are based on the assumption that the distribution of intelligence scores in the population is ____________.
5. The revised Stanford-Binet test analyzes individual's responses into four separate area scores, and a ____________ score that reflects overall intelligence.
6. The other widely used individual test, developed by David ___________ , includes both verbal and ____________ or performance components.
7. Howard Gardner theorized that there are ___________ kinds of intelligence, or frames of mind.
8. Robert Sternberg developed the __________ theory of intelligence.
9. Although the infant-testing movement grew out of the tradition of IQ testing, infant scales focus on perceptual motor skills and ___________ interactions.
10. One controversy about intelligence concerns the relative contributions of ________ and environment to an individual's intelligence.
11. Arthur Jensen argued that intelligence is primarily _____________ , and that environment and culture play a ___________ role in intelligence.
12. Contrary to Jensen's claim, most researchers contend that hereditary and environment each contribute about _______ percent to the determination of intelligence.

13. Early intervention programs are designed for children who are __________ .

14. Studies of _______________ objects indicate that intelligence is expressed differently in different cultures.

15. Another controversy about intelligence concerns the use and _________ of intelligence tests.

16. An IQ score below ______ is the usual criterion for mental retardation.

17. Mental ___________ can result from organic or cultural factors.

18. Individuals with above-average IQ scores or superior talent for something are deemed as _____________ .

19. The ______________ thinker typically selects the correct answer required by many intelligence tests.

20. ______________ is the ability to think about in novel and unusual ways and produce unique solutions to problems.

D. MATCHING KEY PEOPLE QUESTIONS

___ 1 The author of a theory of intelligence that assumes eight frames of mind.

___ 2. The individual who encourages a child's natural curiosity and cautions adults not to overcontrol a child's creativity.

___ 3. The author of the triarchic theory of intelligence.

___ 4 The author of two-factor theory of intelligence that assumes there is a general intelligence and a number of specific intelligence.

___ 5 The individual who developed the concept of mental age in his effort to devise a method for determining which students would not benefit from typical school instruction.

___ 6. The individual who developed the infant development assessment.

___ 7. The author of the most widely used individual intelligence test other than revised versions of the Stanford-Binet.

___ 8. The individual who initiated revisions of Binet's intelligence test, and longitudinal research on 1,500 gifted persons.

A. Alfred Binet

B. David Wechsler

C. Charles Spearman

D. L.L. Thurston

E. Howard Gardner

F. Robert J. Sternberg

G. Arnold Gesell

H. Nancy Bayley

I. Robert McCall

J. Lewis Terman

K. J. P. Guillford

L. Mihaly Csikszentmihalyi

M. Teresa Amabile

E. MULTIPLE CHOICE KNOWLEDGE QUESTIONS

1. The psychometric approach to intelligence

    a. focuses on intellectual changes that shape the organization of adolescent intelligence.

    b. ignores individual differences and emphasizes the dynamic nature of intelligence.

    c. is not concerned with predicting intelligence at a later point in development.

    d. focuses on individual differences and seeks to measure them.

2. ____________ is the extent to which a test yields a consistent, reproducible measure of a child's performance.

   a. Standardization
   b. Reliability
   c. Concurrent validity
   d. Criterion validity

3. Joe has a mental age of 8 and a chronological age of 10. Joe's IQ is

   a. 80.
   b. 100.
   c. 125.
   d. 160.

4. Which is *not* an important area in the latest edition of the Standford-Binet test?

   a. verbal reasoning
   b. short-term memory
   c. perceptual speech
   d. visual reasoning

5. One of the main advantages of the Wechsler scales over the Binet test is that the Wechsler scales include measures that are

   a. progressive.
   b. culturally specific.
   c. not verbal.
   d. screens for brain damage.

6. Howard Gardner is known for

   a. his emphasis on multiple intelligences.

   b. revising the original Binet test for use in the United States.

   c. devising the formula for IQ.

   d. his arguments that intelligence consists only of verbal and mathematical abilities.

7. In Robert Sternberg's theory, it is the kind of practical knowledge that allows one to be successful in life.

   a. explicit intelligence

   b. contextual intelligence

   c. componential intelligence

   d. experiential intelligence

8. In addition to the question of whether intelligence is primarily inherited, another important question about intelligence concerns

   a. the reliability of the testing instrument.

   b. cultural and ethnic differences in test scores.

   c. using the computer as a model for information-processing.

   d. the emotional and social adjustment of gifted individuals.

9. Most modern attempts to improve the intellectual environments of impoverished children have focused on

   a. prevention.

   b. educational remediation.

   c. providing money to families.

   d. all of the above techniques.

10. Some intelligence tests have been constructed without any verbal items in an attempt to make them

    a. more reliable.

    b. better able to predict school success in normal schools.

    c. culture-fair.

    d. better able to identify children with strong psychomotor skills.

11. The smallest numbers of mentally retarded individuals are in the category of _____________ retardation.

    a. mild

    b. moderate

    c. severe

    d. profound

12. Which of the following forms of mental retardation is caused by the presence of an extra chromosome?

    a. Down syndrome

    b. cretinism

    c. PKU

    d. cultural-familial retardation

13. Gifted individuals

    a. have above-average intelligence.

    b. have a superior talent.

    c. have academic aptitude.

    d. All of the above are correct.

14. Producing novel responses to problems

    a. is creativity.

    b. may be the product of high intelligence.

    c. is convergent thinking.

    d. All of the above are correct.

15. A psychology professor asks his students to think of as many uses as possible for a paper clip. The professor is encouraging

    a. brainstorming.

    b. divergent thinking.

    c. convergent thinking.

    d. ideational originality.

F. CRITICAL THINKING QUESTIONS

1. What is the difference between Multiple Intelligences and talent or ability?

2. Given the limitations, why even bother to use IQ tests?

G. APPLICATION QUESTIONS

To stimulate the mind and encourage curious learners, individuals need opportunities for experimentation and reflection. The pressure to cover the material in curriculum guides and the sameness of classroom routines can limit such experiences. All too often teachers seek the "right" answer rather than asking probing questions to understand and further a student's thinking. This weakens mental muscles. Challenging students to construct meaning—to develop perspectives, to think independently, to take risks with problem-solving and decision-making—these dispositions can encourage intellectual autonomy and curiosity.

1. Describe a situation from your schooling where you were hindered from intellectual exploration.

2. Describe a situation from your schooling where you were helped towards intellectual exploration.

H. COGNITIVE MAPS

WHAT IS INTELLIGENCE?

- (1)______ ability
- problem (2)_____ skills
- ability to (3)_____ and learn
- individual differences

INTELLIGENCE TESTS

How Tests are Constructed and Evaluated

- reliability
  - test-retest reliability
  - alternate forms reliability
  - split-half reliability
- validity
  - content validity
  - criterion validity
  - concurrent validity
  - predictive validity
- standardization
  - norms

The Binet and Wechsler Tests

- The Binet Test

KEY PERSON
(1)_____ _______
- mental age

William Stern
- intelligence
  (2)_______- IQ
- normal distribution
- The Wechsler Scales

David Wechsler

Do Children Have a Single Intelligence of Multiple Intelligences

KEY PEOPLE
Charles (3)_______
- two-factor theory
- L.L. Thurston
multiple factor theory
- Howard (4)_______
eight frames of mind/intelligences
- Robert J. (5)_______
triarchic theory

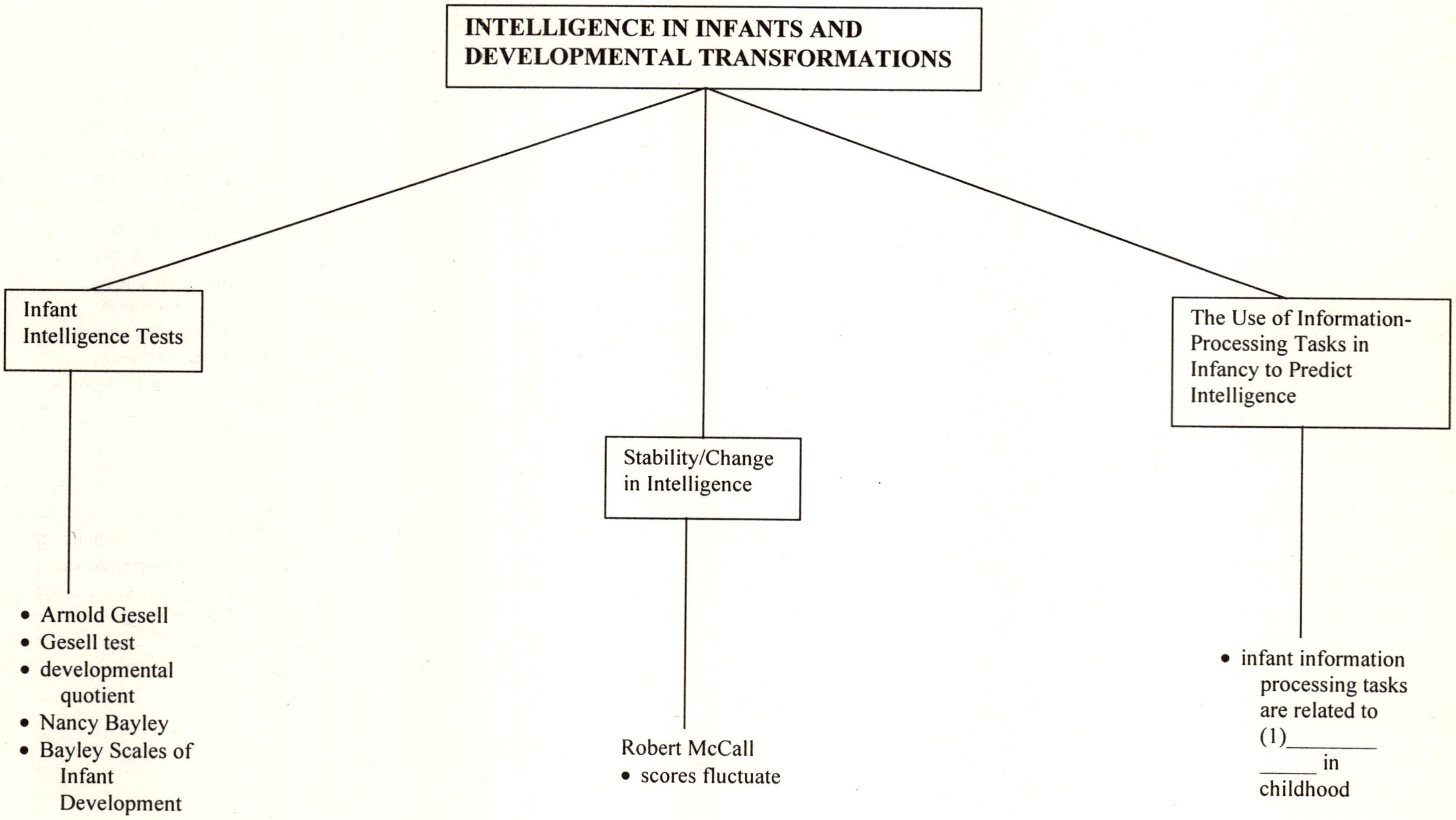

INTELLIGENCE IN INFANTS AND DEVELOPMENTAL TRANSFORMATIONS
Infant Intelligence Tests
• Arnold Gesell
• Gesell test
• developmental quotient
• Nancy Bayley
• Bayley Scales of Infant Development
Stability/Change in Intelligence
Robert McCall
• scores fluctuate
The Use of Information-Processing Tasks in Infancy to Predict Intelligence
• infant information processing tasks are related to (1)________ _____ in childhood

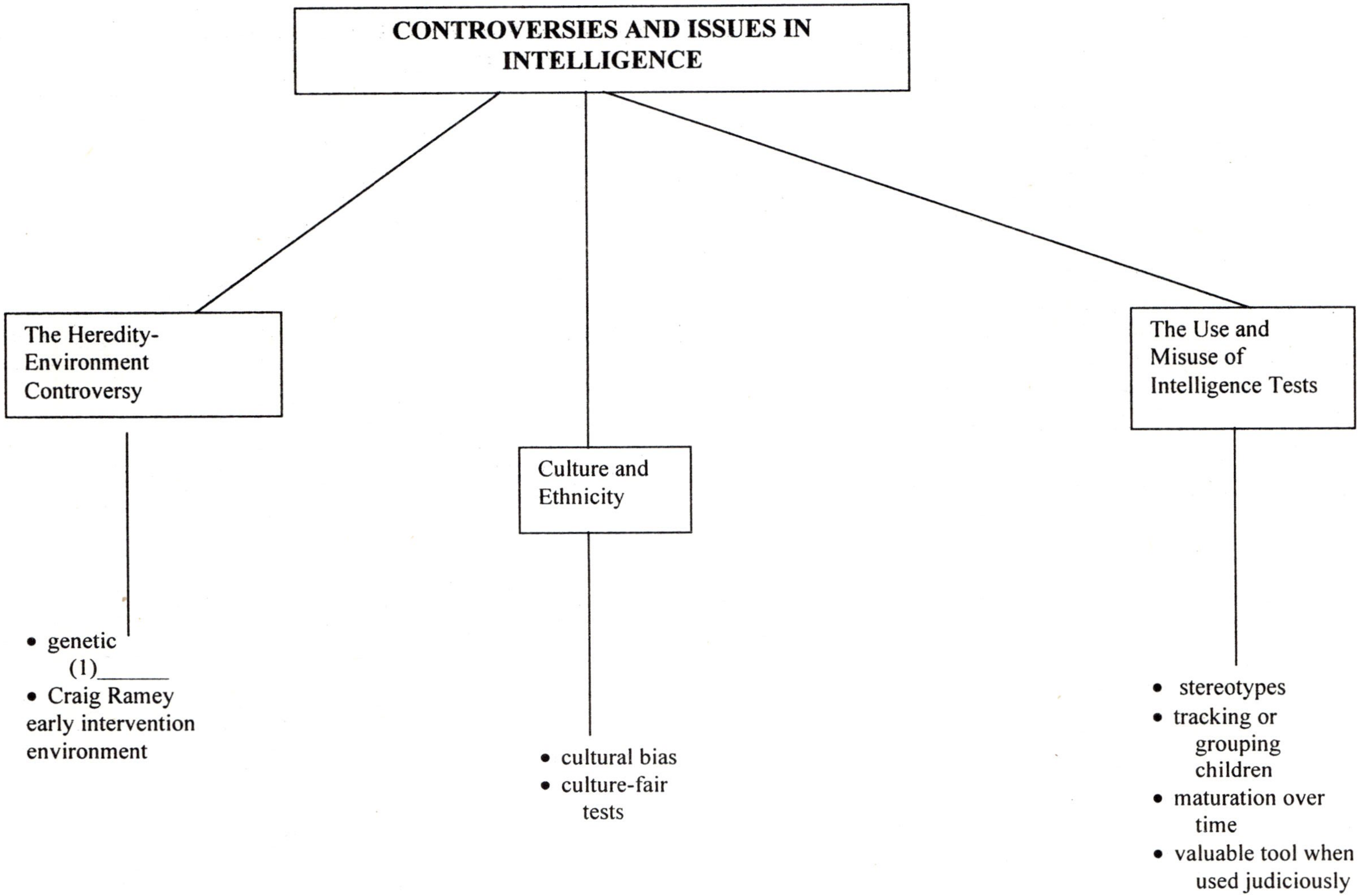
CONTROVERSIES AND ISSUES IN INTELLIGENCE
The Heredity-Environment Controversy
• genetic
(1)______
• Craig Ramey early intervention environment
Culture and Ethnicity
• cultural bias
• culture-fair tests
The Use and Misuse of Intelligence Tests
• stereotypes
• tracking or grouping children
• maturation over time
• valuable tool when used judiciously

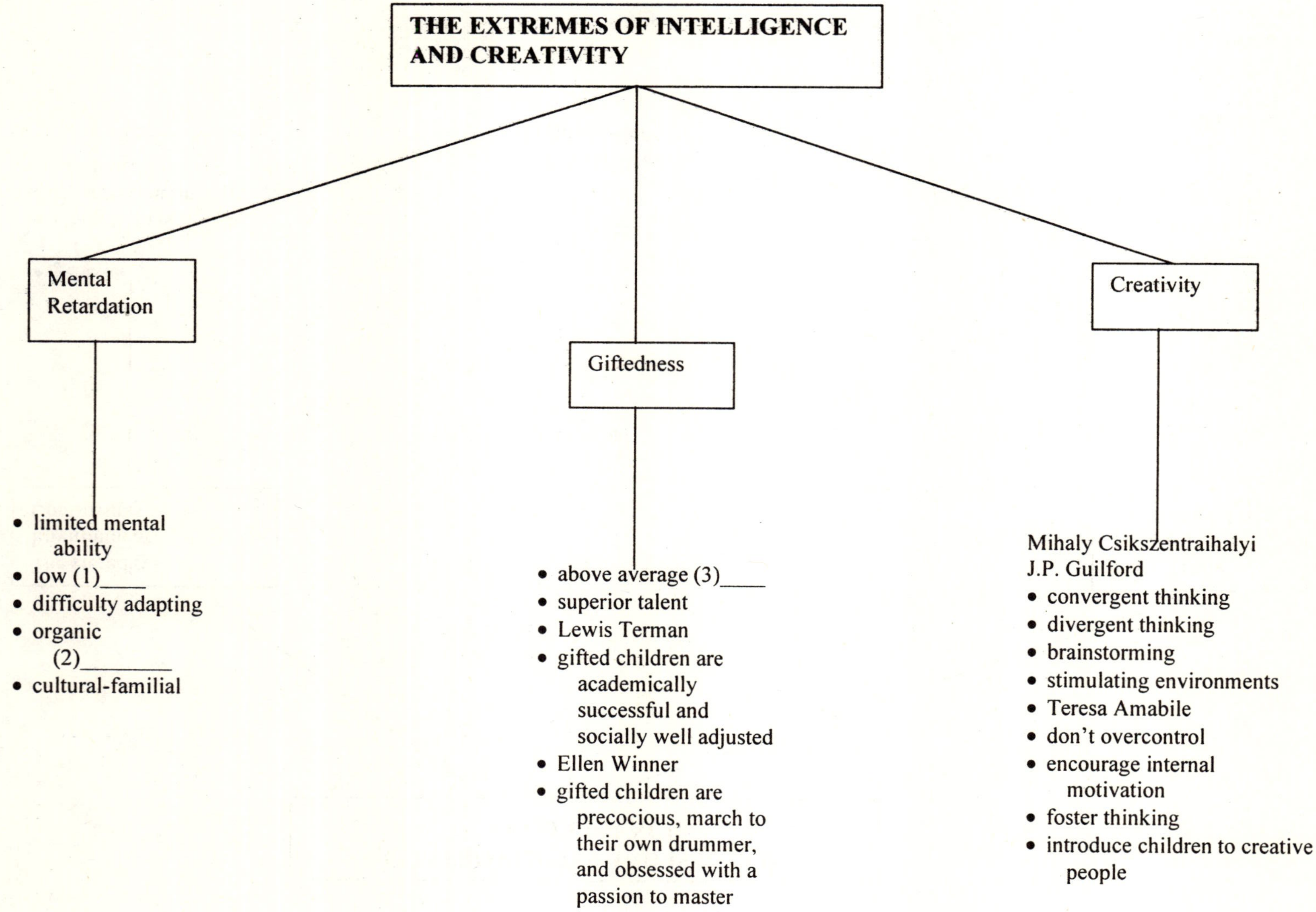
THE EXTREMES OF INTELLIGENCE AND CREATIVITY
Mental Retardation
• limited mental ability
• low (1)____
• difficulty adapting
• organic
(2)________
• cultural-familial
Giftedness
• above average (3)____
• superior talent
• Lewis Terman
• gifted children are academically successful and socially well adjusted
• Ellen Winner
• gifted children are precocious, march to their own drummer, and obsessed with a passion to master
Creativity
Mihaly Csikszentraihalyi
J.P. Guilford
• convergent thinking
• divergent thinking
• brainstorming
• stimulating environments
• Teresa Amabile
• don't overcontrol
• encourage internal motivation
• foster thinking
• introduce children to creative people

I. REVIEW PRIORITIES

Assess your present understanding of the material in this chapter by rating yourself for each heading using the following scale:

1 – I thoroughly understand material and its context to other sections

2 – I understand most of the material and have a basic grasp of the context to other sections

3 –I have a shaky understanding of the material and a poor grasp of the context

4 –I have an inadequate understanding of the material

What is Intelligence? _____

Intelligence Tests

- How Tests Are Constructed _____
- The Binet & Wechsler Tests _____
- Do Children have Single or Multiple Intelligences? _____

Intelligence in Infancy and Development Transformations

- Infant Intelligence Tests _____
- Stability/Change in Intelligence _____
- The Use of Information Processing Tasks in Infancy To Predict Intelligence _____

Controversies and Issues in Intelligence

- The Heredity/Environment Controversy _____
- Culture and Ethnicity _____
- The Uses and Misuse of Intelligence Tests _____

The Extremes of Intelligence and Creativity

- Mental Retardation ______
- Giftedness ______
- Creativity ______

ANSWER KEY

B. TRUE OR FALSE KEY CONTENT QUESTIONS

1. T
2. T
3. F
4. F
5. F
6. T
7. T
8. T
9. F
10. T
11. F
12. F
13. F
14. T
15. F

C. FILL IN THE BLANK KEY TERMS

1. intelligence
2. Reliability
3. validity
4. normal
5. composite
6. Wechsler; nonverbal
7. eight
8. triarchic
9. social
10. heredity
11. inherited; minimal
12. 50
13. at risk
14. sorting or spatial
15. misuse
16. 70
17. retardation
18. gifted
19. convergent
20. Creativity

D. MATCHING KEY PEOPLE QUESTIONS

1. E
2. M
3. F
4. C
5. A
6. H
7. B
8. J

E. MULTIPLE CHOICE KNOWLEDGE QUESTIONS

1. d
2. b
3. a
4. c
5. c
6. a
7. b
8. b
9. a
10. c
11. d
12. a
13. d
14. a
15. b

F. CRITICAL THINKING QUESTIONS

1.

- Gardner characterizes intelligence as Frames of the Mind. These domains (verbal, math, spatial, movement, music, interpersonal, intrapersonal, and naturalistic) represent different mental domains. Multiple Intelligences is being applied in pilot projects in select schools. The emphasis seems to be using Multiple Intelligences to further skill development. However, like talent or ability, it is very difficult to measure Multiple Intelligences. Presently, the value of educational applications of Multiple Intelligence is suggestive rather than prescriptive. Much more research is needed.

2.

- Three significant challenges to standardized testing were reviewed in the text. Controversies continue in defining intelligence by heredity or environment, measuring intelligence in a culturally and ethnically fair manner, and using the results of intelligence tests appropriately. Despite these limitations, intelligence tests are still widely used. However, intelligence tests were never meant to be the only source of assessment. Intelligence tests can provide specific information about an array of mental abilities. IQ tests are most effective when used in conjunction with an individual's medical background, developmental history, and family experiences.

H. COGNITIVE MAPS

A.

1. verbal
2. solving
3. adapt

B.

1. Alfred Binet
2. quotient
3. Spearman
4. Gardner
5. Sternberg

C.

1. standardized tests

D.

1. loading

E.

1. IQ
2. Retardation
3. IQ

CHAPTER 10: LANGUAGE DEVELOPMENT

A. LEARNING OBJECTIVES

What is Language?

1. Define *language* using common characteristics.
2. Define and give examples of each language rule system: *phonology, morphology, syntax, semantics*, and *pragmatics*.

Biological and Environmental Influences

3. State the roles and interaction of each side of the brain in language.
4. Define Noam Chomsky's concept of a *language acquisition device* (LAD).
5. Define *motherese, recasting, echoing, expanding,* and *labeling*.

Language and Cognition

6. Describe the two separate questions concerning language and cognition.

How Language Develops

7. Define Roger Brown's concept of *mean length of utterance* (MLU).
8. Define and contrast the whole language approach to the basic skills and phonics approach to reading.

Bilingualism

9. Explain the recommendations regarding linguistic and cultural diversity made by the National Association for the Education of Young Children.

B. *TRUE OR FALSE KEY CONTENT QUESTIONS*

What is Language?

1. T F Language is a system of symbols used to communicate.

2. T F Infants know how to read lips.

3. T F Syntax involves the meaning of words and sentences.

Biological and Environmental Influences

4. T F Humans acquired language about 10,000 years ago.

5. T F Children throughout the world develop language milestones at different times due to the variation in language.

6. T F Damage to Broca's area often causes problems in speech production, whereas damage to Wernick's area often causes problems in language comprehension.

7. T F The critical period for language acquisition occurs between 18 months and puberty.

8. T F Language development is orderly and sequential despite vast individual differences.

9. T F Children from poor economic backgrounds hear about the same number of words from their parents as do children from middle class economic backgrounds.

Language and Cognition

10. T F Cognition is necessary for language development.

How Language Develops

11. T F A child's first words are spoken between 12 and 18 months.

12. T F The basic skills and phonics approach to reading emphasizes whole and meaningful instruction.

13. T F Children who enter school with less verbal skill and less phonological awareness are most at risk for reading.

Bilingualism

14. T F Critics of bilingualism argue that bilingualism interferes with the performance of both languages.

15. T F Success in learning a second language is greater in childhood than in adolescence.

C. FILL IN THE BLANK KEY TERMS

1. Human languages possess a creative aspect called infinite ____________.
2. The study of basic speech sounds is ______________.
3. ______________ is the study of rules that govern the combining and sequencing of morphemes.
4. ______________ refers to the rules for combining words into acceptable phrases and sentences.
5. The sentence, "The car looked at the mechanic," is semantically correct/incorrect even though it is syntactically correct/incorrect.
6. Pragmatics deals with rules for the ______________ of language in an appropriate conversation and knowledge underlying the use of language in ______________.
7. _________ refers to an inability to articulate and/or comprehend ideas that result from brain damage.
8. The part of the left side of the brain essential to the muscle movements involved in speech production is _____________ area, whereas the part of the left side of the brain involved in language comprehension is ____________ area.
9. Speaking _____________ entails talking in a higher-than-normal frequency, greater-than-normal pitch, and using simple words in short sentences.
10. _____________ is phrasing the same meaning of a sentence in a different way.
11. Repeating what the child has said to you is called _____________.
12. Restating a child's utterance in another, more sophisticated form is called __________.

13. The process of ______________ via the great word game may account for a large part of a child's early vocabulary.

14. Jerome Bruner argues that the sociocultural ___ ______________ is fundamental to an understanding of children's language development.

15. The mean length of utterance is a(n) ____________ of language development based on the number of words per sentence that a child will produce in a sample of 50 to 100 sentences.

16. Children acquire _______ to ________ new words per day between the ages of one and six.

17. During middle and late childhood, children make gains understanding ___________, as evidenced by their use of comparative and subjective phrases.

18. The debate about how to teach reading focuses on the ____________ -language approach versus the basic-skills-and-___________-approach.

19. Early _____________ is important for children who have reading problems.

20. In bilingual education programs, children learn concepts in their _____________ language part of the time while they begin to learn things in ____________.

D. MATCHING KEY PEOPLE QUESTIONS

___ 1. The individual who proposed that there is a critical period for learning language.

___ 2. The individual who devised mean length of utterance to measure children's language maturity.

___ 3. The individual who proposed that children are born with an innate grammatical ability that underlies all languages.

___ 4. The researcher who studied the ability of infants to understand speech sounds.

___ 5. The individual who identified an area of the left hemisphere of the brain that allows articulation and comprehension.

___ 6. The psychologist who developed the concept of language acquisition support system (LASS).

___ 7. Studied the relationship between income level and language acquisition

___ 8. Individual who identified three sequential frameworks of language development in infants and toddlers.

A. Patricia Kuhl

B. Paul Broca

C. Noam Chomsky

D. Eric Lenneberg

E. Roger Brown

F. Naomi Baron

G. Jerome Bruner

H. Janellen Huttenlocher

I. Lois Bloom

J. Betty Hart and Todd Risley

K. Lois Bloom

E. MULTIPLE CHOICE KNOWLEDGE QUESTIONS

1. All languages share which of the following characteristics?

   a. words and sequencing

   b. infinite generativity and multiple levels of rules

   c. words and displacement

   d. meaning and structure

2. Phonology is the study of

   a. use of language.

   b. order of the words of a language.

   c. associations of the words of a language.

   d. sounds of a language.

3. How many morphemes does the word "worker" have?

   a. one

   b. two

   c. three

   d. four

4. The statement, "My car was hit by a speeding lamp post"

   a. is grammatically incorrect.

   b. demonstrates improper pragmatics.

   c. suffers from poor displacement.

   d. violates syntactical restrictions.

5. Japanese children must learn to say thank you with "arigato" in formal settings, with "domo" to a social inferior, and with "arigato gazaimasu" to a social superior. These variations reflect a ____________ aspect of language.

   a. pragmatic

   b. phonetic

   c. syntactical

   d. grammatical

6. The most important factor distinguishing the speech of two-year-old Patty from that of six-year-old Fred is

   a. semantics.

   b. pragmatics

   c. overgeneralizations.

   d. syntax.

7. The idea that human infants come into the world with something like a "language acquisition device" pre-wired in their brains is a characteristic of a ____________ view of language acquisition.

8. Chomsky's view of language argues that

   a. language is innate.
   b. language is acquired through reinforcement.
   c. language results from sensorimotor knowledge.
   d. language acquisition relies both on built-in structures and on principles of learning and cognition.

9. Timmy says to his father, "More milk, Daddy." The father says back to his child, "Shall I get you some more milk?" This is an example of

   a. prompting.
   b. echoing.
   c. expanding.
   d. recasting.

10. The finding that deaf children, who have no command of written or sign language, perform the same on some problem-solving tasks as peers without hearing problems supports the view that

    a. language is an important foundation for thinking.
    b. perception and experience must give rise to language functions in humans.
    c. cognition is an important foundation of language.
    d. cognition is universal; language is irrelevant to its function.

11. In teaching children to read, the currently accepted method is the

a. ABC method alone.

b. whole-word method with the phonics method.

c. whole-word method alone.

d. phonics method alone.

F. CRITICAL THINKING QUESTIONS

1. Compare and contrast "print rich environments" with Vygotsky's concept of zone of proximal development.

2. Discuss the challenges faced in bilingual education.

G. APPLICATION QUESTIONS

Are you aware of the difference between praise and encouragement? Praise is a type of reward. It is another form of behavior management. Praise can make children dependent on others to judge the value of their work. It inhibits self-evaluation and self-confidence. On the other hand, encouragement helps children identify their own feelings of pride or success. Encouraging comments allow children to self-evaluate without damaging their autonomy. Praise fosters external judgment. Encouragement fosters internal satisfaction. Notice the examples below.

1. Can you add your own?

<u>Praise</u>	<u>Encouragement</u>
I am proud of you.	I'll bet you feel good about that.
Good work!	How did you figure that out? The end of the story made me laugh.
I like how Billy is sitting.	Thank you for your help.
You did a super job.	

H. COGNITIVE MAPS

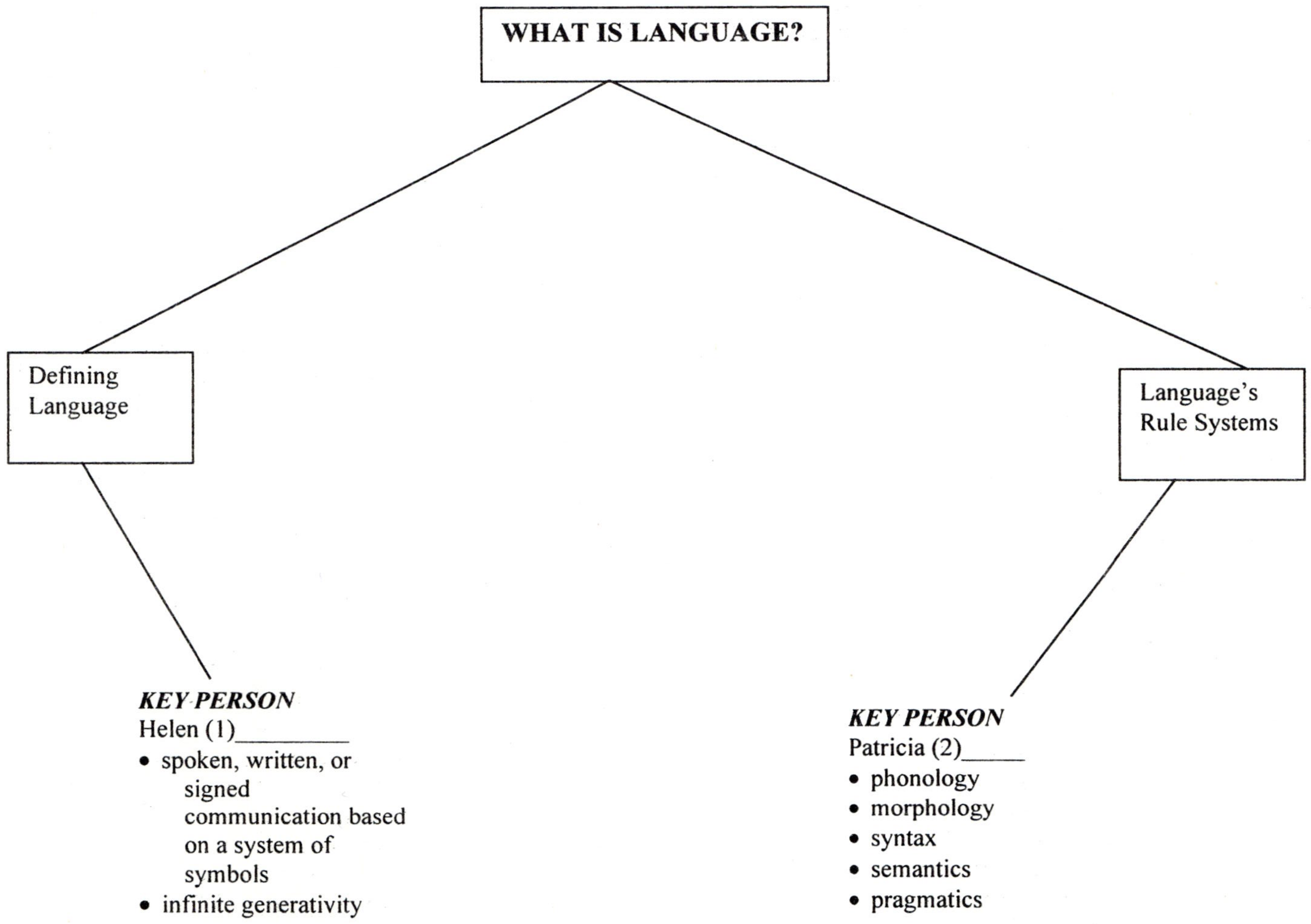
WHAT IS LANGUAGE?
Defining Language
KEY PERSON
Helen (1)________
• spoken, written, or signed communication based on a system of symbols
• infinite generativity
Language's Rule Systems
KEY PERSON
Patricia (2)_____
• phonology
• morphology
• syntax
• semantics
• pragmatics

BIOLOGICAL AND ENVIRONMENTAL INFLUENCES

Biological Influences

Paul Broca

- language milestones occur at about the same time developmentally
- brain's left hemisphere
- aphasia
- Broca's area
- Werniche's area
- language acquisition device (LAD)

KEY PERSON

(1)______ _________

- critical period

Eric Lenneberg

Behavioral and Environmental Influences

Roger Brown

- behavioral
  - language reinforcement and imitation
- environmental
  - motherese
  - recasting
  - echoing
  - expanding
  - labeling

Betty Hart
Todd Risley

- parents influences

Naomi Baron

An Interactionist View of Language

- biological base LAD
- worldwide similar language milestones
- sociocultural context

KEY PERSON

Jerome (2)_______
Language acquisition support system (LASS)

LANGUAGE AND COGNITION

- considerable (1)_____________ between language and cognition

HOW LANGUAGE DEVELOPS

Infancy

- babbling
- earliest communication is pragmatic
- holophrase hypothesis
- overextension
- underextension
- telegraphic speech
- mean length of utterance (MLU)

Early Childhood

KEY PERSON
Janellen (1)________

- advances in
  - phonology
  - morphology
  - syntax
  - semantics
  - pragmatics

Overview of Early Language Development

KEY PERSON
Louis (2)______

- emergence of words
- simple sentences
- complex sentences

Middle and Late Childhood

KEY PERSON
Catherine (3)______

- reading
- whole language approach
- basic-skills-and-phonetics approach
- a combination of the two approaches is the best strategy
- writing
- literacy

BILINGUALISM

- teach academic subjects to children in their (1)______ language while gradually adding English
- bilingualism does not interfere with (2)_________ in either language
- success in learning a second language is greater in (3)___________

I. REVIEW PRIORITIES

Assess your present understanding of the material in this chapter by rating yourself for each heading using the following scale:

1 – I thoroughly understand material and its context to other sections

2 – I understand most of the material and have a basic grasp of the context to other sections

3 – I have a shaky understanding of the material and a poor grasp of the context

4 – I have an inadequate understanding of the material

What is Language?

- Defining Language ____
- Language's Rule System ____

Biological and Environmental Influences

- Biological Influences ____
- Behavioral and Environmental Influences ____
- An Interactionist View ____

Language and Cognition/How Language Develops

- Language and Development in Infancy ____
- Language Development in Early Childhood ____
- Overview of Early Language Development ____
- Language Development in Middle/Late Childhood ____

Bilingualism ____

ANSWER KEY

B. TRUE OR FALSE KEY CONTENT QUESTIONS

1. T
2. T
3. F
4. F
5. F
6. T
7. T
8. T
9. F
10. F
11. T
12. F
13. T
14. F
15. T

C. FILL IN THE BLANK KEY TERMS

1. generativity
2. phonology
3. Morphology
4. Syntax
5. incorrect; correct
6. use; context
7. Aphasia
8. Broca's; Wernicke's
9. motherese
10. Recasting
11. echoing
12. expanding
13. labeling
14. context
15. index
16. five; eight
17. grammar
18. whole; phonetic
19. intervention
20. native; English

D. MATCHING KEY PEOPLE QUESTIONS

1. D
2. E
3. C
4. A
5. B
6. G
7. J
8. K

E. MULTIPLE CHOICE KNOWLEDGE QUESTIONS

1. a
2. d
3. b
4. d
5. a
6. b
7. b
8. a
9. c
10 c
11. b

F. CRITICAL THINKING QUESTIONS

1.

- Language acquisition is complex and interactive. Literacy depends on the interplay between biological and environmental influences. Jerome Bruner stresses the sociocultural role of parents and teachers in modeling reading and writing. Parents structure and nurture their child's exploration of language through naturalistic reading (newspaper, magazines, books), reading bedtime stories, writing letters, etc. This print rich environment sets a norm for children to emulate.
- Vygotsky believed that language plays a key role in cognition. The zone of proximal development (ZPG) is an apt framework for learning how to read and write. Skillful guidance and assistance by adults helps give children the confidence to tackle the complexity and mystery of the written word. When the printed word permeates a classroom (a stop sign, North/East/South/West markers identifying a cardinal direction on each wall, and signs labeling supplies and resources) children can more easily accept print as a natural part of their environment.

2.

- The goal of bilingual education is to teach academic subjects in their native language concurrently with English instruction. Bilingual educators must grapple with two issues: Language acquisition and basic literacy.
- Language acquisition takes time. Verbal proficiency in a second language takes about two or three years. The standard of proficiency in the second language is just the same as the first language: 1) Am I competent enough to communicate? 2) Am I confident enough to express myself naturally?
- Literacy, the skills to understand academic content through reading and writing, can take four or more years. Children who do not become proficient in their second language after two or three years suffer learning deficiencies in their first language.

H. COGNITIVE MAPS

A

1. Keller
2. Kuhl

B

1. Noam Chomsky
2. Bruner

C

1. connectedness

D

1. Huttenlocker
2. Bloom
2. Snow

E

1. native
2. performance
3. childhood

SECTION 4: SOCIOEMOTIONAL DEVELOPMENT

CHAPTER 11: EMOTIONAL DEVELOPMENT

A. LEARNING OBJECTIVES

Exploring Emotion

1. Define *emotion*.

Development of Emotion

2. Define *positive affectivity* and *negative affectivity*.
3. List the developmental sequence for emotional expression in infants.

Emotional Problems, Stress, and Coping

4. Compare and contrast Seligman's learned helplessness with Lazarus' cognitive appraisal as a way to understand childhood depression.
5. Define *acculturation.*

Emotional Intelligence

6. Define *emotional intelligence*.

Temperament

7. Describe the three temperament styles advanced by Chess and Thomas.

Attachment

8. Define *secure attachment* and *insecure attachment.*

B. TRUE OR FALSE KEY CONTENT QUESTIONS

Defining Emotion

1. T F One characteristic of nearly all classifications of emotion are active affectivity and passive affectivity. Positive and negative.

2. T F The three functions of emotion are 1) adaptation and survival, 2) regulation, and 3) communication.

3. T F Research indicates that emotions play a small role in whether a child's peer relations are successful or unsuccessful.

4. T F As a child gets older emotional regulation shifts from self-initiated sources to external sources.

Development of Emotion

5. T F Based on Izard's MAX coding system, interest, distress, and disgust are present at birth.

6. T F Social referencing means reading emotional cues to determine how to act in a particular situation.

7. T F Moodiness in early adolescence reduces an individual's chance to become a competent adult.

Emotional Problems, Stress, and Coping

8. T F Seligman believes that learned helplessness, caused by prolonged exposure to negative experiences over which there is no control, leads to depression.

9. T F Lazarus' cognitive appraisal is a way children interpret stress as either harmful, threatening, or challenging.

10. T F Firsthand contact between two different cultural groups can cause stress.

11. T F Measures of emotional intelligence have received widespread acceptance.

Temperament

12. T F Most parents believe in the importance of temperament with the birth of their first child.

13. T F Children who have a difficult temperament are at risk for problem behavior.

Attachment

14. T F Feeding is more important than contact comfort in establishing attachment.

15. T F Caregivers of secure babies are sensitive to their signals and are consistently available to meet their needs.

16. T F A mother's role to the child is largely caregiving; a father's role is largely playful interaction.

17. T F In stressful circumstances, infants often prefer their mother than their father.

18. T F More than 12 million young children currently attend licensed day care.

19. T F The NICHD study showed that child care adversely affected the security of infants' attachment to their mother.

20. T F The recommended ratio of children to adult caregivers for three year olds is 15:1.

C. FILL IN THE BLANK KEY TERMS

1. Although it is difficult for researchers to define emotion, the accepted definitions encompass feelings, physiological __________, and overt behavior.
2. Emotions can be classified as either positive __________ or __________ affectivity.
3. Carroll Izard developed the _____________, or Maximally Discriminative Facial Movement Coding System, to study the ____________ expressions of infants.
4. Infants display at least __________ types of cries that differ in frequency, intensity, and pause.
5. Mary Ainsworth and John Bowlby believe that prompt attention by the caregiver contributes to a __________ attachment between the infant and the caregiver.

6. The new functionalism in emotion view indicates that emotion is __________ rather than intrapsychic.

7. Depression is ____________ common during adolescence than during childhood, and is a ___________ common problem for females than males.

8. Martin Seligman proposed a(n) ___________ account of children's depression that focuses on uncontrolled events and experiences.

9. Adolescent depression is also associated with poor __________ relationships, and with difficult changes or challenges.

10. Richard Lazarus hypothesized that our experience of stress is related to our ________ appraisal and interpretation of events.

11. The current view is that daily hassles and life events may be culprits in __________.

12. The negative consequence of acculturation is called ____________ stress, a problem for many ethnic minority group members.

13. __________ refers to an individual's behavioral style and characteristic pattern of responding.

14. Chess and Thomas found that about ____ percent of the children they studied could be classified as easy, _____ percent could be classified as difficult, and ____ percent could be classified as slow-to-warm-up.

15. __________ is the tendency to prefer the tendency of others.

16. Developmentalists define attachment as a close emotional bond between infants and ____________.

17. Harlow and Zimmerman concluded that the object of attachment is the individual who provides _________ comfort rather than oral satisfaction.

18. Ainsworth attributes the nature of an infant's attachment to the __________ and responsiveness of the primary _________ .

19. In stressful situations, infants appear more attached to their _____________

20. The quality of day care received by most children in the United States is ________ and can have _______ developmental outcomes for the children.

D. MATCHING KEY PEOPLE QUESTIONS

___ 1. The creator of Maximally Discriminative Facial Movement Coding System.

___ 2. The researcher who devised the Strange Situation to measure attachment.

___ 3. Either of two researchers who identified the basic temperaments as the easy child, the difficult child, and the slow-to-warm-up child.

___ 4. The individual who studied nontraditional gender roles in Swedish families.

___ 5. One of the two researchers who used monkeys to test the Freudian hypothesis that oral satisfaction promotes attachment to the caregiver.

___ 6. The researcher whose work illustrates the new functionalism in emotion.

___ 7. The psychologist who believes that emotional intelligences matters more than standardized intelligence tests when it comes to predicting competence.

___ 8. The psychiatrist who believed that an infant and its mother instinctively form an attachment.

A. Nancy Eisenberg

B. John Bowlby

C. Carroll Izard

D. Martin Seligman

E. Daniel Goleman

F. Alexander Chess and Stella Thomas

G. Harry Harlow and Robert Zimmerman

H. Konrad Lorenz

I. Mary Ainsworth

J. L. Alan Stroufe

K. Michael Lamb

E. MULTIPLE CHOICE KNOWLEDGE QUESTIONS

1. A classic study by Harry Harlow and Robert Zimmerman found that __________ was (were) most important in infant attachment.

    a. contact comfort

    b. oral satisfaction

    c. sex drive reduction

    d. reinforcers

2. Erik Erikson says that the key time for attachment is within the first _____ after birth.

    a. few minutes

    b. few hours

    c. day

    d. year

3. Mary Ainsworth says attachment security depends on

    a. how sensitive and responsive the caregiver is to infant signals.

    b. the mother's love and concern for the welfare of the child.

    c. the consistency of parental responses during the child-care routine.

    d. reinforcement if attachment behaviors by the caregiver.

4. Which of the following techniques describes use of the Strange Situation to investigate attachment?

    a. watching children as they are separated from and then reunited with their parents

    b. asking parents to describe how emotionally involved they are with their children

    c. watching children play with dolls representing adults and children to see what kind of interactions they create

    d. asking baby-sitters about how infants behave when their parents are gone

5. Temperament is best defined as

   a. the way an individual reacts to a special person in the environment.

   b. an individual's general behavioral style.

   c. the emotions experienced by infants and children.

   d. the reaction displayed by a parent when a child engages in an unwanted activity.

6. Emotion is a mixture of

   a. physiological arousal and cognitions.

   b. cognitions and behaviors.

   c. physiological arousal and behaviors.

   d. None of the alternatives is correct.

7. Early social smiles tend to be toward

   a. food.

   b. faces.

   c. genital stimulation.

   d. random external stimuli.

8. According to John Bowlby, children become depressed as a result of

   a. self-devaluing cognitive schema.

   b. exposure to prolonged uncontrollable negative experiences.

   c. insecure attachments.

   d. living with depressed parents.

9. African Americans living in Dubuque, Iowa who found burning crosses in their yards at night in the fall of 1991 were experiencing

   a. daily hassles.

   b. life events.

   c. frustration.

   d. acculturative stress.

10. The major problem in assessing the impact of day care on child development lies in the

    a. wide variety of "types of day care."

    b. lack of interest in the issue.

    c. fact that so few children attend day care.

    d. lack of theoretical basis for predicting negative outcomes.

F. CRITICAL THINKING QUESTIONS

1. How can emotional intelligence issues be introduced into schools predisposed to an almost exclusive cognitive curriculum?

2. How can parents help their children learn to control their emotions?

G. APPLICATION QUESTIONS

Coping with stress invariably involves anger management. Anger, per se, is not the problem. Mindless attachment to the anger is. An oversimplified view of this complex phenomenon distinguishes between episodic anger, involving a particular situation and chronic anger, which is a more permanent and pervasive. Note the options in dealing with each type of anger and some relaxation exercises to help vent the tension.

Individuals with *situational anger* identify more with their perceived loss than their opportunities for gain. The tension between competing perspectives can be painful and oppressive. An "either/or" outcome personalizes the conflict: "If *THIS* happens, I will be happy, but if *THAT* happens I will not be happy. Since my enemy (nemesis) did *THAT*, then he/she/they must be responsible for my unhappiness. To break this compulsive cycle, to move to a "both/and" outcome and become more responsible for your own thoughts, feelings and actions, consider the following responses to coping with uncontrolled anger:

- Identify situations that trigger anger
- Become aware of body warning signs
- Discuss feelings with friends
- Communicate directly and nonjudgementally
- Learn to assess needs and limits
- Practice mediation

Individuals with *chronic anger* find most things unjust and are mad most of the time. Such responses are defensive and judgmental. Their perspective is self-absorbed; it is almost impossible for them to see another side of the story. Some warning signs to indicate chronic anger are:

- Labeling and blaming—disclaiming personal responsibility in conflict
- Mindreading—invents motives in others for their perceived irresponsibility

- Exaggeration—magnify trivial incidents to boost self-importance
- Inappropriate expectations—unrealistic or unaware expectancy

What can an individual do to deal constructively with anger? Consider the following relaxation technique. Practice these simple steps whenever anger closes down your awareness:

1. How does my body feel?
2. Calm down
    - Take three deep breaths.
    - Count backwards slowly.
    - Think calming thoughts.
    - Conscious positive self-talk.
3. Think out loud how to solve the problem
4. Think about it later
    - Why was I angry?
    - What did I do?
    - What worked?
    - What didn't work?
    - What would I do differently?

H. COGNITIVE MAPS

EXPLORING EMOTION

Defining Emotion

- a feeling or affect
- (1)________ ________ (PA)
- (2)________ ________ (NA)

Functionalism and Emotion

- adaptation and survival
- regulation
- communication

Relational Emotion

- parent-child relationships
- peer relationships

Regulation of Emotion

- gradual shift from external sources for controlling emotions to self-initiated sources
- cognitive strategies gradually increase
- gradually develop capacity to modulate emotional arousal
- become more adept at managing situations
- become more capable at selecting effective ways to (3)_____

DEVELOPMENT OF EMOTION

Infancy

- (1)____________ ____________ ________ __________ Coding System (MAX) Developmental timetable
- Crying
  - basic crying
  - anger cry
  - pain cry
- smiling
  - reflexive smile
  - social smile
- stranger anxiety
- social referencing

Early Childhood

- more adept at talking about emotions
- increase in number of terms to describe emotions
- awareness to control and manage emotions

Middle and Late Childhood

- understand (2)________ emotions like pride and shame
- understand more than one emotion can be expressed in a particular situation
- suppress and conceal emotions
- use strategies to redirect emotions

Adolescence

- emotional highs and lows increase
- moodiness is (3)______

EMOTIONAL PROBLEMS, STRESS, AND COPING

Depression

John Bowlby
- developmental
- Aaron Beck
- cognitive
- Martin Seligman
- learned helplessness theory

Stress and Coping

KEY PERSON
Richard (1)__________
- cognitive appraisal
  - primary appraisal
  - secondary appraisal
- life events and hassles
- sociocultural factors
  - acculturation
  - poverty
- coping
  - remove one stressor
  - use coping strategies

Michael Rutter
- death

EMOTIONAL INTELLIGENCE

- ability to monitor one's own feelings and the feelings of others and use this information to guide thinking and actions

KEY PERSON

- Daniel (1)_______
- emotional self-awareness
- managing emotions
- reading emotions
- handling relationships

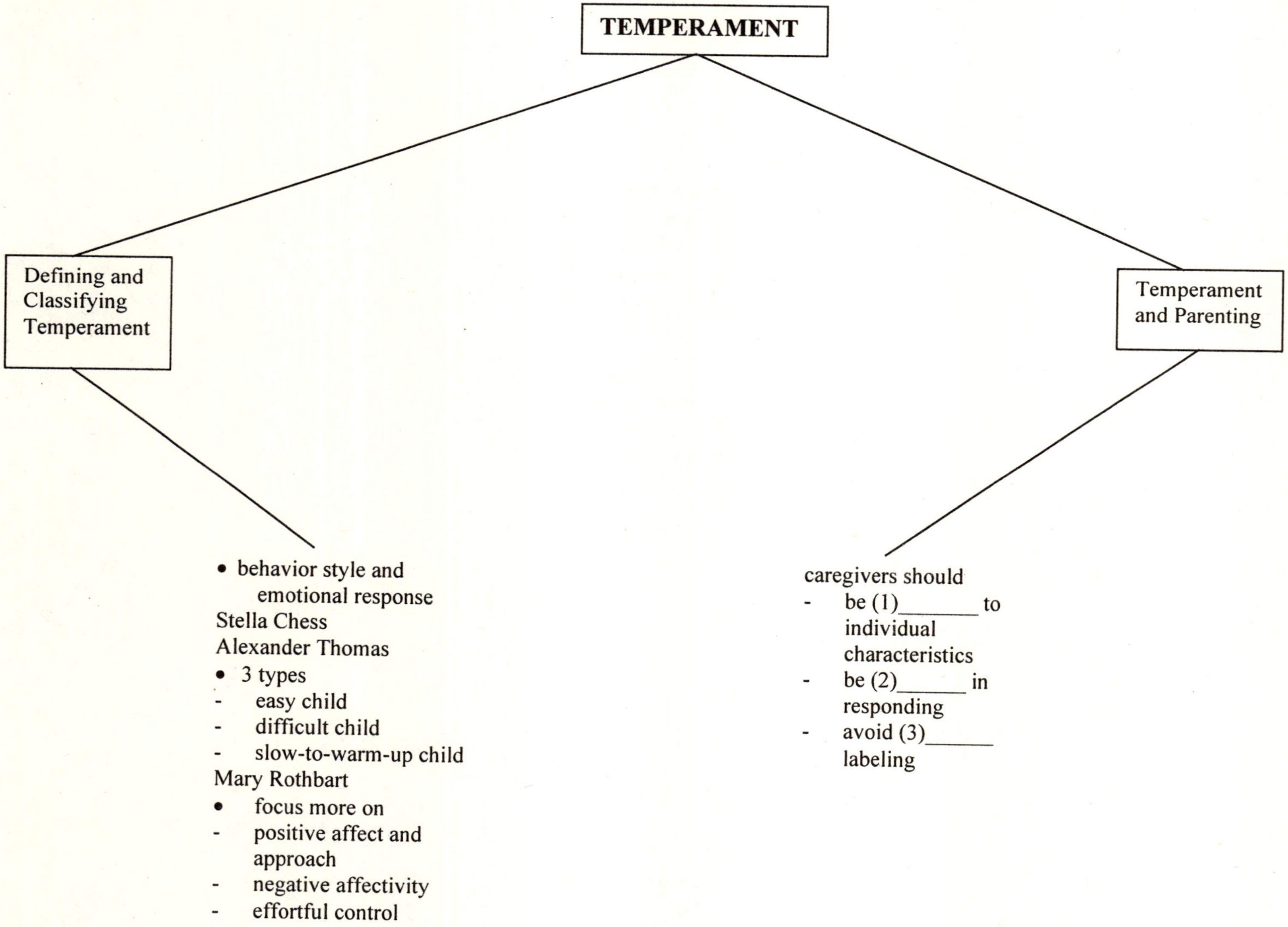
TEMPERAMENT
Defining and Classifying Temperament
• behavior style and emotional response
Stella Chess
Alexander Thomas
• 3 types
- easy child
- difficult child
- slow-to-warm-up child
Mary Rothbart
• focus more on
- positive affect and approach
- negative affectivity
- effortful control
Temperament and Parenting
caregivers should
- be (1)_______ to individual characteristics
- be (2)______ in responding
- avoid (3)______ labeling

ATTACHMENT

What Is Attachment?

- close emotional bond between infant and caregiver
- contact comfort, familiarity, and trust are important

Konrad Lorenz
Erik Erikson
John Bowlby

Individual Differences

KEY PEOPLE

Mary (1)______
L. Alan (2)______

- type B babies - secure
- type A babies - avoidant
- type C babies – ambivalent-resistant
- type D babies - disorganized

Caregiving Styles and Attachment

- secure babies – caregivers are sensitive and consistently available
- avoidant babies – caregivers are unavailable and rejecting
- ambivalent-resistant babies – caregivers are inconsistently available and not affectionate
- disorganized babies – caregivers are neglectful and abusive

Measurement of Attachment

Mary Ainsworth

- strange situation

Attachment, Temperament, and the Wider Social World

- consider biological factors – heredity and temperament
- consider social agents and contexts
- cultural variations

Ross Thompson
Jerome Kagan

Fathers as Caregivers of Infants

KEY PERSON

Michael (3)______

- increased interaction with children
- father – playful interaction

mother - caregiving

Day Care

- need of American families
- quality
- quality affects (4)______

I. REVIEW PRIORITIES

Assess your present understanding of the material in this chapter by rating yourself for each heading using the following scale:

1 – I thoroughly understand material and its context to other sections

2 – I understand most of the material and have a basic grasp of the context to other sections

3 – I have a shaky understanding of the material and a poor grasp of the context

4 – I have an inadequate understanding of the material

Exploring Emotion

- Defining Emotion ____
- Functionalism in Emotion ____
- Relational Emotion ____
- Regulation of Emotion ____

Development of Emotion

- Infancy ____
- Early Childhood ____
- Middle and Late Childhood ____
- Adolescence ____

Emotional Problems, Stress, and Coping

- Depression ____
- Stress and Coping ____

Emotional Intelligence ____

Temperament

- Defining and Classifying Temperament ______
- Temperament and Parenting ______

Attachment

- What is Attachment? ______
- Individual Differences ______
- Caregiving Styles & Attachment Styles ______
- Measurement of Attachment ______
- Attachment, Temperament & Wider Social World ______
- Fathers as Caregivers of Infants ______
- Daycares ______

ANSWER KEY

B. TRUE OR FALSE KEY CONTENT QUESTIONS

1. F
2. T
3. F
4. F
5. T
6. T
7. F
8. T
9. T
10. T
11. F
12. F
13. T
14. F
15. T
16. T
17. T
18. F
19. F
20. F

C. FILL IN THE BLANK KEY TERMS

1. arousal
2. affectivity; negative
3. MAX; facial
4. three
5. secure
6. relational
7. more; more
8. environmental
9. peer
10. cognitive
11. stress
12. acculturative
13. Temperament
14. 40; 10; 15
15. Sociability
16. caregivers
17. contact
18. sensitivity; caregiver
19. mothers
20. poor; negative

D. MATCHING KEY PEOPLE QUESTIONS

1. C
2. I
3. F
4. K
5. G
6. J
7. E
8. B

E. MULTIPLE CHOICE KNOWLEDGE QUESTIONS

1. a
2. d
3. a
4. a
5. c
7. b
8. c
9. d
10. a

F. CRITICAL THINKING QUESTIONS

1.

- Traditional curriculum responds to the 3 R's—Reading, 'Riting, and 'Rithmetic. Given the needs and challenges of 21st century education, that dictum may be expanded to include the 5 R's—Reading, 'Riting, 'Rithmetic, *Respect, and Responsibility*. If this concept is broadly accepted by parents and policy makers as well as administrators and teachers, then a more holistic education can emerge. Increasingly, schools are tackling social problems as part of an emerging "life skills" curriculum. This response to the "whole child" can focus on the ABC's of learning: Affective, Behavioral, and Cognitive.

2.

- As they get older, children gradually shift from external sources for controlling their emotions to self-initiated sources, i.e., moving from pleasing authority (or fighting authority) to learning self-control. Parents play a critical role in helping their children regulate their emotions. They can teach their children problem-solving approaches for regulating emotions, model healthy ways to deal with emotional arousal, and choose effective ways to cope with stress.
- An *emotion-coaching* parent monitors their children's emotions and views their children's negative emotions as a "teachable moment." They assist children in naming the emotion they are experiencing and coach them on how to effectively deal with the emotion.
- An *emotion-dismissing* parent denies or ignores their children's negative emotions. These children do not learn how to regulate their emotions, cope with stress and have more behavioral problems.

H COGNITIVE MAPS

A

1. positive affectivity
2. negative affectivity
3. cope

B

1. Maximally Discriminative Facial Movement
2. complex
3. normal

C

1. Lazarus

D

1. Goleman

E

1. sensitive
2. flexible
3. negative

F

1. Ainsworth
2. Sroufe
3. Lamb
4. attachment

CHAPTER 12: THE SELF AND IDENTITY

A. LEARNING OBJECTIVES

The Self

1. Define *self-understanding, self, esteem,* and *self-concept.*
2. Describe ways to increase children's self-esteem.
3. Compare and contrast children's and adolescent's self-understanding with respect to social comparison, preoccupation, self-protection, and self-integration.
4. Describe Selman's five stages of *perspective-taking.*

Identity

5. Compare and contrast *identity* versus *identity confusion.*
6. Compare and contrast between *crisis* and *commitment* and explain James Marcia's identity statuses theory (identity *diffusion,* identity *foreclosure*, identity *moratorium*, and identity *achievement*).
7. How does parenting relate to identity outcomes?
8. Explain how cultural and ethnicity influences the development of identity.
9. Explain how gender influences the development of identity.

B. *TRUE OR FALSE KEY CONTENT QUESTIONS*

The Self

1. T F Self-understanding is the cognitive representation of the child's self-concept.
2. T F John Watson's research demonstrated that self-awareness emerges after the child is three years old.
3. T F Infants develop a rudimentary form of self-recognition at approximately 18 months old.
4. T F The physical and active self is characteristic of middle and late childhood.
5. T F Contradictory self-descriptions among adolescents dramatically increases between seventh and ninth grades.
6. T F Adolescents are less likely than children to be self-conscious and preoccupied with their self-understanding.
7. T F Children's perspective-taking abilities can improve peer status and the quality of their friendships.
8. T F Self-esteem refers to the domain-specific evaluations of the self.

Identity

9. T F Two core ingredients in Erickson's theory of identity development are personality and role reversal.
10. T F Identity formation begins with adolescence.
11. T F Most adolescents follow a previewing adolescence/postponement achievement (PAPA) cycle.
12. T F College juniors and seniors are more likely to be identity achieved than high school students.
13. T F Both individuality and connectedness in family relations are necessary for identity development.

14. T F James Marcia's theory identifies four identity statuses that focus on the adolescent tension between crisis and commitment.

15. T F Many ethnic minority adolescents have bicultural identities, identifying with both their ethnic minority culture as well as with the majority culture.

16. T F The task for identity exploration is more complex for males than females.

C. TRUE OR FALSE KEY CONTENT QUESTIONS

1. The concept of self-understanding refers to a child's___________ representation of the self.
2. Human infants demonstrate a rudimentary self-understanding at about ____ months old.
3. Young children describe themselves on the basis of ____________ characteristics, whereas elementary-school-age children describe themselves in terms of _________ characteristics and social comparisons.
4. Adolescents use _________ that are more abstract and ___________ than those used by children to describe themselves.
5. The concept of the fluctuating self refers to the characteristic ___________ of self that persists until late adolescence or early adulthood.
6. Substantial discrepancy between one's actual self and one's ideal self can produce _____________ .
7. Compared with children, adolescents are <u>more/less</u> self-conscious and preoccupied with their self-understanding.
8. Robert __________ has proposed a developmental theory of perspective taking.
9. Self-esteem refers to a ____________ evaluation of the self, whereas self-concept refers to a __________-specific evaluation of the self.
10. There are __________ methods for increasing children's self-esteem.
11. According to Erikson, the adolescent enters a psychological ____________ during which he or she tries several __________.

12. Adolescents who cope with the conflicting identities develop a new sense of _______; however, adolescents who do not successfully resolve their identity _________ remain confused and may withdraw from society or lose themselves in the _________.

13. Identity development minimally entails a ____________ direction, ideological stance, and a ________ orientation.

14. Marica's four statuses of identity are defined by the extent of an adolescent's __________ and ___________.

15. Democratic parenting encourages identity _____________, autocratic parenting fosters identity foreclosure, and permissive parenting encourages identity __________ .

16. Identity formation is ___________ by family relationships that are both individuated and connected.

17. Research has shown that identity exploration is __________ among ethnic minority than White American college students.

18. The contemporary view is that identity formation precedes the stage of intimacy for ________ , whereas intimacy precedes identity for __________ .

D. MATCHING KEY PEOPLE QUESTIONS

___ 1. The individual who studied the role of individuality and connectedness in the development of identity.

___ 2. The first theorist to develop a comprehensive theory of identity development.

___ 3. The developmentalist who proposed that the concepts of crisis and commitment could be used to classify individuals according to four identity statuses.

___ 4. The researcher who developed the Self-Perception Profile for Adolescents.

___ 5. Researchers who studied youth organizations dedicated to building a sense of ethnic pride among inner-city youth.

___ 6. The investigator who studied adolescent ethnic group identification in a predominately White American culture.

___ 7. A developmental theorist who studies children's perspective-taking.

___ 8. The researcher who demonstrated that self-awareness emerges very early in infancy and develops over the first three to four months.

A. Susan Harter

B. John Watson

C. Hazel Markus

D. Robert Selman

E. Erik Erikson

F. James Marcia

G. Alan Waterman

H. Catherine Cooper

I. Jean Phinney

J. Shirley Heath & Milbrey McLaughlin

E. MULTIPLE CHOICE KNOWLEDGE QUESTIONS

1. After placing a dot of rouge on an infant's nose, a researcher notes that while looking in the mirror, the infant repeatedly touches her nose. The researcher is studying

   a. visual self-recognition.

   b. cognitive self-understanding.

   c. rational self-esteem.

   d. representative self-conception.

2. When eight-year-old Cory says, "I'm faster than most kids in my class," he is

   a. engaging in self-recognition.

   b. indicating positive affectivity.

   c. displaying identity diffusion.

   d. making a social comparison.

3. Over the course of adolescence, your son becomes more likely to admit inconsistencies in his behavior. This is probably due to his increasing success at

   a. achieving his ideal self.

   b. egocentrism.

   c. self-absorption.

   d. self-integration.

4. Children exhibiting high levels of perspective-taking have been found to

   a. have less self-esteem.

   b. interact more effectively with their peers.

   c. experience more "false" selves.

   d. have more idealistic self-understanding.

5. Which of the following parental characteristics is associated with self-esteem in children?

   a. expression of affection

   b. setting permissive rules

   c. conflicted family environments

   d. parental intelligence

6. Your daughter's high school offers a new course that emphasizes the importance of both academic and social abilities. This course is a sneaky way to try to enhance

   a. identity achievement.

   b. patience during the moratorium.

   c. self-esteem.

   d. harmonious family relationships.

7. According to Erik Erikson, a richer identity can be achieved when the adolescent grows up in a culture

   a. where vocational choices are limited.

   b. that allows a longer period of time for moratorium.

   c. that is ethnically and racially diverse.

   d. where parents hand down decisions in an authoritarian way.

8. James Marcia's concept of identity has been criticized for

   a. ignoring the effects of culture on the development of identity.

   b. reducing Erik Erikson's complex ideas to simply asking whether a person has made a decision or not.

   c. rejecting the importance of commitment.

   d. assuming that parents play no part in the development of their children's identities.

9. Concerning parenting and identity development, autocratic is to foreclosure as

    a. democratic is to achievement.
    b. permissive is to foreclosure.
    c. authoritarian is to diffusion.
    d. neglecting is to connectedness.

10. Catherine Cooper and her colleagues have suggested that connectedness within the family has two dimensions, which are

    a. bonding and respect.
    b. crisis and commitment.
    c. self- and other-connectedness.
    d. mutuality and permeability.

F. CRITICAL THINKING QUESTIONS

1. How do the dimensions of real and ideal, true and false, and possible selves influence adolescents' socioemotional development?

2. Explain why "many ethnic minority youth must bridge 'multiple worlds' in constructing their identity" (Catherine Cooper).

G. APPLICATION QUESTIONS

Damage to pride or self-esteem generally is expressed in some undesirable behavior. Bad feelings usually beget bad actions. How can a power struggle be avoided? One answer is to respect both self and others during conflictual situations. Mutual respect helps prevent discipline problems. Mutual respect involves accepting another for who they are instead of trying to make them into what you want. Many adults have trouble accepting children's reasoning. They try to get children to accept adult reasoning.

1. Describe a childhood situation where you were not fully "heard" by an adult. Were you forced to accept the adult's interpretation of your situation? How did this affect your trust for that adult?

2. Describe an interpersonal conflict that ended with a win/win outcome. What allowed for mutual respect to occur?

H. COGNITIVE MAPS

THE SELF

Self-(1)_________

- •cognitive representation of self
- John Watson
- infancy
- early childhood
- middle and late childhood
- Susan Harter
- Earl Rogers
- adolescence
- Hazel Marcus
- possible self
- Robert Selman
- perspective taking

Self-(2)_____ and Self-(3)________

- self esteem – global self evaluation
- self concept – domain self evaluation
- assessment
- parent-child relationships
- consequences of low self-esteem
- increasing self-esteem

Susan Harter

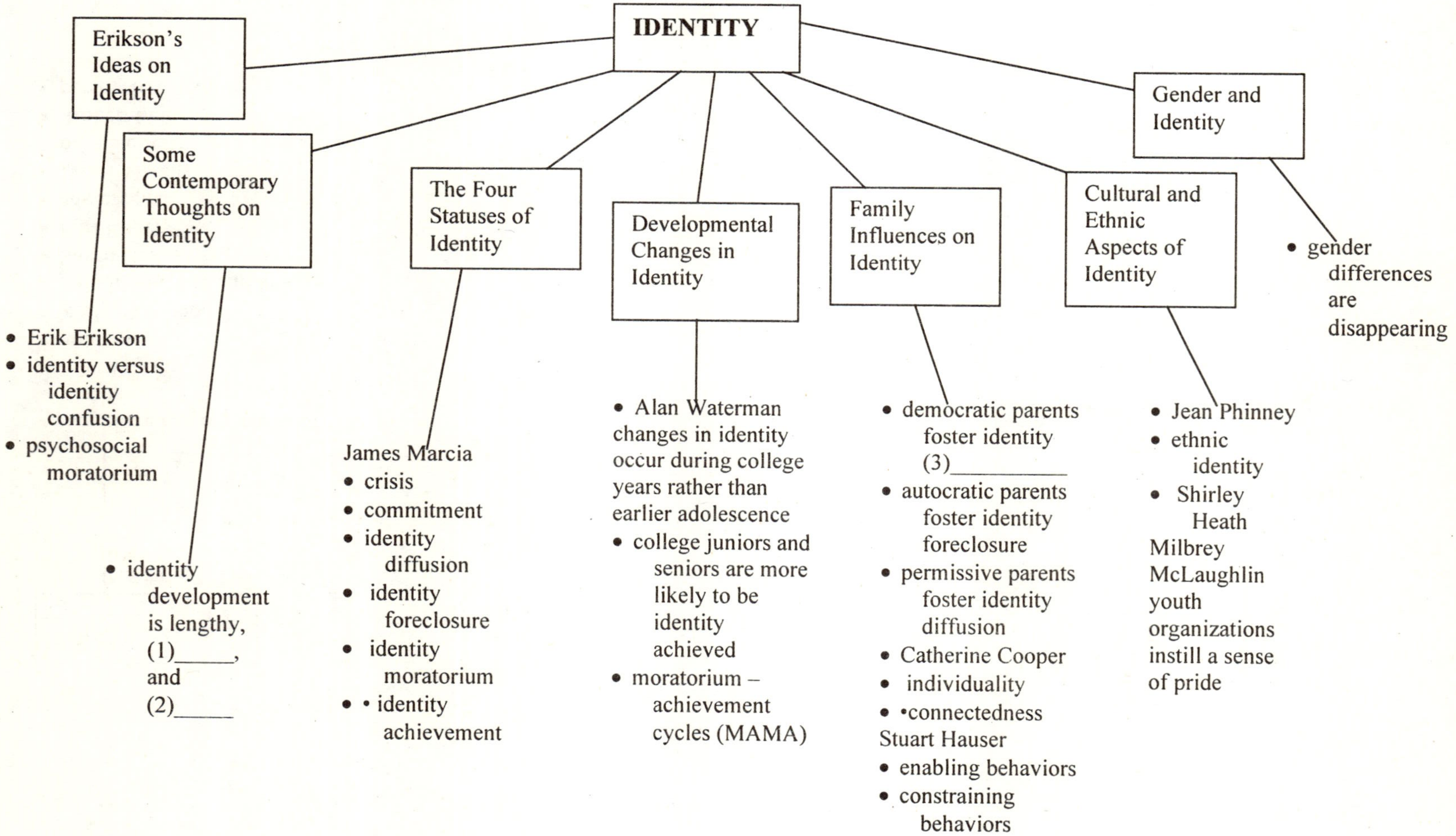
IDENTITY
Erikson's Ideas on Identity
• Erik Erikson
• identity versus identity confusion
• psychosocial moratorium
Some Contemporary Thoughts on Identity
• identity development is lengthy, (1)_____, and (2)_____
The Four Statuses of Identity
James Marcia
• crisis
• commitment
• identity diffusion
• identity foreclosure
• identity moratorium
• • identity achievement
Developmental Changes in Identity
• Alan Waterman changes in identity occur during college years rather than earlier adolescence
• college juniors and seniors are more likely to be identity achieved
• moratorium – achievement cycles (MAMA)
Family Influences on Identity
• democratic parents foster identity (3)__________
• autocratic parents foster identity foreclosure
• permissive parents foster identity diffusion
• Catherine Cooper
• individuality
• •connectedness
Stuart Hauser
• enabling behaviors
• constraining behaviors
Cultural and Ethnic Aspects of Identity
• Jean Phinney
• ethnic identity
• Shirley Heath
Milbrey McLaughlin
youth organizations instill a sense of pride
Gender and Identity
• gender differences are disappearing

I. REVIEW PRIORITIES

Assess your present understanding of the material in this chapter by rating yourself for each heading using the following scale:

1 – I thoroughly understand material and its context to other sections

2 – I understand most of the material and have a basic grasp of the context to other sections

3 – I have a shaky understanding of the material and a poor grasp of the context

4 – I have an inadequate understanding of the material

The Self

- Self-Understanding _____
- Self-Esteem and Self-Concept _____

Identity

- Erickson's Ideas on Identity _____
- Contemporary Thoughts on Identity _____
- The Four Statuses of Identity _____
- Developmental Changes _____
- Family Influences on Identity _____
- Cultural and Ethnic Aspects of Identity _____
- Gender and Identity Development _____

ANSWER KEY

B. TRUE OR FALSE KEY CONTENT QUESTIONS

1. T
2. F
3. T
4. F
5. T
6. F
7. T
8. F
9. F
10. F
11. F
12. T
13. T
14. T
15. T
16. F

C. FILL IN THE BLANK KEY TERMS

1. cognitive
2. 18
3. physical; social
4. labels; idealistic
5. instability
6. depression
7. more
8. Selman
9. global; domain
10. four
11. moratorium; roles
12. self; crisis; crowd
13. vocational; sexual
14. crisis; commitment
15. achievement; diffusion
16. enhanced
17. greater
18. males; females

D. MATCHING KEY PEOPLE QUESTIONS

1. H
2. E
3. F
4. A
5. J
6. I
7. D
8. B

E. MULTIPLE CHOICE KNOWLEDGE QUESTIONS

1. a
2. d
3. d
4. b
5. a
6. c
7. b
8. b
9. a
10. d

F. CRITICAL THINKING QUESTIONS

1.

- Adolescents develop their self-understanding by exploring their multiple selves. An adolescent can distinguish between their *real self* (who they are with friends and their *ideal self* (who they are on a date). An adolescent can distinguish between their *true self* and *false self* (who they imagine themselves to be) as well as *possible self* (who they want to be).
- This differentiation helps them to see the multidimensional possibilities before them. They can describe themselves in terms of connections to others (family, friends, peers, etc.) as well as in the context of current selves (living with parents and participating in high school athletics) and future selves (living independently while away at college). Ironically, their ability to navigate these multiple worlds helps them develop the stability and integration needed for adulthood.

2.

- Most ethnic minority youth *consciously* confront their ethnicity for the first time in adolescence. The messages of identity markers for ethnic minority adolescents can be challenging and confusing. Which cultural mandates to follow: his or her own ethnic group or the ethnic group of the dominant culture?
- Many ethnic minority youth have to confront issues of prejudice and discrimination. Such barriers are often invisible, yet potent, and can limit their goals and aspirations. It is even more difficult to establish a positive identity if they live in impoverished environments where exposure to drugs, gangs, and crime is more prevalent.
- Organizations offering positive role models and effective channels for the needs and interests of adolescents can help ethnic minority youth develop a positive identity.

H. COGNITIVE MAPS

A

1. understanding
2. esteem
3. concept

B

1. gradual
2. complex
3. achievement

CHAPTER 13: GENDER

A. LEARNING OBJECTIVES

What is Gender?

1. Define *gender, gender identity,* and *gender role.*

Biological, Social, and Cognitive Influences

2. Summarize the views of Freud and Erikson about the influence of genitals on gender specific behavior.
3. Compare and contrast the *identification theory* and *social learning theory* regarding gender development.
4. Define *gender schema.*

Gender Stereotypes, Similarities, and Differences

5. Compare and contrast achievement orientations of males and females.
6. Define *rapport talk* and *report talk.* How do they relate to gender differences in talking?

Gender-Role Classification

7. Define *androgyny.* Describe the Bem Sex-Role Inventory.
8. List the characteristics of an androgynous individual.

Development Windows Of Gender Opportunity And Asymmetric Gender Socialization

9. Describe how the intensity of gender socialization is different for boys and girls.
10. When is the developmental window of opportunity in learning gender roles?

B. TRUE OR FALSE KEY CONTENT QUESTIONS

What is Gender?

gender

1. T F Gender role is the sense of being male or female, which most children acquire by the time they are three years old.

Biological, Social, and Cognitive Influences

2. T F Sex hormones are related to some cognitive abilities.
3. T F Violent male criminals and professional football players have higher levels of testosterone than ministers do.
4. T F Freud's theory promotes the idea that anatomy is destiny.
5. T F Children's gender orientation is due to the interaction of biological and environmental factors.
6. T F In the social roles view, women and men have equal power and status due to gender hierarchy and sexual division of labor.
7. T F Social cognitive theory argues that sexual attraction to parents is involved in gender development.
8. T F Girls are encouraged to be more nurturant and emotional than boys, and fathers are more likely to engage in aggressive play with sons than daughters.
9. T F Peers reinforce gender-appropriate behavior.
10. T F Elementary children show a clear preference for being with and liking same-sex peers.
11. T F Pressure to achieve in school is more likely put on girls than boys.
12. T F Studies reveal that nonsexist television programming such as "Freestyle" reduces stereotypical gender attitudes.
13. T F Gender schema theory suggests that a child's gender identification is guided by internal motivation to conform to sociocultural standards and stereotypes.

Gender Stereotypes, Similarities, and Differences

14. T F Gender stereotypes are widespread around the world, especially emphasizing male's power and female's nurturance.

15. T F Physical and biological differences between males and females are substantial.

16. T F Males are more physically aggressive and active than females, while females are more likely to focus on social relationships.

Gender-Role Classification

17. T F In traditional gender roles, a well-adjusted male was suppose to show instrumentalist traits, and the well-adjusted female was suppose to show expressive traits.

18. T F Androgyny education programs have been equally successful with males and females, and both children and adolescents.

Development Windows Of Gender Opportunity And Asymmetric Gender Socialization

19. T F Girls receive gender socialization earlier and more intensely than boys do.

20. T F The only developmental window in learning gender roles comes during the toddler years.

C. FILL IN THE BLANK KEY TERMS

1. Biological, social, and cognitive ___________ affect gender.
2. According to the social learning theory of gender, boys and girls learn gender _______ through __________ and imitation of gender behavior, and through the rewards and punishments they experience for _________ appropriate and inappropriate behaviors.
3. Parents __________ their children's gender development.
4. Fathers are _______ likely than mothers to act differently toward their sons and daughters.
5. Peer demands for conformity to gender roles are especially intense during __________.

6. Despite greater __________ to portrayal of males and females on television shows, programs during the 1990s still portray females as _______ competent than males.

7. A ________ schema is a construct that organizes the world according to sex, and reflects an understanding of ____________ standards.

8. Broad categories that reflect impressions about what behavior is appropriate for males and females are termed gender-role ____________.

9. As sexual equality increases, gender stereotypes and behavioral differences may __________ .

10. A classic review of cognitive gender differences by Eleanor Maccoby and Carol Jacklin indicated that females have better _________ skills than males, and males have better ____________ skills and better ___________ skills than females.

11. One consistent socioemotional finding is that males are more ___________ than females.

12. Males are more likely than females to display _________ toward strangers.

13. Females are more likely than males to include emotional descriptions of their __________ relationships.

14. The traditional masculine orientation was labeled _____________ , and focused on the attainment of goals and emphasized a person's accomplishments.

15. The traditional feminine orientation was labeled ___________ , and emphasized the facilitation of social interaction, interdependence, and relationships.

16. Sandra Bem developed the Bem Sex-Role Inventory that classifies gender-orientation of individuals into four categories: masculine, _________ , androgynous, and __________ .

17. An ____________ individual is a female or male who has a high degree of both feminine and masculine traits, whereas an individual that has neither masculine nor feminine characteristics is said to be ____________.

18. Individuals who are _____________ are the least competent, whereas _____________ individuals are more flexible and more mentally healthy than either masculine or feminine orientated individuals.

D. MATCHING KEY PEOPLE QUESTIONS

___ 1. A communication sociolinguist who has distinguished rapport talk from report talk.

___ 2. A developmentalist who published the classic review of gender differences and criticized Carol Gilligan for overemphasizing differences in gender.

___ 3. An adolescence developmentalist who favors replacing the term androgyny with gender-role transcendence.

___ 4. A developmentalist who created the gender measure called Bem Sex-Role Inventory.

___ 5. A social scientist who argued that sex differences were due to the different restrictions and opportunities society provides for males and females.

___ 6. Researcher(s) who studied gender discrimination in schools.

___ 7. A researcher who challenged the belief of cognitive differences between males and females.

___ 8. A psychologist who argues that the sexes are psychologically similar except in those areas requiring adaptive responses to evolutionary challenges.

A. Stephanie Shields

B. Sandra Bem

C. Eleanor Maccoby

D. Myra and David Sadker

E. Lawrence Kohlberg

F. Carol Jacklin

G. Janet Shibley Hyde

H. Deborah Tannen

I. David Buss

J. Alice Eagly

K. Joseph Pleck

L. Carol Beal

E. *MULTIPLE CHOICE KNOWLEDGE QUESTIONS*

1. __________ refers to a set of expectations about sex-appropriate behavior.

   a. Stereotype

   b. Gender role

   c. Gender intensification

   d. Sexism

2. Which statement is most accurate?

   a. Fathers want their firstborn to be a boy, but mothers want their firstborn to be a girl.

   b. Neither fathers nor mothers express a preference regarding the sex of their firstborn child.

   c. Both fathers and mothers want their firstborn to be a boy.

   d. Fathers want their firstborn to be a girl, but mothers want their firstborn to be a boy.

3. In which area are parents *unlikely* to treat their sons and daughters differently?

   a. the types of toys they are encouraged to play with

   b. the emotional traits that are rewarded and punished

   c. the extent of freedom from supervision

   d. the need to conform to cultural norms

4. On the playground, girls teach girls and boys teach boys about their gender behaviors. This has been called

   a. gender school.

   b. gender intensification.

   c. peer socialization.

   d. peer genderization.

5. Adolescent females watching television are likely to find

   a. fewer role models than their brothers will.

   b. accurate representations of women's roles.

   c. important lessons on managing relationships.

   d. little to identify with in terms of sexual intimacy.

6. Gender schema theory predicts that adolescents are drawn to sources of information that enable them to

   a. conform to stereotypes.

   b. learn about sexuality.

   c. learn about relationships.

   d. think idealistically.

7. In some ways, the culture defines the stereotypes. For example, in contrast to people living in less-developed nations, people living in more highly developed countries tend to see the role of males as

   a. similar to females.

   b. more assertive.

   c. less emotional.

   d. more competent.

8. A relatively clear gender difference has been found in the areas of

   a. aggression and activity level.

   b. susceptibility to mental disorder.

   c. nurturance and helping behavior.

   d. verbal and math abilities.

9. Pat feels embarrassed when making a mistake in public and has experienced episodes of jealousy and love. What gender is Pat likely to be?

   a. male

   b. female

   c. equally likely to be male or female

   d. There is no research on which to base an answer.

10. According to Bem Sex-Role Inventory, an adolescent is androgynous if she scores

   a. high on masculinity and high on femininity.

   b. high on masculinity and low on femininity.

   c. low on femininity and low on masculinity.

   d. halfway between masculinity and femininity.

F. CRITICAL THINKING QUESTIONS

1. Describe the gender differences in beliefs about emotions and emotional responses.

2. Identify significant social influences of gender development.

G. APPLICATION QUESTIONS

Words have a powerful effect on how we think and act. Such semantics are especially striking in the use of words that define the relationship of men and women.

For example, the generic use of the term *mankind* can unconsciously condition men to think in male-centered ways and women to think that they are secondary or do not count. The changing norms of gender equality, within the legal system and the marketplace, have caused a renewed attention to sexist language. However, linguistic habits are learned early and are difficult to break.

1. Consider nonsexist substitutes to the following terms in common usage:

    a. mankind to *humankind or humanity*

    b. chairman to *chairperson or chair*

    c. spokesman to *spokesperson or speaker or representative*

    d. manpower to

    e. statesman to

    f. craftsman to

    g. brotherhood to

    h. common man to

    i. Dear Sir to

H. COGNITIVE MAPS

WHAT IS GENDER?

KEY PERSON

Stephanie (1)________

- sociocultural dimension of being female or male
- gender identity
- gender role

BIOLOGICAL, SOCIAL, AND COGNITIVE INFLUENCES

Biological Influences

Sigmund Freud
Erik Erikson

- heredity – 23rd pair of chromosomes determines anatomical sex
- hormones
  - estrogens
  - androgens
- evolutionary psychology
- interactionist view

Social Influences

KEY PERSON
Alice (1)_______

- social roles view
- identification theory
- social cognitive theory of gender
- parental influences
- peer influences

Eleanor Maccoby
Myra and David Sadker

- school influences
- media influences

Cognitive Influences

KEY PERSON
Lawrence (2)_____

- cognitive developmental theory of gender
- schema
- gender schema
- gender schema theory
- language

GENDER STEREOTYPES, SIMILARITIES, AND DIFFERENCES

Stereotyping

- gender stereotypes
  - male's power
  - female's nurturance

Similarities and Differences

- physical/biological factors
- Carol Jacklin
- Janet Shibley Hyde
- cognitive factors
- socioemotional factors
- Deborah Tannen
- rapport talk
- report talk
- •gender controversy

KEY PERSON

David (1)_____

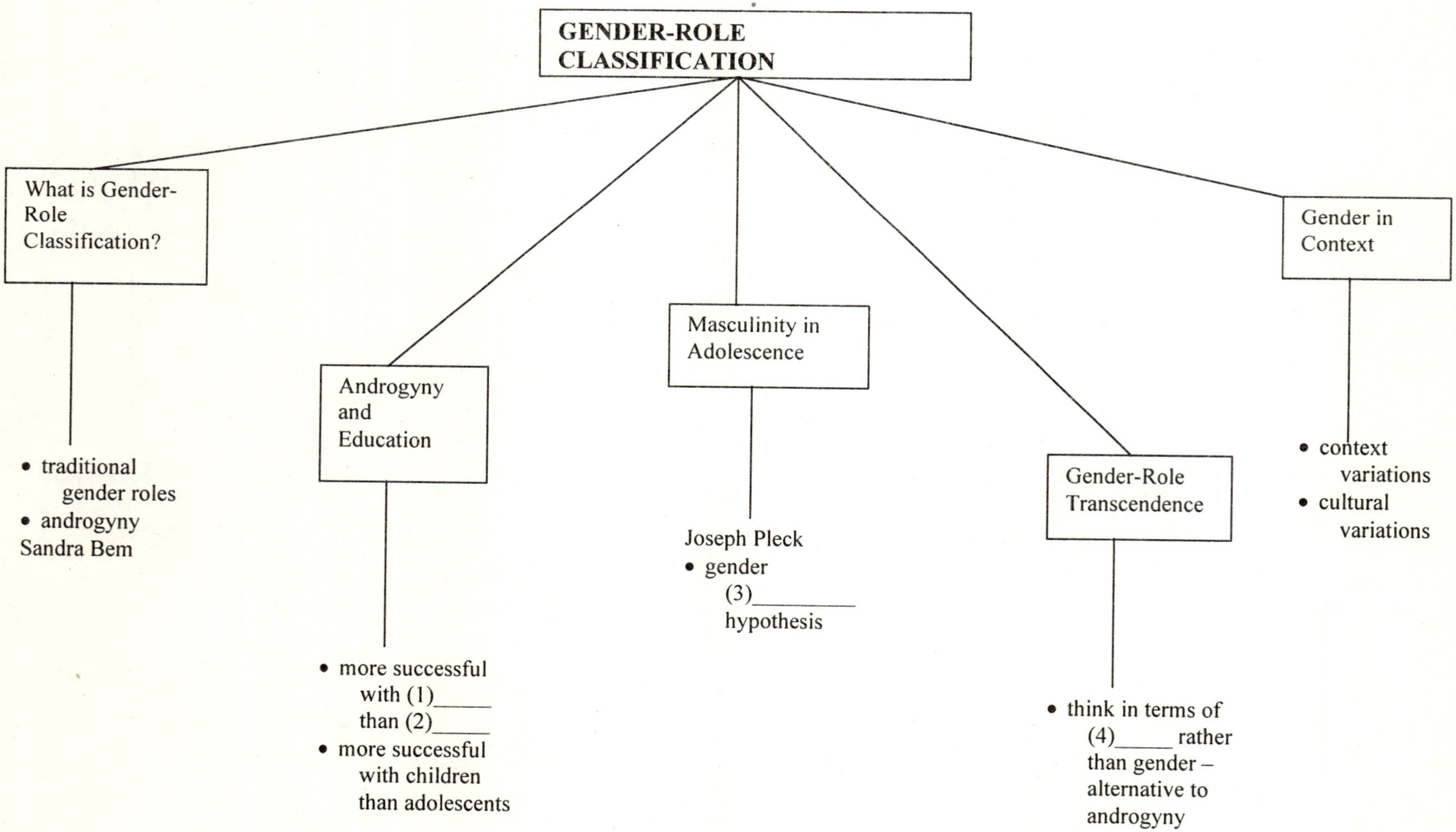
GENDER-ROLE CLASSIFICATION
What is Gender-Role Classification?
• traditional gender roles
• androgyny
Sandra Bem
Androgyny and Education
• more successful with (1)_____ than (2)_____
• more successful with children than adolescents
Masculinity in Adolescence
Joseph Pleck
• gender (3)_________ hypothesis
Gender-Role Transcendence
• think in terms of (4)_____ rather than gender – alternative to androgyny
Gender in Context
• context variations
• cultural variations

DEVELOPMENTAL WINDOWS OF GENDER OPPORTUNITY AND ASYMMETRIC GENDER SOCIALIZATION

Developmental Windows

KEY PERSON
Carol (1)_____
- toddler years
- early adolescence

Asymmetric Socialization

- amount, timing, and intensity of gender socialization
- boys gender socialization is earlier and more intense
- boys have more difficulty learning male gender roles

I. REVIEW PRIORITIES

Assess your present understanding of the material in this chapter by rating yourself for each heading using the following scale:

1 – I thoroughly understand material and its context to other sections

2 – I understand most of the material and have a basic grasp of the context to other sections

3 – I have a shaky understanding of the material and a poor grasp of the context

4 – I have an inadequate understanding of the material

What is Gender? ____

Biological, Social, and Cognitive Influences

- Biological Influences ____
- Social Influences ____
- Cognitive Influences ____

Gender Stereotypes, Similarities, and Differences'

- Stereotyping ____
- Similarities and Differences ____

Gender-Role Classification

- What is Gender-Role Classification ____
- Androgny ____
- Masculinity in Adolescence ____
- Gender-Role Transcendence ____
- Gender in Context ____

Development Windows Of Gender Opportunity And Asymmetric Gender Socialization

- Developmental Windows _____
- Asymmetric Socializations _____

ANSWER KEY

B. TRUE OR FALSE KEY CONTENT QUESTIONS

1. F
2. T
3. T
4. F
5. T
6. F
7. F
8. T
9. T
10. T
11. F
12. F
13. T
14. T
15. T
16. T
17. T
18. F
19. F
20. F

C. FILL IN THE BLANK KEY TERMS

1. influences
2. development; observation; gender
3. influence
4. more
5. adolescence
6. sensitivity; less
7. gender; sociocultural
8. stereotypes
9. diminish
10. verbal; mathematical; visuospatial
11. aggressive
12. anger
13. interpersonal
14. instrumental
15. expressive
16. feminine; undifferentiated
17. androgynous; undifferentiated
18. undifferentiated; androgynous

D. MATCHING KEY PEOPLE QUESTIONS

1. H
2. C
3. K
4. B
5. J
6. D
7. G
8. I

E. MULTIPLE CHOICE KNOWLEDGE QUESTIONS

1. b
2. c
3. d
4. a
5. a
6. a
7. a
8. a
9. c
10. a

F. CRITICAL THINKING QUESTIONS

1.

- Deborah Tannen's research reports that girls are more relationship-oriented than are boys. In a girl's peer group intimacy is pervasive. Girls tend to take turns more often than boys when playing games.
- Boy's talk tends to be more informational. Boys tend to be more competitive when playing games. They boast of their skill and argue who is best.
- Males usually show less self-regulation of emotions than do females.

2.

- Parental influences—Mothers tend to nurturance and physical care; fathers engage in play; both parents emphasize conformity to existing social norms.
- Peer influences—Elementary age children prefer same sex activities; greater social mixing occurs during adolescence, however, peer pressure is strong to maintain culturally-determined gender roles.
- Media—Males are depicted as more competent and powerful than are females in television programming. Females are usually shown to be sexually provocative in rock music videos. Males are more often depicted as clever, industrious, and brave, and females are shown as passive and dependent in print media and children's books.

H. COGNITIVE MAPS

A

1. Shields

B

1. Eagly
2. Kohlberg

C

1. Buss

D

1. females
2. males
3. identification
4. people

E

1. Beal

CHAPTER 14: MORAL DEVELOPMENT

A. LEARNING OBJECTIVES

What is Moral Development?

1. Define *moral development*.

Moral Thoughts

2. Define and contrast *heteronomous morality* and *autonomous morality.*
3. Explain the three levels of Kohlberg's moral reasoning. Describe the criticism of this theory.
4. Compare and contrast the *justice perspective* and the *care perspective*.

Moral Behavior

5. Compare and contrast the behavioral perspective (reinforcement, punishment, and imitation) with the social cognitive perspective (resistence to temptation and self-control) affect moral behavior.

Moral Feelings

6. Define *empathy*. How does empathy relate to *perspective taking*?

Altruism

7. Define *altruism*. Identify how equality, merit, and benevolence develop in William Damon's view of altruism.

Parenting and Moral Development

8. Define *love withdrawal*, *power assertion*, and *induction* child-rearing techniques. Which technique does Martin Hoffman recommend as the best way to support moral development in children? Why?

Moral Education

9. Define *hidden curriculum, character education,* and *values clarification.*

10. Define James Rest's concepts of *moral sensitivity, moral judgment, moral motivation*, and *moral character.*

Juvenile Delinquency

11. Explain how family experiences and peer associations affect juvenile delinquency.

B. TRUE OR FALSE KEY CONTENT QUESTIONS

What is Moral Development?

1. T F Moral development has three components: an interpersonal dimension, an intrapersonal dimension, and ethics.

Moral Thoughts

2. T F Piaget's concept of autonomous morality, beginning around 10 years old, concerns the unchangeable properties of justice and rules.
3. T F Kohlberg's stages of moral reasoning assumes an internalization whereby moral behavior is controlled by internal, self-generated principles.
4. T F Both Piaget and Kohlberg believed that the mutual give and take of peer relations teaches perspective-taking and gives children a sense that rule-making is democratic.
5. T F Kohlberg's theory is criticized for overlooking moral behavior, the justice perspective, and the overestimation of the cultural role.
6. T F Gilligan advocates a stronger care perspective with emphasis on positive modeling for early adolescent girls.

Moral Behavior

7. T F Reinforcement, punishment, imitation, and situational variability defines moral development from the behaviorist point of view.
8. T F The child's ability to resist temptation and develop self-control defines moral development from the social cognitive view.
9. T F Social cognitive theory equates moral competence (moral behaviors) and moral performance (moral behaviors in specific situations).

Moral Feelings

10. T F The contemporary perspective suggests that positive feelings, such as empathy, contribute more to children's moral development than do negative feelings, such as guilt.

Altruism

11. T F After four years old, sharing is considered an act of altruism.

12. T F According to Piaget and Kohlberg, the primary role in a child's moral development comes from peers.

Parenting and Moral Development

13. T F The parental discipline technique of induction, using reason and explanation of consequences, works better with elementary age children than with pre-school age children.

14. T F The internalization of society's moral standards is more likely among lower social economic status (SES) children than among middle class SES children.

15. T F Children's moral development advances when parents are warm and supportive, and involve children in family decision-making.

Moral Education

16. T F Nearly 60 years ago, John Dewey identified the "hidden curriculum" in American schools whereby values of democracy and capitalism were inculcated.

17. T F Values clarification is a direct instruction that teaches students a basic moral literacy that prevents doing harm to self or others.

18. T F Among adolescents, service learning can improve grades, decrease alienation, and increase self-esteem and motivation.

Juvenile Delinquency

19. T F Self-reported patterns suggest that less than 10 percent of adolescents engage in delinquent behavior.

20. T F Youth violence can be reduced by effective parenting and a collaborative support among families, schools, and communities.

C. FILL IN THE BLANK KEY TERMS

1. The development of the rules and conventions regarding how people should behave in their interactions with others is called ____________ development.
2. The concept of immanent justice is a characteristic of Piaget's moral stage of ______________ rather than ______________ morality.
3. According to Piaget, children advance their moral reasoning skills through _________ rather than _________________ relations.
4. Lawrence Kohlberg said that moral development is based on moral ______________ and unfolds in three ___________ , each of which entails two ____________.
5. Factors that influence an individuals' movement through the moral stages include modeling, ______________ conflict, peer relations, and ___________-taking opportunities.
6. The first criticism of Kohlberg's work is that he did not pay enough attention to moral _______________ .
7. A related criticism of Kohlberg's method for the assessment of moral reasoning is that his dilemmas focused on family and __________ rather than on everyday dilemmas concerned with ____________ relationships.
8. Kohlberg's approach exemplifies the ____________ perspective, whereas Gilligan's approach exemplifies the _________ perspective.
9. ____________ influence whether adolescent girls silence their "voice."
10. Behaviorists and __________ learning theorists believe that the basic processes affecting moral development include reinforcement, punishment, and _____________ .

11. A key aspect of moral development is the ability to resist _______________ and to develop self-___________ .

12. Moral ________________ depends on cognitive-sensory processes, whereas moral ______________ depends on an individual's motivation, and the rewards and incentives obtained from specific actions.

13. Empathy depends on the development of the cognitive skill of _____________ taking.

14. Altruism involves both ______________ and exchange.

15. Although parents may encourage sharing, children _____________ their own fairness standards through daily interactions with peers.

16. The child-rearing technique of _________ is a disciplinary procedure in which parents use reason to explain the consequences of children's action for others.

17. The ____________ character education approach either emphasizes values or character traits during specific time periods, or integrates values and character traits into the curriculum.

18. Prominent examples of indirect moral education include values clarification and ____________ moral education.

19. James Rest contends that moral development builds the four processes of moral sensitivity, moral ___________, moral motivation, and moral _____________ .

20. Interventions that can reduce or prevent youth violence should include involvement from _____________, supportive families, and youth and community _____________ .

D. MATCHING KEY PEOPLE QUESTIONS

___ 1. The psychologist who studied why youth kill and what can be done to prevent it.

___ 2. The developmentalist who proposed a comprehensive approach to moral education based on his observations of children and adolescents.

___ 3. Either of two individuals who studied 11,000 children and adolescents who were given an opportunity to lie, cheat, and steal in a variety of circumstances.

___ 4. The individual who advocates the use of parent induction to promote moral development of their children.

___ 5. The developmentalist who proposed a three-level theory of moral development: pre-conventional reasoning, conventional reasoning, and post-conventional reasoning.

___ 6. The psychologist who proposed a two-stage theory of moral development: heteronomous morality and autonomous morality.

___ 7. The individual who criticized Kohlberg's theory as being biased against women and distinguished between justice perspective and care perspective.

___ 8. Educational theorist who identified the hidden curriculum of the moral atmosphere of a school.

A. Jean Piaget

B. Lawrence Kohlberg

C. James Rest

D. Carol Gilligan

E. Hugh Hartshorne and Mark May

F. Walter Mischel

G. William Damon

H. Nancy Eisenberg and Brigett Murphy

I. Martin Hoffman

J. John Dewey

K. Gerald Patterson

L. James Garbarino

D. MULTIPLE CHOICE KNOWLEDGE QUESTIONS

1. Jean Piaget indicates that the heteronomous thinker

    a. believes that rules can be changed because they are merely agreed-upon conventions.

    b. recognizes that punishment for wrongdoing is not inevitable.

    c. judges the goodness of behavior by focusing on the consequences of behavior.

    d. is usually a child between 10 and 12 years old.

2. Lawrence Kohlberg argues that the distinctions between the three levels of moral reasoning have to do with

    a. the degree of internalization.

    b. the immediacy of the consequences for moral actions.

    c. the severity of punishments experienced.

    d. the social pressure of peers.

3. Which theory distinguishes between moral competence and moral performance?

    a. psychosocial

    b. moral development

    c. cognitive social learning

    d. behavioral moral reasoning

4. According to psychoanalytic theory, children internalize and parental moral standards in order to

    a. eliminate the distinction between moral thought and moral behavior.

    b. develop self-recognition skills.

    c. maintain a balance between parental and peer group influence.

    d. reduce anxiety and maintain parental affection.

5. If a person can experience another's feelings and respond in a similar way, this is called

a. pity.

b. empathy.

c. sympathy.

d. understanding.

6. Which of the following actions is an example of altruism?

a. sharing possessions

b. resisting temptation

c. saying thank you

d. not eating food with one's fingers

7. Martin Hoffman recommends that parents promote the moral development of their children and adolescents through

a. love withdrawal.

b. power assertion.

c. induction.

d. altruism.

8. An adolescent is asked to describe his attitudes toward premarital sexual activity and then to think about the consequences of sexual activity and its alternatives. He is probably involved in a moral education program emphasizing

a. cooperation and altruism.

b. a bag of moral values.

c. direct tuition of moral values.

d. a values-clarification approach.

9. Which approach to reducing youth violence appears to be the most promising?

   a. anger management programs

   b. having police talk to youth at school

   c. using scare tactics in the home and at school

   d. using an "awareness" approach on television

10. One of the best ways to get adolescents to volunteer in a community activity is to

   a. model volunteerism.

   b. encourage them to volunteer.

   c. have them read about community need.

   d. have public service announcements on television.

F. CRITICAL THINKING QUESTIONS

1. What strategies can promote impulse control?

2. Describe the predictors of youth violence and effective recommendations for reducing youth violence.

G. APPLICATION QUESTIONS

Risk taking is an essential part of the learning process. Unless individuals are willing to consider other viewpoints, they can fall victim to rote learning and limit their innate curiosity. Behavioral risk-taking means extending, without danger, one's physical prowess. Intellectual risk-taking in science means generating and testing hypotheses. Artistic risk-taking means engaging one's creativity. What do you do to encourage risk taking in your own life?

1. Describe moral risk-taking in your own life. Examine the tensions you struggled with that encouraged your moral development.

2. How have you dealt with fear as you have learned when it is appropriate to take risks?

H. COGNITIVE MAPS

MORAL DEVELOPMENT

What is Moral Development

- thoughts, feelings, and behaviors regarding the standards of right and wrong – (1)____
- (2)_________ dimensions
- (3)_________ dimensions

MORAL DEVELOPMENT

Moral Thoughts

Piaget's Theory

Jean Piaget
- (1)_______ morality
- (2)______justice
- autonomous morality

Kohlberg's Theory

Lawrence Kohlberg
- internalization
- 3 levels and 6 stages

Level 1 – Preconventional Reasoning
  - Stage 1 – heteronomous morality
  - Stage 2 – individualism, instrumental purpose, and exchange

Level 2 – Conventional Reasoning
  - Stage 3 – interpersonal norms
  - Stage 4 – social system morality

Level 3 – Postconventional Reasoning
  - Stage 5 – social contract or utility are individual rights
  - stage 6 – universal ethical principles

- influences on moral reasoning

Lawrence Walker
- criticisms

James Rest
- (3)_________ perspective
- (4)______ perspective

Carol Gilligan

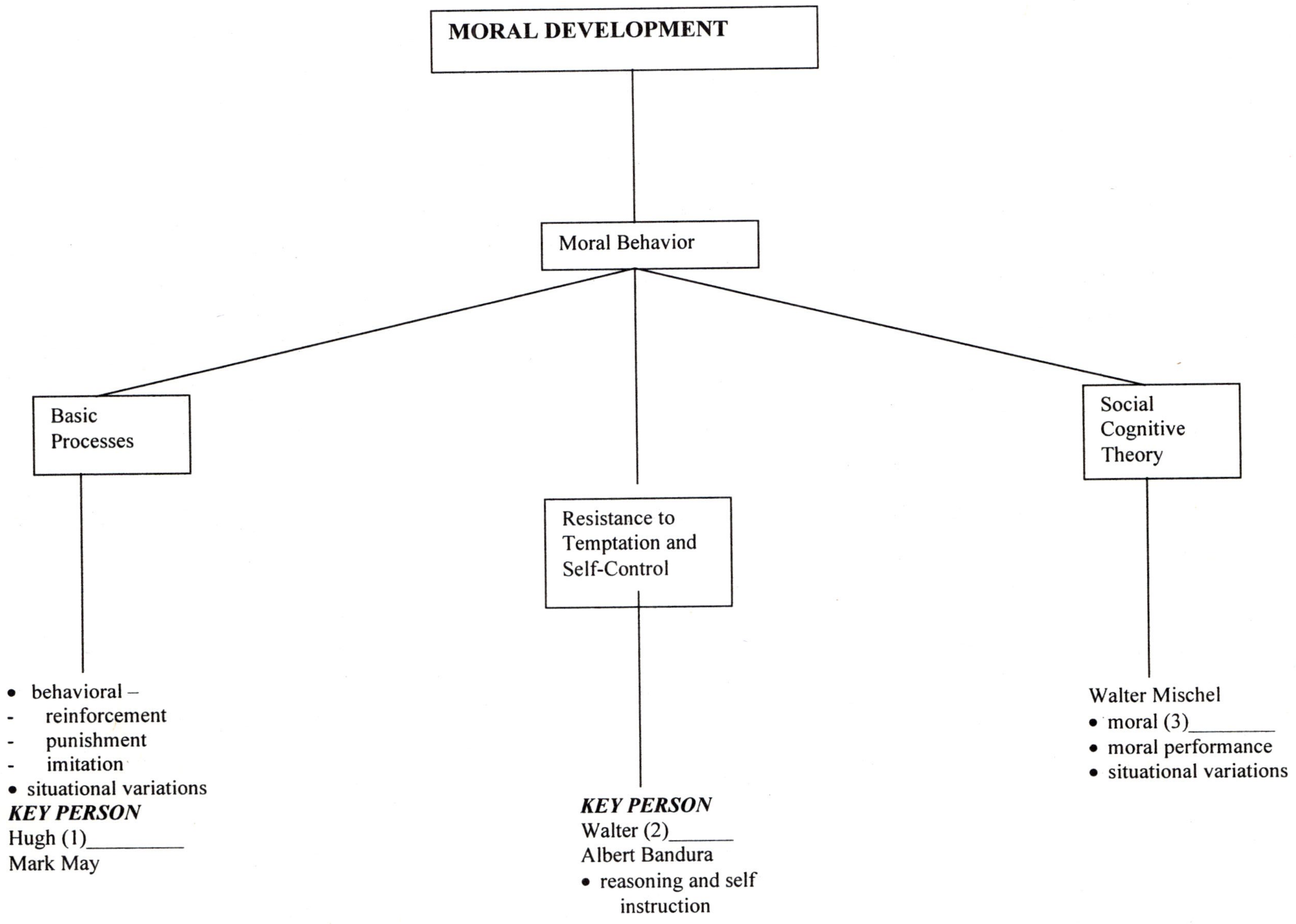

MORAL DEVELOPMENT
Moral Behavior
Basic Processes
Resistance to Temptation and Self-Control
Social Cognitive Theory
• behavioral –
- reinforcement
- punishment
- imitation
• situational variations
KEY PERSON
Hugh (1)_________
Mark May
KEY PERSON
Walter (2)______
Albert Bandura
• reasoning and self instruction
Walter Mischel
• moral (3)________
• moral performance
• situational variations

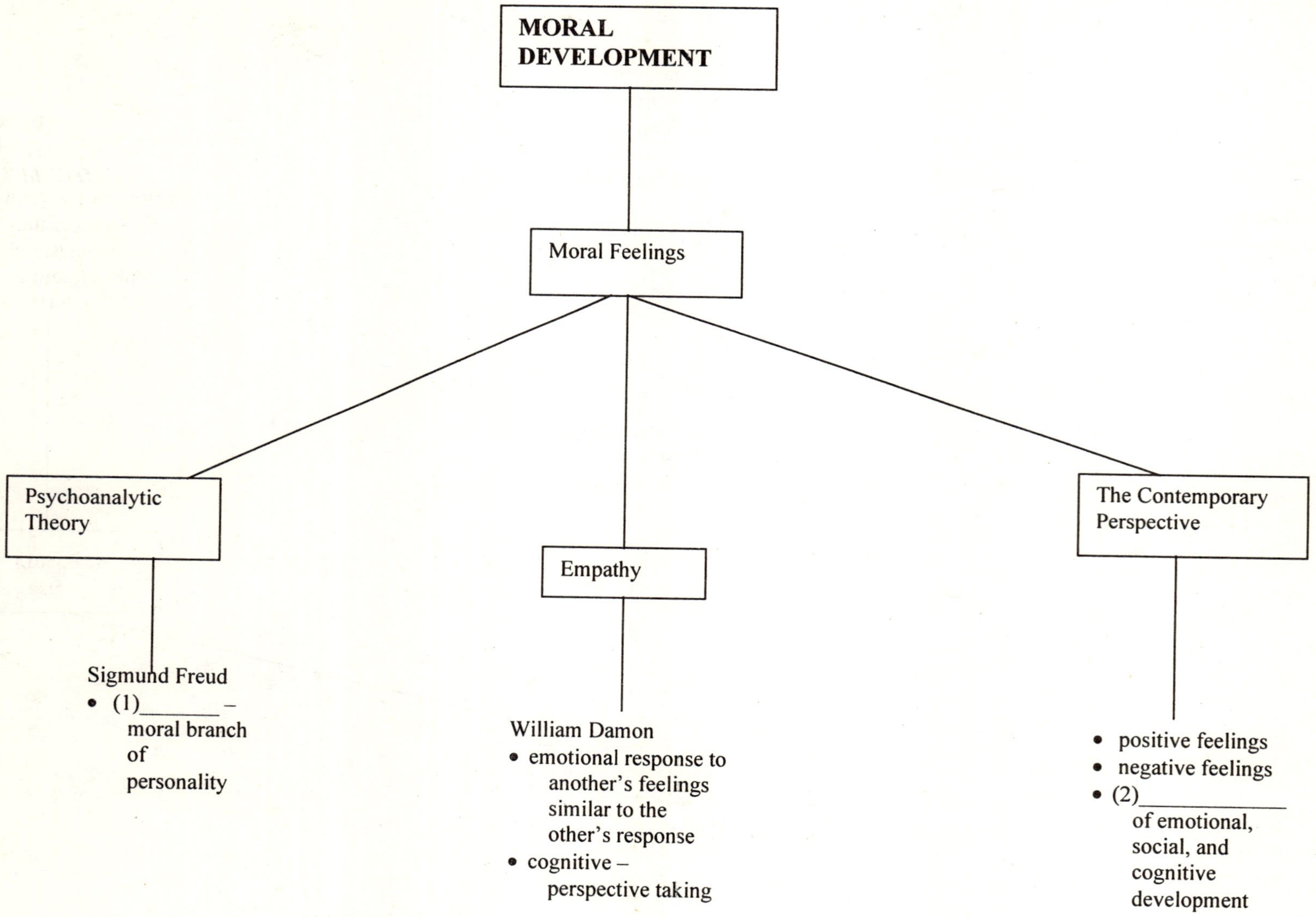
MORAL DEVELOPMENT
Moral Feelings
Psychoanalytic Theory
Sigmund Freud
• (1)_______ – moral branch of personality
Empathy
William Damon
• emotional response to another's feelings similar to the other's response
• cognitive – perspective taking
The Contemporary Perspective
• positive feelings
• negative feelings
• (2)____________ of emotional, social, and cognitive development

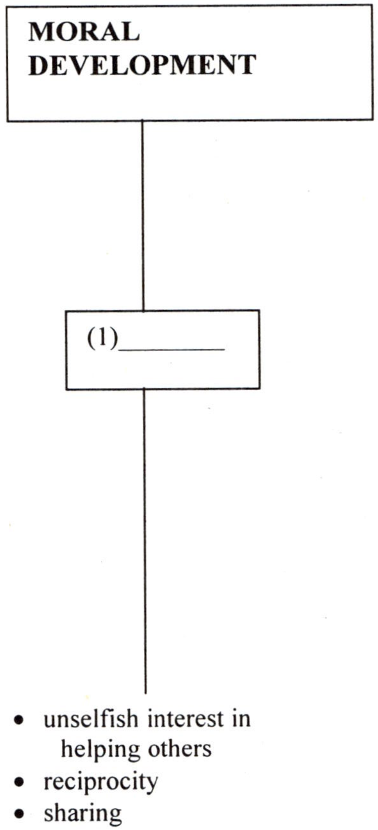
MORAL DEVELOPMENT
(1)________
• unselfish interest in helping others
• reciprocity
• sharing

MORAL DEVELOPMENT

Parenting and Moral Development

Parental Discipline

- love (1)________
- power assertion
- induction

Martin Hoffman

Some Conclusions

- parents are warm and supportive
- perspective taking
- involve children in decision-making
- modeling

KEY PERSON

Nancy (2)________

Brigett Murphy

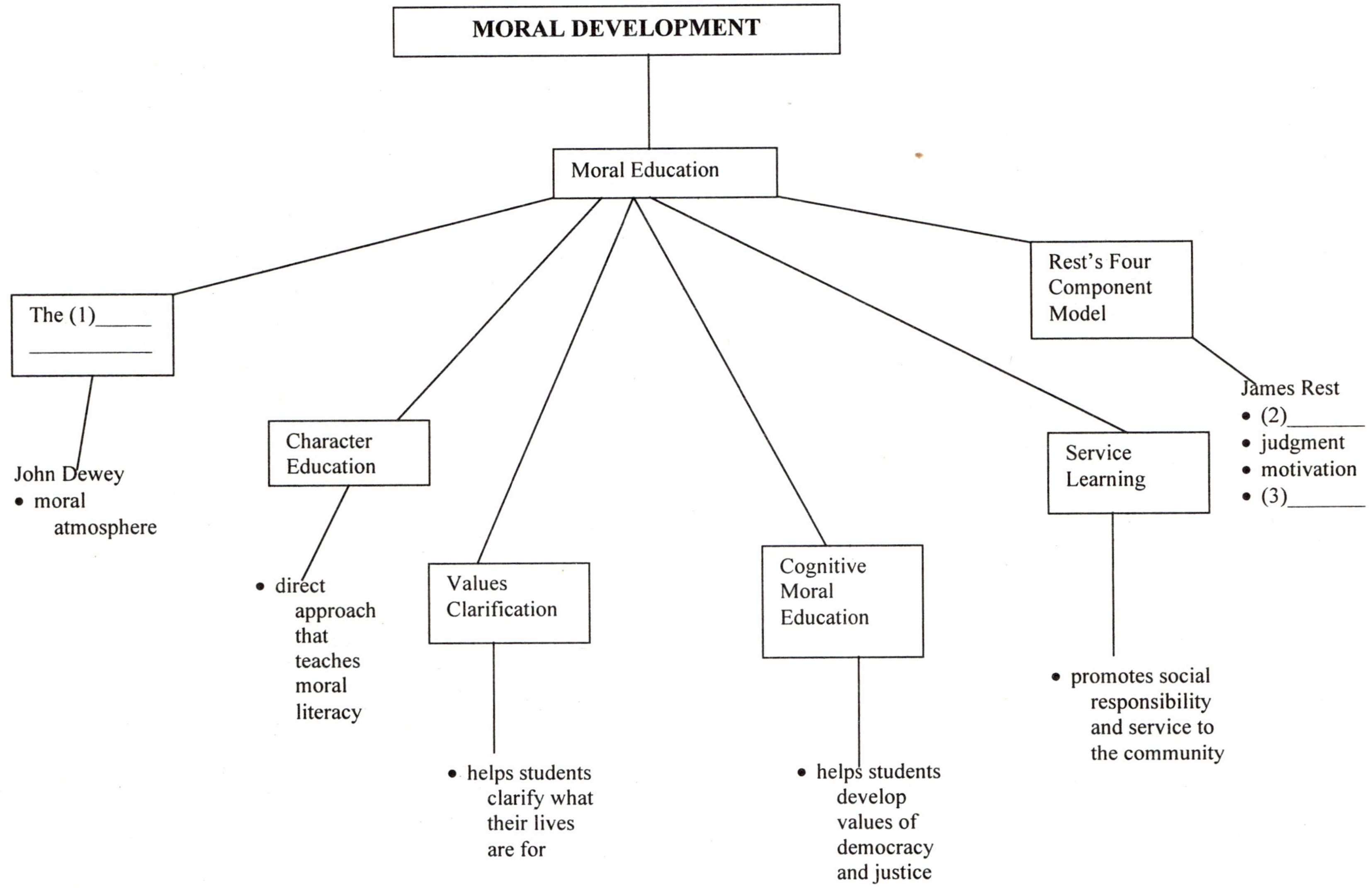
MORAL DEVELOPMENT
Moral Education
The (1)_____ ___________
John Dewey
• moral atmosphere
Character Education
• direct approach that teaches moral literacy
Values Clarification
• helps students clarify what their lives are for
Cognitive Moral Education
• helps students develop values of democracy and justice
Service Learning
• promotes social responsibility and service to the community
Rest's Four Component Model
James Rest
• (2)_______
• judgment
• motivation
• (3)_______

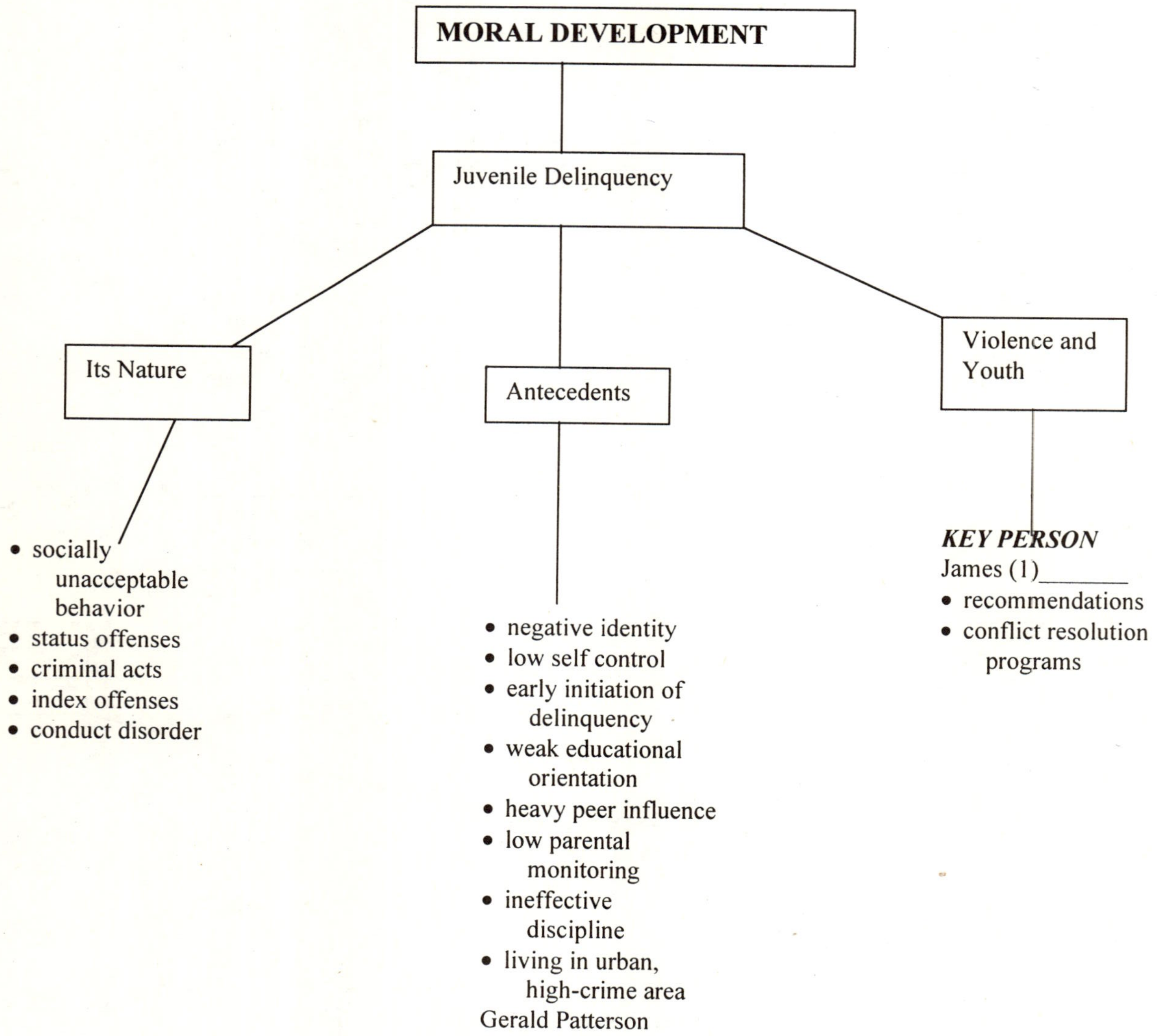
MORAL DEVELOPMENT
Juvenile Delinquency
Its Nature
Antecedents
Violence and Youth
• socially unacceptable behavior
• status offenses
• criminal acts
• index offenses
• conduct disorder
• negative identity
• low self control
• early initiation of delinquency
• weak educational orientation
• heavy peer influence
• low parental monitoring
• ineffective discipline
• living in urban, high-crime area
Gerald Patterson
KEY PERSON
James (1)________
• recommendations
• conflict resolution programs

I. REVIEW PRIORITIES

Assess your present understanding of the material in this chapter by rating yourself for each heading using the following scale:

1 – I thoroughly understand material and its context to other sections

2 – I understand most of the material and have a basic grasp of the context to other sections

3 – I have a shaky understanding of the material and a poor grasp of the context

4 – I have an inadequate understanding of the material

What is Moral Development? ____

Moral Thoughts

- Piaget's Theory ____
- Kohlberg's Theory ____

Moral Behavior

- Basic Processes ____
- Resistence to Temptation & Self-Control ____
- Social Cognitive Theory ____

Moral Feelings

- Psychoanalytic Theory ____
- Empathy ____
- The Contemporary Perspective ____

Altruism ____

Parenting and Moral Development

- Parental Discipline ______
- Some Conclusions ______

Moral Education

- The Hidden Curriculum ______
- Character Education ______
- Values Clarification ______
- Cognitive Moral Education ______
- Service Learning ______
- Rest's Four Component Model ______

Juvenile Delinquency

- Its Nature ______
- Antecedents ______
- Violence and Youth ______

ANSWER KEY

B. TRUE OR FALSE KEY CONTENT QUESTIONS

1. F
2. F
3. T
4. T
5. F
6. T
7. T
8. T
9. F
10. F
11. T
12. T
13. T
14. F
15. T
16. F
17. F

18. T
19. F
20. T

C. FILL IN THE BLANK KEY TERMS

1. moral
2. heteronomous; autonomous
3. peer; parent-child
4. reasoning; levels; stages
5. cognitive; perspective
6. behavior
7. authority; interpersonal
8. justice; care
9. Contexts
10. social; imitation
11. temptation; control
12. competence; performance
13. perspective
14. reciprocity
15. construct
16. induction
17. direct
18. cognitive
19. judgment; character
20. schools; organizations

D. MATCHING KEY PEOPLE QUESTIONS

1. L
2. G
3. E
4. I
5. B
6. A
7. D
8. J

E. MULTIPLE CHOICE KNOWLEDGE QUESTIONS

1. c
2. a
3. c
4. d
5. b
6. a
7. c
8. d
9. a
10. b

F. CRITICAL THINKING QUESTIONS

1.
   - Self-control can be learned. The behavioral perspective emphasizes external motivators such as rewards and punishment. The social cognitive perspective emphasizes internal motivators, such as reasoning and self-reinforcement.

- Self-regulation also involves a balance of high principles (moral reasoning) and high ego strength (moral convictions). This emphasis on moral competence depends on moral knowledge, awareness of moral rules and regulations and the motivation to "do right."

2.

- Predictors include:
  - -early involvement with drugs and alcohol
  - -easy access to weapons, especially handguns
  - -association with antisocial peers
  - -pervasive exposure to violence in the media
- Reduction efforts include:
  - -nonpunitive and fair parental discipline
  - -consistent parental involvement in the child's daily life
  - -paying nonjudgmental attention to the child's perception of experiences
  - -give support to schools to teach interpersonal problem-solving strategies
  - -create a partnership among families, schools, and community (social-service organizations, churches, media, etc.) that provide opportunities for positive development.

H. COGNITIVE MAPS

A

1. ethics
2. intrapersonal
3. interpersonal

B

1. heteronomous
2. immanent
3. justice
4. care

C

1. Hartshorne
2. Mischel
3. competence

D

1. superego
2. interrelatedness

E

1. Altruism

F

1. withdrawal
2. Eisenberg

G.

1. Hidden Curriculum
2. sensitivity
3. character

H

1. Garbarino

SECTION 5: SOCIAL CONTEXTS OF DEVELOPMENT

CHAPTER 15: FAMILIES

A. LEARNING OBJECTIVES

The Nature of Family Processes

1. Define *reciprocal socialization.*
2. Define *scaffolding.*
3. Compare and contrast the *continuity view* and *discontinuity view* of the developmental construction of relationships.

Parenting

4. Define and contrast these four parenting styles: *authoritarian, authoritative, neglectful,* and *indulgent.*
5. Explain the influences that may lead to child abuse or maltreatment.

Sibling Relationships and Birth Order

6. Discuss firstborn children's relationships with later-born siblings.
7. Characterize the effects of only children.

Family Processes in Adolescence

8. What is a developmentally appropriate parental response to an adolescent's need for autonomy, which promotes parent-adolescent connectedness.

The Changing Family in a Changing Social World

9. What are the main effects of divorce on children and adolescents?

10. Define *boundary ambiguity* and explain how it applies to stepfamilies.

11. In what ways does parenting of White families differ from ethnic minority families?

12. Describe how fathers' involvement with their children has changed over time in the United States.

B. *TRUE OR FALSE KEY CONTENT QUESTIONS*

The Nature of Family Processes

1. T F Eye contact between mother and infant positively affects the child's social competence.
2. T F The continuity view of the developmental construction of relationships emphasizes change and growth in relationships over time.
3. T F Parents spend more time with their child during the middle to late childhood years.
4. T F Co-regulation describes the transition period during middle to late childhood where some control is transferred from parent to child.
5. T F Parental comforting of children when they experience negative emotions is linked with constructive anger reactions.

Parenting

6. T F Children have fewer playmates when parents arrange peer contacts when their children are young.
7. T F The authoritative parenting style is restrictive and punitive and allows little verbal exchange.
8. T F Experts contend that child abuse is mostly caused by the individual personality characteristics of parents.

Sibling Relationships and Birth Order

9. T F Due to age similarities, children interact more positively with siblings than parents.
10. T F The oldest sibling is more antagonistic and more nurturant toward their younger siblings.

Family Processes in Adolescence

11. T F A child's attachment to parents remains strong during adolescence.

12. T F Moderate parent-adolescent conflict facilitates the adolescent's transition from being dependent on parents to becoming autonomous.

The Changing Family in a Changing Social World

13. T F The United States has the highest percentage of single-parent families in the world; one out of four children spend part of their childhood in a stepparent family.

14. T F Restabilization often takes longer in stepfamilies than in divorced families.

15. T F High-income families tend to use discipline that promotes externalization while low-income families tend to use discipline that promotes internalization.

C. FILL IN THE BLANK KEY TERMS

1. Reciprocal socialization means that parents socialize their children and that children socialize their children.
2. Studies of reciprocal socialization during infancy reveal that eye mutual gaze plays an important role in socialization.
3. The family can be viewed as a social system defined in terms of generation, gender, and role.
4. In parent-child relationships, parents exert unilateral authority over children, whereas peer relationships entail a more equal basis.
5. Competent parents adapt to children's developmental changes.
6. Middle and late childhood is a time of coregulation, a condition in which parents maintain supervision, but begin to allow children to engage in self-regulation.
7. Diana Baumrind identified three types of parenting: authoritarian, authoritative, and permissive, each of which influences the social behavior of children.

8. Although child abuse refers to both abuse and neglect, experts often use the term child _____________ to describe both phenomena.

9. Maltreated children display poor peer relations characterized by excessive physical and verbal _____________ and avoidance.

10. In comparison to parents, siblings may provide _____________ socializing influences on adolescents.

11. Parents have higher expectations for __________-born children, place more responsibility on them than later-born children.

12. Older siblings are both more antagonistic and _____________ toward younger siblings.

13. Only children are _____________ orientated, and often display a desirable personality, especially in comparison to _____________ children.

14. Parents can foster autonomy in adolescents by relinquishing _____________ in areas in which _____________ decision can be made and guiding decisions in areas in which the adolescent's knowledge is more limited.

15. The _________ model of parent adolescent relations emphasizes that conflict is moderate and may facilitate the development of autonomy.

16. One important factor is the _________ of the child at the time of the divorce.

17. _____________ parenting is the most effective parenting style for children and adolescents in stepfamilies.

18. Lois Hoffman argues that working mothers are more _____________ models for the socialization of today's children than are full-time mothers, especially in the case of daughters/sons.

19. Interviews of latchkey children indicate that a majority had negative experiences related to a lack of limits and _____________ during the latchkey hours.

20. The father's role in parenting has changed from being the _____________ teacher in colonial American times to being _____________ and actively involved with children in contemporary times.

D. MATCHING KEY PEOPLE QUESTIONS

F 1. The developmentalist who established the concept of authoritative parenting and studied the relationship between parent responsiveness and adolescent social competence.

E 2. The developmentalist who studied children and adolescents six years after the divorce of their parents.

D 3. The scholar who studied how historical and cultural events, such as war or mass migrations, affects family lifestyle.

___ 4. The individual who wrote about the effects of working mothers on the development of their children.

___ 5. Authors of a study investigating hour-by-hour emotional realities lived by families with adolescents

___ 6. This individual coined the term *co-regulation* to describe the gradual transfer of control from parent to child during the preadolescent years.

___ 7. A child advocate who documented the problems and challenges of latchkey children.

___ 8. The researcher who conducted a longitudinal study supporting the discontinuity view of relationships.

A. Jean Piaget

B. Andrew Collins

C. Eleanor Maccoby

D. Ross Parke

E. Joseph Allen

F. Diana Baumrind

G. Reed Larson and Marsye Richards

H. G. Stanley Hall

I. Lois Hoffman

J. Joan Lipsitt

K. E. Mavis Hetherington

L. Laurence Steinberg and Ann Levine

E. MULTIPLE CHOICE KNOWLEDGE QUESTIONS

1. An adolescent and her father are engaged in a freewheeling discussion as they walk through the park. Their discourse is smooth and comfortable, coordinated and sensitive. It gives the impression that they are "waltzing" together verbally. This situation is an example of

   a. reciprocity.

   b. synchrony.

   c. idealistic notions of parent-child relationships.

   d. socialization.

2. Compared to younger children, parents of elementary school children use more

   a. physical affection.

   b. physical manipulation.

   c. routine caregiving.

   d. withholding of special privileges.

3. Diane Baumrind describes authoritative parents as

   a. restrictive, punitive, and allowing little verbal guide.

   b. encouraging independence and placing limits on the actions of children and adolescents.

   c. power assertive, rejecting, unresponsive, and parent centered.

   d. undemanding, rejecting, uninvolved, and controlling.

4. Bill's parents have few rules for household conduct or academic expectations. They do not punish Bill when he violates rules, but merely accept his behavior. Bill is likely to develop

   a. social competence because his parents unconditionally accept him.

   b. anxiety about social comparisons and social inferiority feelings.

   c. self-reliance, social responsibility, and autonomy.

   d. little impulse control and disregard for rules.

5. Firstborn children are

   a. more achievement-orientated than those born later.

   b. less achievement-orientated than those born later.

   c. more psychologically well adjusted than those born later.

   d. on the average, less socially responsible than those born later.

6. Adolescents who are securely attached to their parents

   a. cannot adequately develop autonomy.

   b. show less secure attachment to peers.

   c. have more difficulty engaging with peers and separating from parents.

   d. have higher self-esteem than insecurely attached peers.

7. You are very depressed because you argue with your daughter about common everyday problems at least once a week, and these arguments last for more than five minutes. Experts on adolescents would tell you that

   a. this high level of conflict with your daughter will lead to latter disturbances.

   b. this type of conflict is well within the normal limits, and you should not be concerned about it.

   c. if you are arguing this much now, your arguments will increase in later adolescence.

   d. these arguments will prevent your daughter from developing an autonomous identity.

8. Which term refers to the confusion in stepfamilies regarding the membership of the family and each individual's responsibility?

   a. family blending

   b. boundary ambiguity

   c. stepfamily dynamism

   d. stepfamily individuation

9. After coming home from school, Jimmy must wait until six o'clock before his parents return home from work. Jimmy would best be described as a

   a. hurried child.
   b. latchkey child.
   c. neglected child.
   d. stepchild.

10. Ethnic families tend to differ from White American families in that the former

   a. are smaller.
   b. show more extended kinship networks.
   c. encourage more autonomy among girls than boys.
   d. have more employed mothers.

F. CRITICAL THINKING QUESTIONS

1. Compare and contrast the direct and indirect effects of the family system on the development of the child.

2. What are the effects on a child if the parents differ in their parenting style?

G. APPLICATION QUESTIONS

Children construct social knowledge as a result of reflecting on their experiences. A child's motivation to experiment and master social skills is directly related to how his or her emotional needs are met. When parents are warm, attentive and help explain limits, children are more likely to be secure, confident and socially competent. Children notice when parents respectfully consider their ideas and feelings. Parents model both verbal and nonverbal ways to express feelings. How do you deal with your emotions? Do you hold them in and hide them when you are upset? Or, are you a "yeller" when things go wrong? How did your parents express their emotions?

1. On a scale of 1–10, equating 1 with no expression of feelings and equating 10 with aggressive expression of feelings, rate how you express the following feelings:
    a. anger
    b. joy
    c. disappointment
    d. surprise
    e. sorrow
    f. nervousness

2. On a scale of 1–10, equating 1 with no expression of feelings and equating 10 with aggressive expression of feelings, rate how your mother (or principle female caretaker) expresses the following feelings:
    a. anger
    b. joy
    c. disappointment
    d. surprise
    e. sorrow
    f. nervousness

3. On a scale of 1–10, equating 1 with no expression of feelings and equating 10 with aggressive expression of feelings, rate how your father (or principle male caretaker) expresses the following feelings:

   a. anger
   b. joy
   c. disappointment
   d. surprise
   e. sorrow
   f. nervousness

4. What is the relationship between how you express feelings and how your parents (or principle caregiver) expresses the same feelings?

H. COGNITIVE MAPS

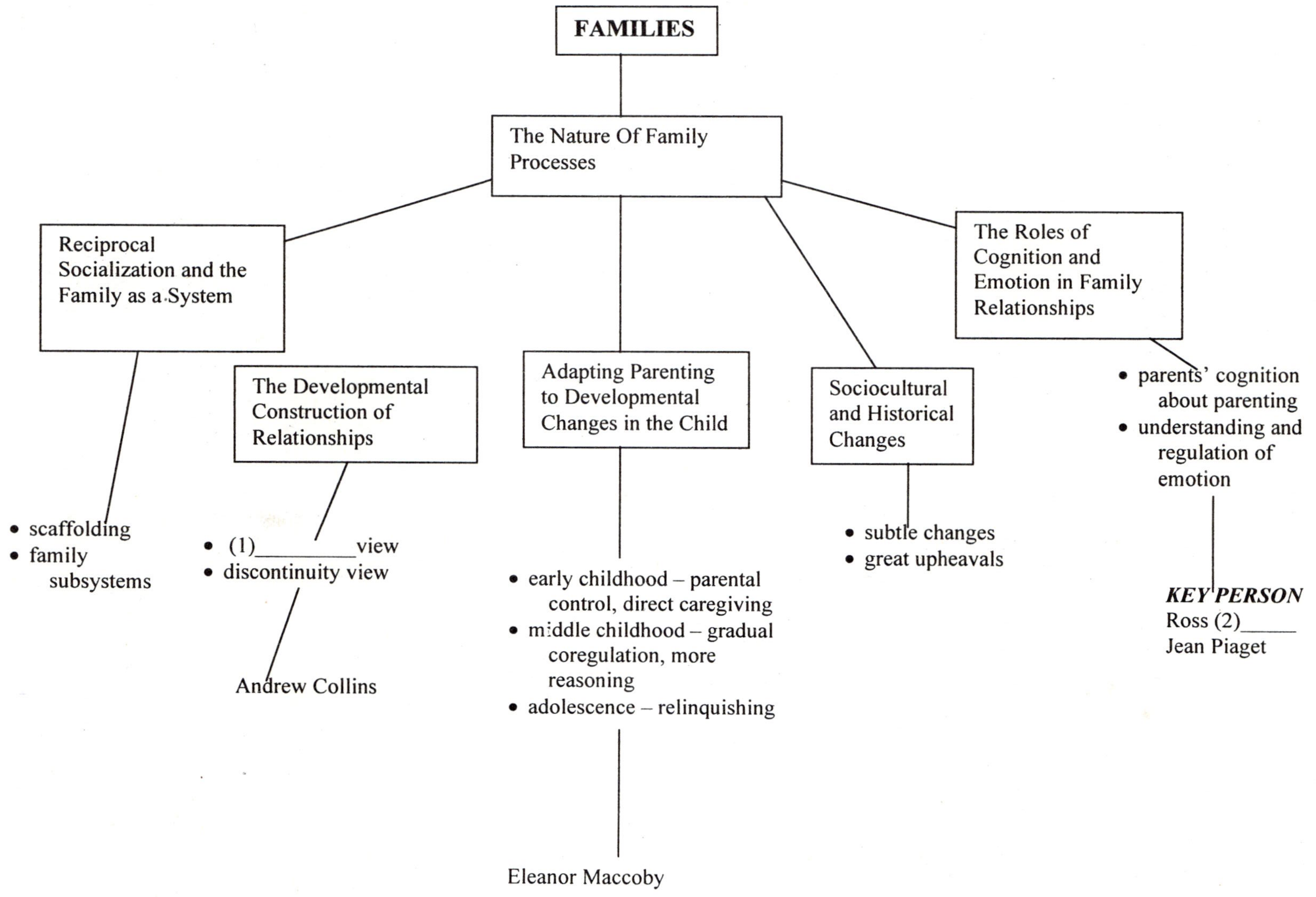
FAMILIES
The Nature Of Family Processes
Reciprocal Socialization and the Family as a System
• scaffolding
• family subsystems
The Developmental Construction of Relationships
• (1)________view
• discontinuity view
Andrew Collins
Adapting Parenting to Developmental Changes in the Child
• early childhood – parental control, direct caregiving
• middle childhood – gradual coregulation, more reasoning
• adolescence – relinquishing
Eleanor Maccoby
Sociocultural and Historical Changes
• subtle changes
• great upheavals
The Roles of Cognition and Emotion in Family Relationships
• parents' cognition about parenting
• understanding and regulation of emotion
KEY PERSON
Ross (2)_____
Jean Piaget

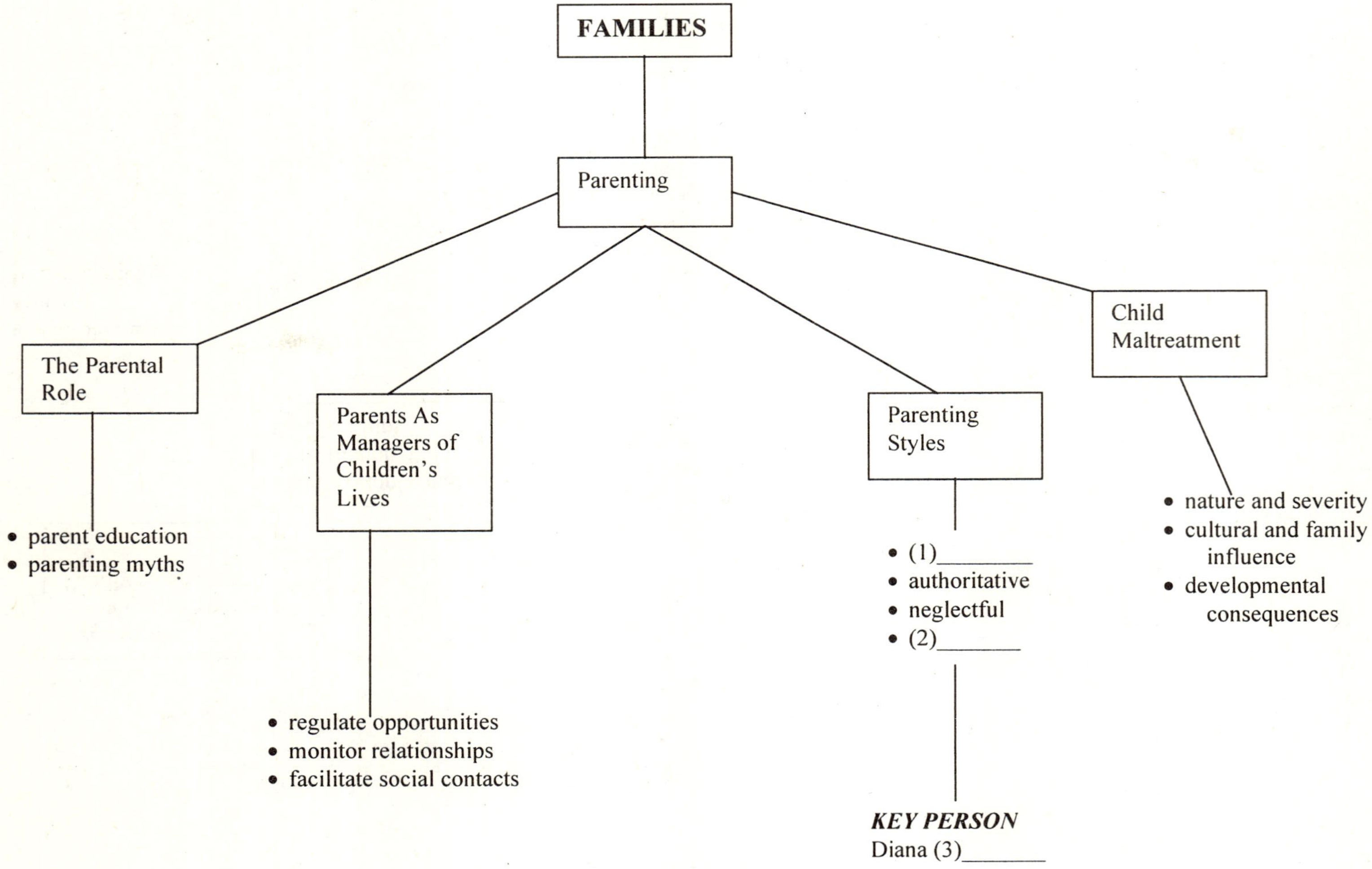
FAMILIES
Parenting
The Parental Role
• parent education
• parenting myths
Parents As Managers of Children's Lives
• regulate opportunities
• monitor relationships
• facilitate social contacts
Parenting Styles
• (1)________
• authoritative
• neglectful
• (2)_______
KEY PERSON
Diana (3)_______
Child Maltreatment
• nature and severity
• cultural and family influence
• developmental consequences

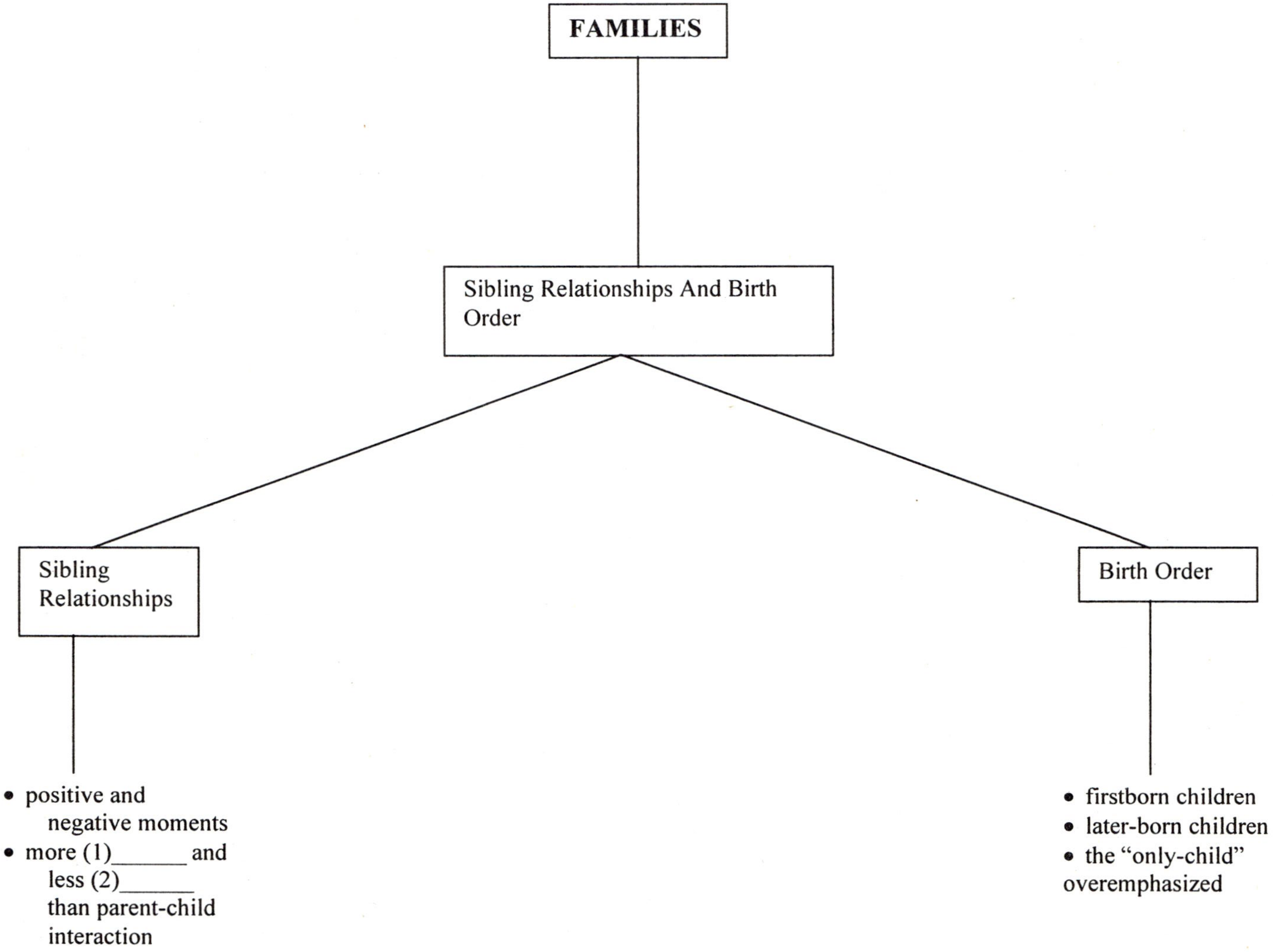
FAMILIES
Sibling Relationships And Birth Order
Sibling Relationships
• positive and negative moments
• more (1)______ and less (2)______ than parent-child interaction
Birth Order
• firstborn children
• later-born children
• the "only-child" overemphasized

FAMILIES

Family Processes In Adolescence

Autonomy and Attachment

- secure attachment
- dismissing/avoidant attachment
- preoccupied/ambivalent attachment
- unresolved/disorganized attachment

KEY PERSON

Joseph (1)_____

Parent-Adolescent Conflict

- increases in early adolescence, decreases in late adolescence
- positive developmental functions
- linked with negative outcomes

Reed Larson and Marsye Richards

G. Stanley Hall

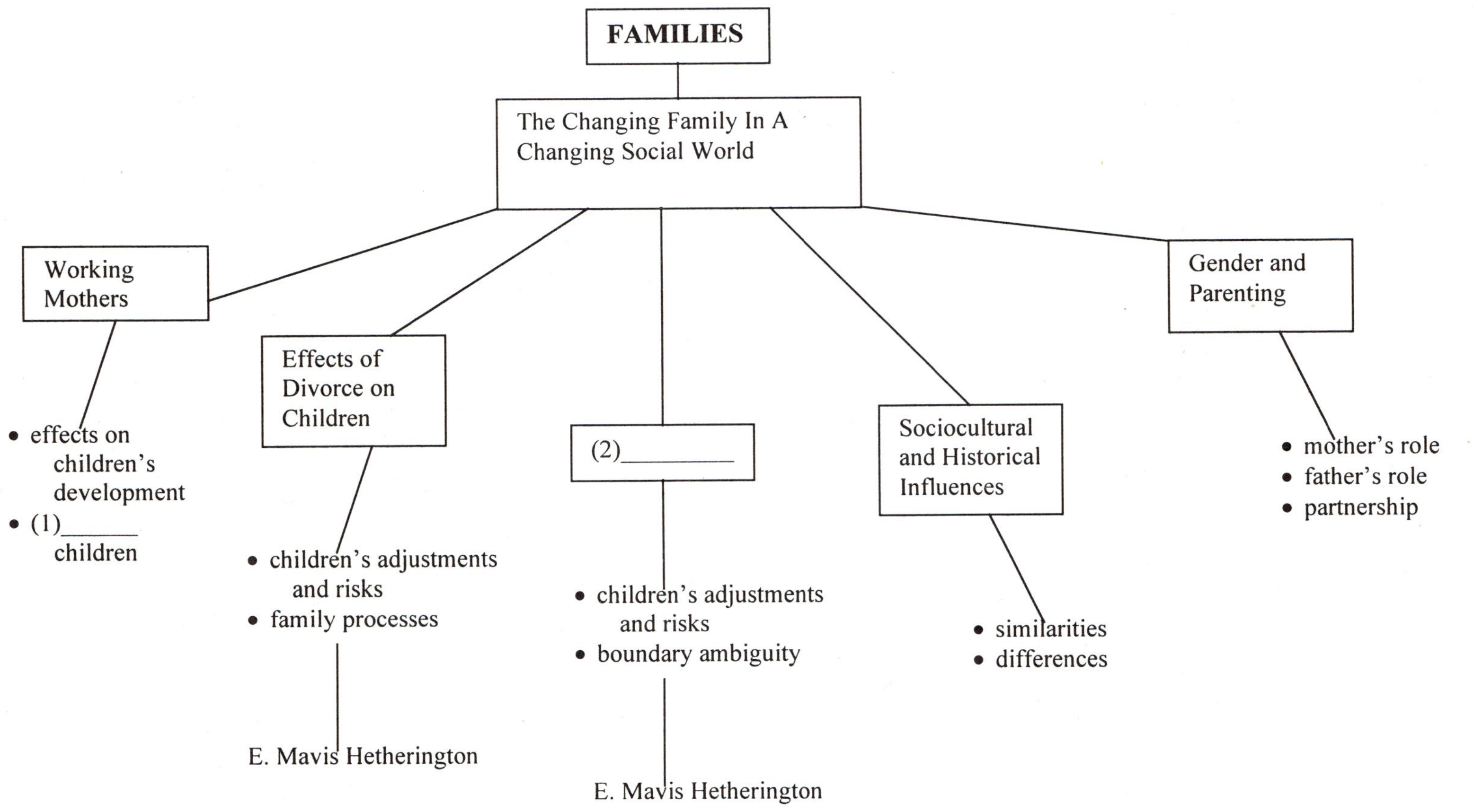
FAMILIES
The Changing Family In A Changing Social World
Working Mothers
• effects on children's development
• (1)______ children
Effects of Divorce on Children
• children's adjustments and risks
• family processes
E. Mavis Hetherington
(2)__________
• children's adjustments and risks
• boundary ambiguity
E. Mavis Hetherington
Sociocultural and Historical Influences
• similarities
• differences
Gender and Parenting
• mother's role
• father's role
• partnership

I. REVIEW PRIORITIES

Assess your present understanding of the material in this chapter by rating yourself for each heading using the following scale:

1 – I thoroughly understand material and its context to other sections

2 – I understand most of the material and have a basic grasp of the context to other sections

3 – I have a shaky understanding of the material and a poor grasp of the context

4 – I have an inadequate understanding of the material

The Nature of Family Processes

- Reciprocal Socialization and the Family as a System ____
- The Developmental Construction of Relationships ____
- Adopting Parenting to Developmental Changes in the Child ____
- Sociocultural and Historical Changes ____
- The Role of Cognition and Emotion in Family Relationships ____

Parenting

- The Parental Role ____
- Parents as Managers of Children's Lives ____
- Parenting Styles ____
- Child Maltreatment ____

Sibling Relationships and Birth Order

- Sibling Relationships ____
- Birth Order ____

Family Processes in Adolescence

- Autonomy and Attachment _____
- Parent-Adolescent Conflict _____

The Changing Family in a Changing Social World

- Working Mothers _____
- Effects of Divorce on Children _____
- Stepfamilies _____
- Sociocultural and Historical Influences _____
- Gender and Parenting _____

ANSWER KEY

B. TRUE OR FALSE KEY CONTENT QUESTIONS

1. T
2. F
3. F
4. T
5. T
6. F
7. F
8. F
9. F
10. T
11. T
12. T
13. T
14. T
15. T

C. FILL IN THE BLANK KEY TERMS

1. parents; parents
2. mutual
3. system
4. authority; equal
5. adapt
6. coregulation; regulation
7. authoritarian
8. maltreatment
9. aggression
10. stronger
11. first
12. nurturant
13. achievement; later-born
14. control; reasonable
15. new
16. age
17. Authoritative
18. realistic; daughters
19. supervision
21. moral; nurturant

D. MATCHING KEY PEOPLE QUESTIONS

1. F
2. K
3. D
4. I
5. G
6. C
7. J
8. B

E. MULTIPLE CHOICE KNOWLEDGE QUESTIONS

1. b
2. d
3. b
4. d
5. a
6. d
7. b
8. b
9. b
10. b

F. CRITICAL THINKING QUESTIONS

1.

- The socialization between parents and children is now viewed as a reciprocal process. For example, the dialogue between mothers and their infants is closely coordinated, like a dance. Mutual eye contact between mother and child involve high interconnection and synchronicity.
- Children also influence parent's behavior. For example, a child's academic or athletic achievement is supported by parent participation in school activities.
- Each family member is a participant in subgroups of a family system. For example, father and mother is one subsystem. Father and daughter is another subsystem. Daughter and other sibling(s) is yet another subsystem. These systems directly and indirectly effect each other. Lack of intimacy between a husband and wife can result in parents investing less emotion in their child's life.

2.

- Note the four classifications of parenting:
  a. *Authoritarian parenting* is restrictive and punitive. The parent places limits and controls on the child. This approach—my way or the highway—creates social incompetence in the child.
  b. *Authoritative parenting* encourages children to be independent. This approach —lots of verbal "give and take" amidst a warm and nurturant atmosphere— creates social competence in children.
  c. *Neglectful parenting* is a style where parents are very uninvolved in a child's life. Children from this parenting style show poor self-control and are socially incompetent.
  d. *Indulgent parenting* is a style where parents are very involved but place few demands or controls on the child. Children from this parenting style do not learn respect for others, have difficulty with self-control and are socially incompetent.

  These four parenting styles approach a tension inherent in parenting: acceptance and responsiveness on one hand, and control and limits on the other. In the family system, one parent may emphasize one role, warmth and acceptance for example, while the other parent emphasizes another role, firm limit setting, for example.

- Consistency is obviously necessary for a child to understand the importance of both combinations

H. COGNITIVE MAPS

A

1. continuity
2. Park

B

1. authoritarian
2. indulgent
3. Baumrind

C

1. negative
2. varied

D

1. Allen

E

1. latchkey
2. Stepfamilies

CHAPTER 16: PEERS

A. LEARNING OBJECTIVES

Peer Relations

1. Define *peer.*
2. Compare and contrast peer and child-parent relationships.
3. What makes children popular with their peers?
4. Describe the characteristics of *bullies* and *whipping boys.*

Play

5. Define *play.* List and describe Mildred Parten's classifications of play.
6. Compare and contrast *symbolic/pretend play* with *social constructive play.*
7. Discuss the ages and nature of children's involvement with games.

Friendship

8. Discuss Harry Stack Sullivan's concepts of how friendships shape children's and adolescent's well-being.
9. Define *intimacy in friendships.*

Adolescence, Peers, and Romantic Relationships

10. Define and compare *crowds* and *cliques.*
11. How do child groups differ from adolescent groups?
12. Define *dating script.* What is the difference between male and female dating script on the first date?

B. TRUE OR FALSE KEY CONTENT QUESTIONS

Peer Relations

1. T F Peer relations are especially important for children who are withdrawn and aggressive.
2. T F Adolescents learn intimacy skills from close friendships with selected peers.
3. T F Peer rejection positively influences a child's social confidence.
4. T F Well adjusted boys are less likely to be involved in peer aggression, especially when their parents promote self-assertion.
5. T F Rough and tumble play occurs more in parent-child interactions than peer relations.
6. T F Peer interactions occur on a less equal basis than parent-child relations.
7. T F The frequency of peer interactions, both positive and negative, increase during the preschool years.
8. T F Rejected children are encouraged to join peers without trying to change what is taking place in the peer group.
9. T F Boys who were bullied in their childhood were more depressed and had lower self-esteem during their twenties.

Play

10. T F Parents should discourage imaginary play in children because it diminishes cognitive development.
11. T F Three year olds engage in more cooperative and associative play; five year olds engage in more solitary and parallel play.
12. T F During the elementary school years, games are especially meaningful because of the presence of a challenge.

Friendship

13. T F Adolescents with superficial friendships or no friends are lonelier and more depressed than adolescents with intimate friendships.

14. T F Boys, more than girls, view friendships as opportunities to develop interpersonal relationships.

15. T F Adolescents who have older friends more often engage in delinquent behavior and early sexual behavior.

Adolescence, Peers, and Romantic Relationships

16. T F Around eleventh and twelfth grades, conformity to peers peaks, especially to their antisocial behavior.

17. T F During adolescence, peer relationships progress from same-sex groups to mixed-sex groups to mixed-sex couples.

18. T F Peer support of achievement during adolescence is relatively high among all ethnic groups.

19. T F Cyberdating is especially popular among middle school students.

20. T F On first dates, males follow a reactive dating script and females follow a proactive dating script.

C. FILL IN THE BLANK KEY TERMS

1. Peers provide a source of ______________ about the world outside the family.
2. Children are more/less likely to engage in rough-and-tumble play with other children; however, children are more likely to approach adults in times of _________ .
3. Highly aggressive boys, or ________ , are likely to have parents who rejected them, were _____________ , and were permissive about their sons' aggression.

4. Recipients of aggression, or ___________ boys, are likely to have parents who were anxious and overprotective.

5. Popular children give out reinforcements to other children, __________ to them, show enthusiasm, and appear self-____________, but not conceited.

6. ______________ children have few friends, but ________________ children are more likely to be disruptive, aggressive, and overtly disliked by peers.

7. The key factor that predicts whether rejected children become delinquents or drop out of school later in adolescence is their ____________ toward peers in elementary school.

8. Training neglected children centers around increasing their ability to attract ____________ in positive ways.

9. Training rejected children centers around decreasing their attempt to _____________ peer interactions.

10. Taking another person's point of view defines the concept of _____________-taking.

11. According to Dodge, inappropriate aggression is frequently the result of misinterpreting another child's ______________ .

12. According to Daniel Berlyne, play satisfies a(n) _______________ drive in all people.

13. Mildred Parten's play categories resemble the contemporary category of __________ play.

14. Preschool children use practice play to improve their physical or mental mastery and ____________ of skills.

15. A preschool child who _______________ a couch is a cruise ship engages in pretend/symbolic play.

16. Games are <u>more/less</u> salient in the preschool than the elementary school years.

17. Childhood friendship requires the ability to ___________ cooperatively, whereas adolescent friendship requires the ability to self-______________ appropriately.

18. Cliques are ____________ , involve greater intimacy, and have more group ___________ than crowds.

19. The classic study by James Coleman found that the leading crowds in high school were likely to be composed of ______________ and ________________ girls.

20. Female adolescents bring a ____________ desire for intimacy and personality exploration to dating than do male adolescents.

D. MATCHING KEY PEOPLE QUESTIONS

___ 1. The individual who performed the classic study of adolescents cliques and crowds.

___ 2. The researcher who performed the study of children's play.

___ 3. The researcher who used naturalistic observation techniques to investigate the function of children groups and adolescent groups.

___ 4. A developmentalist who identified a five-step process about how children and adolescents decode social cues.

___ 5. A psychoanalytic theorist who believed that friendships more than parent-child relationships were fundamental to the development of adolescents.

___ 6. A researcher who described play as exciting and pleasurable because it satisfied the exploratory urge toward curiosity.

___ 7. An observer of young children at play who found that pretend play involved props, plot, and roles.

___ 8. The individual who studied peer relations for four decades, especially how much easier school transitions are negotiated with children who have friends.

A. Anna Freud

B. Harry Stack Sullivan

C. Catherine Garvey

D. John Coie

E. Kenneth Dodge

F. Daniel Berlyne

G. Mildred Parten

H. Jean Piaget

I. Willard Hartup

J. James Coleman

K. Brad Brown and Jane Lohr

L. Dexter Dunphy

E. MULTIPLE CHOICE KNOWLEDGE QUESTIONS

1. The main function of the peer group is to

    a. foster love and understanding.

    b. act as a surrogate for the parents.

    c. teach the importance of friendship.

    d. teach about the world outside the family.

2. All of the following children will be popular with their peers *except*

    a. those who give out lots of reinforcement.

    b. those who listen carefully to what other have to say.

    c. those who try to please others even if it means compromising themselves.

    d. those who are self-confident.

3. Samantha has few friends at school. Other children pay little attention to her and no one invites her home. Samantha is probably a(n)

    a. rejected child.

    b. neglected child.

    c. latchkey child.

    d. controversial child.

4. When Bonnie informs Connie that she is afraid of boys and has never been on a date, by definition she is

    a. violating accepted gender norms.

    b. modeling for her parents.

    c. increasing the intimacy of the relationship.

    d. assessing the trust versus mistrust level of the relationship.

5. In 1961, James Coleman found that high-school leaders were most often

   a. athletes.

   b. females.

   c. intelligent.

   d. rich.

6. Compared to children's cliques, adolescents' cliques are more likely to

   a. be made up of many types of individuals.

   b. have both male and female members.

   c. contain individuals who are not friends.

   d. be smaller.

7. Developmentalists characterize play as

   a. pleasurable activity.

   b. engaged in for its own sake.

   c. the work of children.

   d. All of the above help define play.

8. Mildred Parten's play categories are examples of increasingly complex and interactive

   a. models of work.

   b. social play.

   c. instructional play.

   d. games.

9. Practice play differs from sensorimotor play in which of the following ways?

   a. It is common in the infancy stage of development.

   b. It involves coordination of skills.

   c. It revolves around the use of symbols.

   d. It is common in adolescence.

10. Ethnic-minority adolescents are more likely than white students to

   a. have school friends separate from home or neighborhood friends

   b. be classified as "popular."

   c. hang around in same-sexed groups.

   d. be unconcerned about their ethnic status.

F. CRITICAL THINKING QUESTIONS

1. How does parental or teaching style contribute to bullying behavior or "whipping boy" outcomes?

2. How has the function of adolescent dating changed in the last 100 years?

G. APPLICATION QUESTIONS

As a parent or teacher, helping children learn how to be accepted by others may be the most important thing you teach. Sometimes it takes more than modeling respect for other people's feelings. How do you respond to someone who does not seem to care, who shows no remorse for anti-social behaviors? Typically, such children have a history of peer rejection. They do not have friends, and they do not expect to have any. Therefore, they believe they have nothing left to lose by offending or hurting other children. Such a response stems from unmet needs for acceptance by peers.

1. How would you help this unwanted child identify and meet his/her needs for acceptance by peers?

2. How might you introduce the notion of forgiveness, to both the perpetrator and the victims? Are there situations when forgiveness is inappropriate?

H. COGNITIVE MAPS

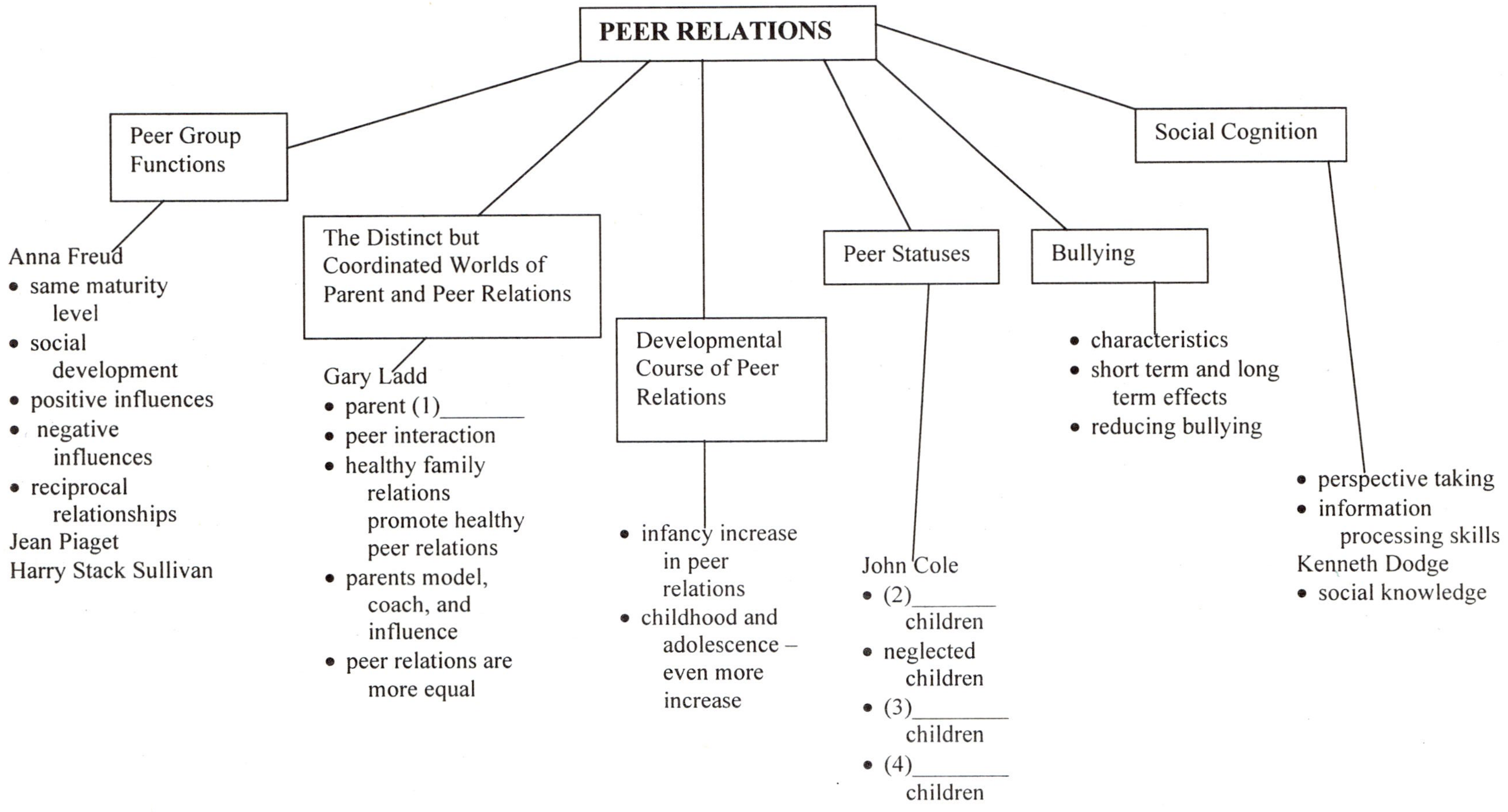

PEER RELATIONS
Peer Group Functions
Anna Freud
• same maturity level
• social development
• positive influences
• negative influences
• reciprocal relationships
Jean Piaget
Harry Stack Sullivan
The Distinct but Coordinated Worlds of Parent and Peer Relations
Gary Ladd
• parent (1)________
• peer interaction
• healthy family relations promote healthy peer relations
• parents model, coach, and influence
• peer relations are more equal
Developmental Course of Peer Relations
• infancy increase in peer relations
• childhood and adolescence – even more increase
Peer Statuses
John Cole
• (2)________ children
• neglected children
• (3)________ children
• (4)________ children
Bullying
• characteristics
• short term and long term effects
• reducing bullying
Social Cognition
• perspective taking
• information processing skills
Kenneth Dodge
• social knowledge

PLAY

Play's Functions

Erik Erikson
Sigmund Freud
Lev Vygotsky
Daniel Berlyne

- play therapy
- increases peer (1)_______
- helps release tension
- enhances (2)______ development
- supports exploration

Parten's Classic Study of Play

KEY PERSON
Mildred (3)_______

- unoccupied play
- solitary play
- onlooker play
- parallel play
- associative play
- cooperative play

Types of Play

- social and cognitive aspects
- sensorimotor play
- practice play
- pretent/symbolic play

Carolee Howes

- social play
- constructive play
- games

Sociocultural Contexts of Play

- modern children
- form and content of play is influenced by culture and socioeconomic factors

FRIENDSHIP

Friendship's Functions

- companionship
- stimulation
- (1)_______ support
- (2)____ support
- social (3)_________
- intimacy/affection

Sullivan's Ideas

Harry Stack Sullivan
Willard Hartup

- basic social needs
  - tenderness/attachment
  - companionship
  - social acceptance
  - intimacy
  - sexual relations
- friendships nurture emotional well-being and social competence
- intimacy intensifies during early adolescence
- adolescents depend on friends for companionship, reassurance of worth, and intimacy

Intimacy and Similarity

- key aspects of friendship
- intimacy in friendship
  - share problems
  - listen
  - understand
- friends are similar
  - age, sex, ethnicity
  - attitudes toward school
  - educational aspirations
  - achievement orientations
  - like same music, clothes, activities

Mixed-Age Friendships

- engage in more (4)_______ behavior
- early maturing girls have older friends

ADOLESCENCE, PEERS, AND ROMANTIC RELATIONSHIPS

Peer Pressure and Conformity

- pressure to conform to peers increases in adolescence
- negative conforming behavior
- positive conforming behavior

Cliques and Crowds

- crowd – largest and least personal group
- clique – smaller, more intimate and cohesive group
- James Coleman
- jocks, populars, normals, druggies, nobodies, independents
- jocks, populars, and independents – high self esteem
- nobodies – lowest self-esteem

Brad Brown
Jane Lohr

Adolescent Groups Versus Child Groups

- adolescent groups – formal, more heterogeneous, and more mixed sex than children's groups

KEY PERSON
Dexter (1)______

Dating and Romantic Relationships

Candice Feiring

- functions
- types of dating
- developmental functions
- dating scripts
- emotion and romantic relationships
- culture

I. REVIEW PRIORITIES

Assess your present understanding of the material in this chapter by rating yourself for each heading using the following scale:

1 – I thoroughly understand material and its context to other sections

2 – I understand most of the material and have a basic grasp of the context to other sections

3 – I have a shaky understanding of the material and a poor grasp of the context

4 – I have an inadequate understanding of the material

Peer Relations

- Peer Group Function _____
- The Distinct Coordinated Worlds of Parent and Peer Relations _____
- Developmental Course of Peer Relations _____
- Peer Statuses _____
- Bullying _____
- Social Cognition _____

Play

- Play's Functions _____
- Parten's Classic Study of Play _____
- Types of Play _____
- Sociocultural Contexts of Play _____

Friendship

- Friendship's Functions _____
- Sullivan's Ideas _____

- Intimacy and Similarity ______
- Mixed-Age Friendships ______

Adolescence, Peers, and Romantic Relationships

- Peer Pressure and Conformity ______
- Cliques and Crowds ______
- Adolescent Groups Versus Child Groups ______
- Dating and Romantic Relationships ______

ANSWER KEY

B. TRUE OR FALSE KEY CONTENT QUESTIONS

1. T
2. T
3. F
4. T
5. F
6. F
7. T
8. T
9. T
10. F
11. F
12. T
13. T
14. F
15. T
16. F
17. T
18. F
19. T
20. F

C. FILL IN THE BLANK KEY TERMS

1. information
2. more; stress
3. bullies; authoritarian
4. whipping
5. listen; confident
6. Neglected; rejected
7. aggression
8. attention
9. dominate
10. perspective

11. intentions
12. exploratory
13. social
14. coordination
15. pretends
16. less
17. play; disclose
18. smaller; cohesion
19. athletes; popular
20. stronger

D. MATCHING KEY PEOPLE QUESTIONS

1. J
2. G
3. L
4. E
5. B
6. F
7. C
8. I

E. MULTIPLE CHOICE KNOWLEDGE QUESTIONS

1. d
2. c
3. b
4. c
5. a
6. b
7. d
8. b
9. b
10. a

F. CRITICAL THINKING QUESTIONS

1.
   - Bullies' parents—Authoritarian and rejecting of their child, yet permissive about son's aggression.
   - Whipping boy's parents—Anxious and overprotective, taking special care to avoid aggression.
   - Well adjusted boy's parents—Promoted self-assertiveness rather than aggression in mediating conflict; they also encouraged their sons to be tolerant and resist peer pressure.
   - Teachers who encourage more cooperative interactions have less peer isolation or aggressive peer behavior.

2.

- During the first half of the 20th Century, the purpose of dating was courtship for marriage.
- Today, the purpose of dating includes:
  a. recreation and enjoyment;
  b. source of status and achievement;
  c. a socialization process to learn how to get along with others;
  d. learning about intimacy and a meaningful relationship;
  e. sexual exploration and experimentation;
  f. helps adolescents separate from families of origin;
  g. courtship for marriage.
- Values and religious beliefs in various cultures often dictate the age that dating begins, how much freedom is allowed, the need for chaperones, and the roles of males and females. Tensions can arise in immigrant families between "new world" adolescents and "old world" parents.

H. COGNITIVE MAPS

A

1. interaction
2. popular
3. rejected
4. controversial

B

1. affiliation
2. cognitive
3. Parten

C

1. physical
2. ego
3. comparison
4. deviant

D

1. Dunphy

CHAPTER 17: SCHOOLS

A. LEARNING OBJECTIVES

The Nature of Children's Schooling

1. Define and compare *direct instruction approach* and *constructivist approach (cognitive & social)* to learning.

Schools and Developmental Status

2. Define *developmentally appropriate practice.*
3. What is the purpose of Project Head Start and Project Follow Through?
4. Describe the characteristics of effective schools for middle school students.
5. Describe the recommendations of the William Grant Foundation Commission to reduce the high school dropout rate.

Socioeconomic Status and Ethnicity in Schools

6. Describe the contributions of James Comer and Eliot Aronson to create better learning environments for impoverished minority students.

Children with Disabilities

7. Define *learning disability* and *Attention Deficit/Hyperactivity Disorder* (ADHD).
8. Define *inclusion.*

Achievement

9. Compare and contrast *extrinsic and intrinsic motivation.*
10. Define and contrast *attribution, mastery orientation,* and *self-efficacy.*
11. How does culture influence achievement among ethnic minority children?

B. TRUE OR FALSE KEY CONTENT QUESTIONS

The Nature of Children's Schooling

1. T F Advocates of direct instruction approach argue that the constructive (cognitive and social) approach makes students passive learners.
2. T F Advocates of the constructive (cognitive and social) approach argue that direct instruction approach does not give enough attention to the content of a discipline.
3. T F A constructivist theme moves instruction away from the teacher and toward the student.

Schools and Developmental Status

4. T F The Montessori approach fosters individual independence and develops cognitive skills but de-emphasizes verbal interaction with the teacher and peers.
5. T F Direct teaching through large group paper-and-pencil activities is believed to be developmentally appropriate.
6. T F At least 40 percent of Head Start programs and 80 percent of early childhood programs are of questionable quality.
7. T F Elementary school teachers "cover the curriculum" because children need to distinguish learning by subject area.
8. T F The Carnegie Corporation Report recommended restructuring middle schools to smaller "communities" in which teacher teams teach in more flexibly designed curriculum blocks and lower the student-to-counselor ratio.
9. T F Over the past 40 years, high school dropouts has increased considerably.
10. T F To reduce the dropout rate schools need to support monitored work experiences, such as apprenticeships and internships.

Socioeconomic Status and Ethnicity in Schools

11. T F Schools in low-income neighborhoods often have fewer resources, have less experienced teachers, and are more likely to encourage rote learning rather than thinking skills.

12. T F Institutional racism permeates many schools because teachers fail to challenge children of color to achieve.

Children with Disabilities

13. T F About three times as many girls as boys are classified as having a learning disability.

14. T F The most common problem for students with a learning disability is reading.

15. T F Attention Deficit/Hyperactivity Disorder (ADHD) decreases in adolescence.

16. T F It is inappropriate to include children with disabilities in a mainstream classroom because it is very costly and time consuming.

Achievement

17. T F One view of extrinsic motivation emphasizes self-determination, personal choice, and responsibility.

18. T F When rewards convey information about mastery, they are more likely to promote student feeling of competence.

19. T F Low self-efficacy students are more likely to expend effort and persist longer at a learning task than high self-efficacy students.

20. T F Asian schools and parents have a much higher expectation for their children's education and achievement than do American schools and parents.

C. FILL IN THE BLANK KEY TERMS

1. The back-to-basics movement believe that children should be taught in a ____________________ approach characterized by mastery of _____________ content.
2. Alternately, the _________________ approach emphasizes the child's active construction of knowledge, which is __________ centered.
3. Child-centered kindergartens emphasize the ____________ of learning rather than what is learned.
4. In Montessori schools, children are given considerable _____________ in choosing activities and allowed to move from one activity to another as they choose.
5. The Reggio Emilia approach views young children as _______________ , encourages them to learn about topics of interest to them, and uses various stimulating media and materials.
6. Schooling that is based on age-appropriate activities emphasizing the hands-on approach to learning exemplifies developmentally _______________ practice.
7. The purpose of Project Head Start was to provide an opportunity for children from low-income families to acquire skills important for success in ___________.
8. Estimates indicate every dollar spent on such programs eventually returns ________ over a lifetime.
9. Children's self-__________ is lower in the latter part of elementary school than earlier in elementary school experience.
10. Puberty makes the transition to junior high school more difficult as does the appearance of formal operational thought, the increase of responsibility and _____________ , the move to a larger school, and an increased focus on _____________ .
11. Reducing the dropout rate requires lowering the barriers between __________ and ____________ .
12. One way to maximize each adolescent's learning potential is to limit class ________ .
13. Eliot Aronson believes that the jigsaw classroom promotes student __________________ through cooperatively striving for the same goal.

14. According to John Ogbu, ethnic minority children have ______________ educational opportunities, are exposed to teachers who have _______ expectations for them, and encounter negative stereotypes about ethnic minority groups.

15. When disabled children are placed in regular school classes with other children, they have been ___________________, although the more current term is _____________.

16. Children of normal intelligence, who have severe difficulty with some but not all academic areas, and who have no health or emotional condition that explains their problems are labeled ___________ disabled.

17. ADHD is frequently treated with amphetamines such as _____________, a widely prescribed and effective treatment for _____ percent of the cases.

18. The desire to accomplish something or reach a standard of excellence is called _______________ motivation.

19. A key factor in understanding internal causes for achievement is ____________.

20. Children with helpless orientations react to challenges by questioning their _________; children with mastery orientations react to challenges by focusing on their learning ________________.

D. MATCHING KEY PEOPLE QUESTIONS

___ 1. A researcher who developed the concept of the jigsaw classroom.

___ 2. An educational researcher who identified the characteristics of outstanding middle schools.

___ 3. An educator who believed that the team approach is the best way to educate children.

___ 4. An anthropologist who proposed the view that ethnic minority students are exploited in American schools.

___ 5. Advanced the concept of a project approach in elementary classrooms where students plan and select their activities.

___ 6. A physician-turned-educator who developed an approach to education emphasizing student freedom and spontaneity.

___ 7. A social cognitive theorist who believes that self-efficacy is a critical factor in student achievement.

___ 8. An educator who documented the effects of poverty on children in their inner-city neighborhoods and schools.

A. Maria Montessori

B. Lillian Katz and Sylvia Chard

C. Jonathan Kozol

D. John Ogbu

E. Margaret Beale Spencer

F. James Comer

G. Eliot Aronson

H. Davis McClelland

I. Joan Lipsitz

J. Carol Dweck

K. Albert Bandura

L. John Nicholls

M. Harold Stevenson

B. MULTIPLE CHOICE KNOWLEDGE QUESTIONS

1. According to the direct-instruction approach, the main function of schools should be to
   a. provide extracurricular activities.
   b. enhance the social and emotional development of adolescents.
   c. be comprehensive and provide a multifaceted curriculum.
   d. develop an intellectually mature person by emphasizing training in basic subjects.

2. Schools that stress both cognitive and social skills based on knowledge of child development use
   a. subject-centered teaching.
   b. developmentally appropriate practices.
   c. Montessori methods.
   d. techniques from Project Preschool.

3. Project Head Start was designed to
   a. provide low-income children a chance to acquire skills that would help them succeed at school.
   b. assess the advantages and disadvantages of preschool educational programs.
   c. give parents an educational daycare center.
   d. determine the feasibility of starting formal education at an earlier age.

4. A trend in adolescent development that has stimulated the creation of middle schools is
   a. an increase in formal operational thinking among early adolescents.
   b. the need for high achievement orientation.
   c. the earlier and highly variable beginning of puberty.
   d. the fact that today's teens spend more time with peers than with parents or adults.

5. Joan Lipsitz said that the common thread among schools that have been successful in diminishing the trauma often associated with middle-school experience was that they all emphasized

   a. gender equity.
   b. curricular flexibility.
   c. discipline.
   d. the importance of high academic standards.

6. During the last 40 years, the dropout rate of American school children has

   a. increased significantly.
   b. increased slightly.
   c. decreased slightly.
   d. decreased significantly.

7. The critical factor in reducing the dropout rate involves

   a. improving the connection between schooling and work.
   b. a significant increase in the amount of money the government is willing to spend on education.
   c. ending racial inequality in the classroom.
   d. increasing the school year.

8. Jack, a second grader, has no trouble with math, science, or art, but cannot spell, read, or write. Jack is likely to be found to have a(n)

   a. vision impairment.
   b. speech disability.
   c. learning disability.
   d. attention deficit.

9. Attention-deficit hyperactivity disorder is usually not diagnosed until children enter the first or second grade. Why?

   a. The disorder does not develop until children reach middle childhood.

   b. Test for the disorder are not given until these grades.

   c. The disorder is often confused with other disorders such as emotional disability or mental retardation.

   d. The syndrome is not noticeable until children must perform structured, organized tasks.

10. Which condition promotes intrinsic motivation?

   a. Children receive rewards for good work.

   b. Children learn that success depends on effort rather than work.

   c. Children are compared to others.

   d. All of these answers are correct.

F. CRITICAL THINKING QUESTIONS

1. How does attribution theory relate to the statement "adolescents are like intuitive scientists, seeking to explain the cause behind what happens?"

2. Describe effective intervention strategies for learning disabled students.

G. APPLICATION QUESTIONS

"Time is used differently in Reggio preschools than in preschools in the United States. Experiences and themes last months, as opposed to the one- or two-week units typical in the United States. The children are never expected to move on to something new until they have exhausted their ideas fully. Often, in Reggio, children were observed painting at easels for an entire morning or working with clay for hours." (Seefeldt, C., 1995, Art—A serious work. Young Children, 50(3), p.42)

Early childhood educators throughout the world realize that the process of learning is more important for children than the product. Since the process is given so much time at Reggio preschools, the children's products are extraordinary. Reflect on what learning experiences were most productive to you during your preschool and elementary years.

1. Describe what learning mode works best for you: visual, auditory, or kinesthetic (manual dexterity). In thinking about your process, picture yourself putting together a barbecue from a kit. Do you *look* at the illustrations? Do you *read* the directions or have someone *tell* you the instructions? Do you just begin *construction* and consult the instructions when you get confused? Or do you get frustrated and have someone else put it together?

2. Imagine you are deeply absorbed in a high interest project, a hobby or an art/craft endeavor, for example. How long can you go without interruption? What keeps you so engaged? Have you ever had a similar situation occur in a school setting? If so, describe. If not, why?

H. COGNITIVE MAPS

THE NATURE OF CHILDREN'S SCHOOLING

Contemporary Approaches to Student Learning

- direct (1)________ approach
- cognitive constructivist approaches
- social constructivist approaches

Schools' Changing Social Developmental Contexts

- preschool – (2)______ setting is the classroom
- elementary – social setting is the classroom
- secondary – social setting is the (3)_____

SCHOOLS AND DEVELOPMENTAL STATUS

Early Childhood Education

- child-centered kindergarten
- Reggio Emilia Approach
- Montessori Approach
- Maria Montessori
- developmentally appropriate practice
- Project (1)_____ Start
- Project Follow Through

The Transition to Elementary School

- concern – negative feedback
- elementary school children should involve active, (2)_________ learning

Lillian Katz
Sylvia Chard

Schools for Adolescents

- Middle Schools/Junior High coincide with (3)______ – physical, cognitive, and socioemotional changes
- top-dog phenomenon
- effective schools stress the importance of (4)_______ development and individual differences
- Joan Lipsitz
- high school drop outs

SOCIOECONOMIC STATUS AND ETHNICITY IN SCHOOLS

The Education of Students from Low Socioeconomic Backgrounds

KEY PERSON

Jonathan (1)_____

- learning barriers at home that children in poverty face
- learning barriers at school that children in poverty face

Ethnicity in Schools

John Ogbu
Margaret Beale Spencer
James Comer
Eliot Aronson

- teachers need to have positive expectations for students of color
- community, team approach
- jigsaw classroom to reduce racial tension

CHILDREN WITH DISABILITIES

Who Are Children with Disabilities?

- (1)___% U.S. children receive special education services
- (2)___% of these children have a learning disability

Learning Disabilities

- have normal intelligence, difficulty in one or more academic areas
- more boys than girls
- most common problem is reading
- intervention

Attention Deficit/Hyperactivity Disorder

- signs
  - inattention
  - hyperactivity/impulsivity
  - difficult to discipline
  - low frustration tolerance
  - problems in peer relations
  - general immaturity
  - clumsiness
- treatment includes academic, behavioral, and medical intervention

Educational Issues Involving Children with Disabilities

- Public Law 94-142
- Individuals with Disabilities Act (IDEA)
- instructional technology
- Individualized Educational Plan (IEP)
- Least Restrictive Environment (LRE)
- inclusion
- mainstreaming

ACHIEVEMENT

Need for Achievement

David McClellend
- achievement motivation
- desire to accomplish something
- reach a standard of excellence
- expend effort to excel
- links between parenting practices and children's achievement

Extrinsic and (1)________ Motivation

- extrinsic motivation – external incentives like rewards and punishments
- internal motivation – internal incentives like self-determination, curiosity, challenge, and effort
- choices and responsibility increases intrinsic motivation
- rewards can undermine motivation

Attribution

Bernard Weiner
- attribution theory

Mastery Orientation

KEY PERSON
Carol (2)________
- helpless orientation
- mastery orientation
- performance orientation

Self-Efficacy

Albert Bandura
Dale Schunk
- master a situation and produce positive outcomes
- low efficacy students avoid challenging tasks
- high efficacy students eagerly work at tasks

Goal-Setting, Planning, and Self-Monitoring

KEY PERSON
John (3)______
- set goals that are specific, proximal, and challenging
- good planning means managing time effectively, setting priorities, and being organized
- self-monitoring benefits learning

Ethnicity and Culture

Sandra Graham
Harold Stevenson
- ethnicity and socioeconomic status
- American children are more achievement oriented than some countries but less achievement oriented than Asian countries

I. REVIEW PRIORITIES

Assess your present understanding of the material in this chapter by rating yourself for each heading using the following scale:

1 – I thoroughly understand material and its context to other sections

2 – I understand most of the material and have a basic grasp of the context to other sections

3 – I have a shaky understanding of the material and a poor grasp of the context

4 – I have an inadequate understanding of the material

The Nature of Children's Schooling

- Contemporary Approaches to Student Learning ______
- Schools' Changing Social Developmental Contexts ______

Schools and Developmental Status

- Early Childhood Education ______
- The Transition to Elementary School ______
- Schools for Adolescents ______

Socioeconomic Status and Ethnicity in Schools

- The Education of Students from Low Socioeconomic Backgrounds ______
- Ethnicity in Schools ______

Children with Disabilities

- Who are Children With Disabilities? ______
- Learning Disabilities ______
- Attention Deficit/Hyperactivity Disorder ______
- Educational Issues Involving Children with Disabilities ______

Achievement

- Need for Achievement ____
- Extrinsic and Intrinsic Motivation ____
- Attribution ____
- Mastery Orientation ____
- Self-Efficacy ____
- Goal-Setting, Planning, and Self-Monitoring ____
- Ethnicity and Culture ____

ANSWER KEY

B. TRUE OR FALSE KEY CONTENT QUESTIONS

1. F
2. F
3. T
4. T
5. F
6. T
7. F
8. T
9. F
10. T
11. T
12. T
13. F
14. T
15. F
16. F
17. F
18. T
19. F
20. T

C. FILL IN THE BLANK KEY TERMS

1. direct instruction; academic
2. constructivist; learner
3. process
4. freedom
5. competent
6. appropriate
7. school
8. $5.73
9. esteem

10. independence; achievement
11. work; school
12. size
13. interdependence
14. inferior; low
15. mainstreamed; inclusion
16. learning
17. Ritalin; 85-95%
18. achievement
19. effort
20. abilities; strategies

D. MATCHING KEY PEOPLE QUESTIONS

1. G
2. I
3. F
4. D
5. B
6. A
7. K
8. C

E. MULTIPLE CHOICE KNOWLEDGE QUESTIONS

1. d
2. b
3. a
4. c
5. b
6. d
7. a
8. c
9. d
10. b

F. CRITICAL THINKING QUESTIONS

1.

- Attribution theory states that individuals are motivated to make sense out of their own behavior by discovering its underlying causes.
- The search for a cause is usually initiated when unexpected and important events end in failure, such as good students getting a poor grade.
- When adolescent (or older) students do poorly on a test or assignment they can generate causal attributes in an attempt to explain the poor performance. By determining the factors that are controllable, the student is motivated to renew goals and expect positive future results.
- Bernard Weiner identified three dimensions of causal attributions:
    a. *Locus*—Is the cause internal or external to the individual?
    b. *Stability*—Does the cause remain the same or change?
    c. *Controllability*—Can the individual control the cause?

2.

- Most interventions focus on improving reading ability. This may include phonological awareness at the kindergarten level, assistance with handwriting and spelling, or attention to listening, concentration, and reasoning.
- Intensive instruction by a competent teacher can improve deficient reading skills in many students. However, early intervention is necessary, but is often unavailable.

H. COGNITIVE MAPS

A

1. instruction
2. social
3. school

B

1. Head
2. constructivist
3. puberty
4. socioemotional

C

1. Kozol

D

1. 10%
2. 50%

E

1. Intrinsic
2. Doveck
3. Nichols

CHAPTER 18: CULTURE

A. LEARNING OBJECTIVES

Culture and Children's Development

1. Define and contrast *ethnocentrism* and *cross-cultural studies.*
2. Define *rites of passage* and explain how the absence of a formal rite of passage can create adult status ambiguity in adolescents.

Socioeconomic Status and Poverty

3. What are the economic and psychological effects of poverty on children and families?

Ethnicity

4. Define prejudice. Explain the opposing views about the progress of eliminating discrimination and bias.
5. Compare and contrast *assimilation* with *pluralism.*

Technology

6. Describe the negative effects of aggression and pro-social behavior on children due to television viewing.
7. Describe the promise and concern of the Internet's influence on children. How does it affect the gap between rich and poor, male and female students, and between instructivist and constructivist teaching?

B. TRUE OR FALSE KEY CONTENT QUESTIONS

Culture and Children's Development

1. T F The future will bring extensive contact between people from varied cultural and ethnic backgrounds.
2. T F In the 21st century, global interdependence is a matter of belief or choice.
3. T F The United States is an achievement-oriented and individualistic culture.
4. T F Americans have distinct rites of passage that mark the transition from adolescence to adulthood.

Socioeconomic Status and Poverty

5. T F Low-income parents are more likely to discipline children with criticism and physical punishment.
6. T F The poverty threshold was originally based on the estimated cost of food multiplied by three.
7. T F There are twice as many American children living in poverty as any other industrial nation.
8. T F More men than women live in poverty.

Ethnicity

9. T F Research on ethnic minority groups often focus on negative and stressful factors.
10. T F Ethnic minority groups are homogeneous.
11. T F Assimilation refers to the absorption of ethnic minority groups into the dominant group at the loss of ethnic group core values.
12. T F For many years, pluralism was thought to be the best course for American society, but assimilation is increasingly being advocated.

Technology

13. T F By high school graduation, American children spend more time watching television than time in the classroom.

14. T F Children can learn aggressive attitudes and behaviors, as well as become desensitized to violence, from watching violence on television.

15. T F Since the number of computers has significantly increased in America's schools, the pedagogy has been dramatically changed through the use of constructive learning activities.

C. FILL IN THE BLANK KEY TERMS

1. The concept of __________ refers to the behavior, patterns, beliefs, and all other products of a particular group of people that are transmitted from generation to generation.
2. _________-cultural studies identify which aspects of development are universal and which aspects are culture-____________ .
3. Placing a priority on personal goals rather than goals of the group defines _____________; whereas ______________ represents an approach in which individuals subordinate their personal goals to serve the group.
4. In the United States, high school _____________ is one candidate for a rite of passage into adulthood; a second candidate is sexual ______________ .
5. Change that results from direct and continuous contact between two distinct cultural groups is called _______________ .
6. The ________________ model indicates that individuals of different cultures can work together to achieve goals while maintaining their distinct identities.
7. The synonym for social class, SES, refers to ________________ status.
8. With regard to child rearing practices, low-income parents value ____________ characteristics in their children, such as obedience and neatness; middle-class parents value ____________ characteristics in their adolescents, such as self-control.

9. With regard to intellectual orientation, middle class children read more/less; and watch television more/less than children of working class parents.

10. Poverty can have ____________ effects on children.

11. A caring ___________ can help a youth overcome the effects of poverty.

12. ____________ refers to such things as one's cultural heritage and national characteristics, whereas ________________ status, or social class, refers to groupings of individuals on the basis of occupational, educational, and economic characteristics.

13. Much research on ethnic minority adolescents does not separate the influences of ethnicity from the influences of __________ class.

14. The failure to recognize diversity and individual variation can result in _______________ of an ethnic minority group.

15. ________________ refers to an ethnic minority group's absorption by the dominant group, whereas ______________ refers to a coexistence between distinct ethnic and cultural groups.

D. MATCHING KEY PEOPLE QUESTIONS

___ 1. A cross-cultural expert who described the characteristics of culture.

___ 2. An Asian American researcher who believes that value conflicts underlie controversies regarding ethnic issues.

___ 3. An anthropologist whose study of Samoan adolescents challenged the "Storm and Stress" view of adolescence.

___ 4. An American social psychologist who indicated that people in all cultures tend to be ethnocentric.

___ 5. The researcher who has investigated many dimensions of the information age, such as television and computers.

___ 6. The researcher who studied the conditions of poverty and stress among single mothers.

___ 7. The social researcher who studies prejudice and believes that ethnicity defines who receives the benefits of citizenship.

___ 8. Television researcher who studied "Sesame Street" programming that taught children how to use positive social skills.

A. Richard Brislin

B. Donald Campbell

C. Margaret Mead

D. Vonnie McLoyd

E. Stanley Sue

F. James Jones

G. David Elkind

H. Sandra Calvert

I. Stanley Sue

J. Aimee Leifer

B. MULTIPLE CHOICE KNOWLEDGE QUESTIONS

1. As a Russian ice-skating judge, Sergi is supposed to remain completely unbiased. Like most individuals, however, he finds that this is virtually impossible and tends to give slightly higher scores to fellow Russians. Sergi's behavior exemplifies
    a. culturalism.
    b. pluralism.
    c. reciprocal socialization.
    d. ethnocentrism.

2. Margaret Mead's studies of adolescent Samoans illustrate the concept of

   a. poverty.

   b. social class.

   c. cross-cultural research.

   d. discrimination.

3. Rituals such as bar mitzvah and confirmation serve the adolescent citizen of the United States as

   a. rites of passage.

   b. cultural transitions of sexuality.

   c. evidence of ethnocentrism.

   d. family traditions.

4. Which of the following models of cultural change assumes that it is possible for an individual to know and understand two different cultures?

   a. acculturation.

   b. alternation.

   c. marginalization.

   d. multicultural.

5. Working class parents place less value on socializing their youth for _________ and a higher value on ___________ and responsibility.

   a. cooperation; competition

   b. self-control; obedience

   c. competition; achievement

   d. achievement; competition

6. The most common measure of economic hardship is

   a. low socioeconomic class.

   b. parental unemployment.

   c. the federal poverty threshold.

   d. inadequate housing and homelessness.

7. The individual raised in a single-parent, female-headed household is more likely than not to be

   a. sexually active.

   b. promiscuous.

   c. in trouble with the law.

   d. poor.

8. Until recently, there has been little research that systematically compares the _____ of different ethnic groups.

   a. sexual patterns

   b. family interactions

   c. sibling relationships

   d. strengths and weakness

9. Concerning the integration of ethnic groups into a culture, assimilation is to pluralism as

   a. discrimination is to prejudice.

   b. absorption is to coexistence.

   c. separate is to combined.

   d. tolerance is to intolerance.

10. Stanley Sue tries to resolve assimilation-pluralism conflicts in education by focusing on

   a. functional skills.

   b. redefining sociocultural issues.

   c. economic issues.

   d. common humanistic values.

F. CRITICAL THINKING QUESTIONS

1. Characterize the following inequalities associated with social class.

   - Occupation
   - Education
   - Economic resources
   - Power

2. Describe the educational advantages and concerns of the Internet.

G. APPLICATION QUESTIONS

It is generally agreed that the overriding goal for schools is to provide purposeful learning experiences for students. However, what happens when the culture of a school does not reflect the economic or ethnic culture of the home? Those children whose homes and family expectations are the least similar to school have the most adjustment to make. How did *you* honor similarities and celebrate differences when school culture was noticeably different from your home or neighborhood culture?

1. Cultural differences affect communication.
    a. How and when is speech used?
    b. What does body language mean?
    c. Is polite to look directly at the speaker.

2. Cultural differences affect relationships too.
    a. How is respect perceived between adults and children?
    b. Does one follow formal or informal behavior when in public?
    c. Is it better to be cooperative or competitive?

H. COGNITIVE MAPS

CULTURE AND CHILDREN'S DEVELOPMENT

The Nature of Culture

KEY PERSON

Richard (1)________

- behavior, patterns, beliefs, and other products of a group of people that are passed on from generation to generation

The Relevance of Culture to the Study of Children

- ethnocentrism
- global interdependence

Donald Campbell

Cross-Cultural Comparisons

KEY PERSON

Margaret (2)_______

- cross-cultural studies
- achievement
- individualism
- collectivism
- rites of passage

SOCIOECONOMIC STATUS AND POVERTY

The Nature of Socioeconomic Status

- grouping of people with similar occupational, educational, and economic characteristics
- inequalities

Socioeconomic Variations in Families, Neighborhoods, and Schools

Vonnie McLoyd

- influences adjustment
- Low (1)_____
  - high value on external characteristics – obedience and neatness
  - parenting – criticize discipline with punishment
  - watch TV more
  - high risk for mental health problems
- Middle and Upper SES
  - high value on internal characteristics – self-control and delay of gratification
  - parenting – explain discipline with reason
  - read more

Poverty

Vonnie McLoyd

- economic hardship
- social and psychological difficulties
- longlasting poverty has adverse effects on children
- (2)_______ of poverty
- two-generation interventions

ETHNICITY

The Nature of Ethnicity

- cultural heritage
- nationality characteristics
- race
- religion
- language

Ethnicity and Socioeconomic Status

Stanley Sac

- ethnic explanations of child development are sometime exaggerated and are really based on socioeconomic status
- poverty contributes to stress
- double disadvantage – prejudice and poverty

Differences and Diversity

James (1)_____

- recognize and respect differences
- strengths of ethnic minority groups
- diversity within ethnic groups
- stereotyping

Prejudice, Discrimination, and Bias

- unjustified negative attitude toward an individual because of the individual's membership group
- classroom contexts, media, interpersonal interactions, daily conversations, crimes, poverty, strangeness, mistakes, and deteriorations

Assimilation and Pluralism

- assimilation – absorption of ethnic minority groups into the dominant group
- pluralism – coexistence of distinct (2)_____ and (3)______ groups in the same society
- assimilation/pluralism conflict

America: A Nation of Blended Cultures

- America is a great receiver of ethnic groups
- mixing of ideologies and identities

TECHNOLOGY

Television

- negative influences
- positive influences
- (1)___ children watch more TV than any other country
- TV violence induces aggression and antisocial behaviors
- TV prosocial behavior is associated with increase in positive behavior
- Aimee Leifer
- TV is negatively related to verbal skills and creativity in children – cognitive development

Computers and the Internet

KEY PERSON

Sandra (2)_________

- Internet – core of computer-mediated communication
- email – electronic mail
- dramatic increase in the use of computers and the internet
- unregulation of internet makes it difficult for parents to monitor
- will technology widen the gap between social issues
- technology alone doesn't improve children's learning – active, constructivist learning is required along with other factors

I. REVIEW PRIORITIES

Assess your present understanding of the material in this chapter by rating yourself for each heading using the following scale:

1 – I thoroughly understand material and its context to other sections

2 – I understand most of the material and have a basic grasp of the context to other sections

3 – I have a shaky understanding of the material and a poor grasp of the context

4 – I have an inadequate understanding of the material

Culture and Children's Development

- The Nature of Culture _____
- The Relevance of Culture to the Study of Children _____
- Cross-Cultural Comparisons _____

Socioeconomic Status and Poverty

- The Nature of Socioeconomic Status _____
- Socioeconomic Variations in Families, Neighborhoods And Schools _____
- Poverty _____

Ethnicity

- The Nature of Ethnicity _____
- Ethnicity and Socioeconomic Status _____
- Differences and Diversity _____
- Prejudice, Discrimination, and Bias _____
- Assimilation and Pluralism _____
- America: A Nation of Blended Cultures _____

Technology

- Television _____
- Computers and the Internet _____

ANSWER KEY

B. TRUE OR FALSE KEY CONTENT QUESTIONS

1. T
2. F
3. T
4. F
5. T
6. T
7. T
8. F
9. T
10. F
11. T
12. F
13. T
14. T
15. F

C. FILL IN THE BLANK KEY TERMS

1. culture
2. Cross; specific
3. individualism; collectivism
4. graduation; intercourse
5. acculturation
6. multicultural
7. socioeconomic
8. external; internal
9. more; less
10. damaging
11. mentor
12. Ethnicity; socioeconomic
13. social
14. stereotyping
15. Assimilation; pluralism

D. MATCHING KEY PEOPLE QUESTIONS

1. A
2. E
3. C
4. B
5. H
6. D
7. F
8. J

E. MULTIPLE CHOICE KNOWLEDGE QUESTIONS

1. d
2. c
3. a
4. b
5. b
6. c
7. d
8. d
9. b
10. b

F. CRITICAL THINKING QUESTIONS

1.

- Occupation
  - ✓ Greater unemployment
  - ✓ Fewer skills needed in the marketplace
  - ✓ Unstable work history
- Education
  - ✓ Poor school readiness—read less and watched more TV
  - ✓ Fewer resources and of poorer quality in low-income schools
  - ✓ Sporadic parent support
  - ✓ More learning disabled students
- Economic resources
  - ✓ High proportion of ethnic minorities live in poverty
  - ✓ High percentage of single-parent families causes strain
  - ✓ Reduced government benefits
- Power
  - ✓ Rarely the decision makers
  - ✓ Low prestige/low self-esteem
  - ✓ Institutional prejudice
  - ✓ Poor access to technology, such as the Internet

2.

- Advantages
  - ✓ With large databases of information, students can gather and integrate knowledge.
  - ✓ Using project-centered activities, students can engage in collaborative learning, such as survey taking or cooperative scavenger hunts.
  - ✓ Students can communicate globally and inexpensively using e-mail.

- Concerns
  - ✓ Disproportionate access to high SES students
  - ✓ Disproportionate access to white students
  - ✓ Disproportionate use by males
  - ✓ Tendency to favor drill and practice to interactive higher thinking

H. COGNITIVE MAPS

A

1. Brislin
2. Mead

B

1. SES
2. Feminization

C

1. Jones
2. ethnic
3. cultural

D

1. U.S.
2. Calvert